HOLY SHIT

A Brief History of Swearing

Melissa Mohr

OXFORD
UNIVERSITY PRESS

OXFORD
UNIVERSITY PRESS

Oxford University Press is a department of the University of Oxford.
It furthers the University's objective of excellence in research,
scholarship, and education by publishing worldwide.

Oxford   New York
Auckland   Cape Town   Dar es Salaam   Hong Kong   Karachi
Kuala Lumpur   Madrid   Melbourne   Mexico City   Nairobi
New Delhi   Shanghai   Taipei   Toronto

With offices in
Argentina   Austria   Brazil   Chile   Czech Republic   France   Greece
Guatemala   Hungary   Italy   Japan   Poland   Portugal   Singapore
South Korea   Switzerland   Thailand   Turkey   Ukraine   Vietnam

Oxford is a registered trademark of Oxford University Press
in the UK and certain other countries.

Published in the United States of America by
Oxford University Press
198 Madison Avenue, New York, NY 10016

© Melissa Mohr 2013

First issued as an Oxford University Press paperback, 2016

Library of Congress Cataloging-in-Publication Data
Mohr, Melissa.
Holy shit : a brief history of swearing / Melissa Mohr.
p.   cm.
Includes bibliographical references.
ISBN 978-0-19-974267-7 (hardcover); 978-0-19-049168-0 (paperback)
1. Swearing—History. 2. English language—Obscene words—History.
3. English language—Slang—History. 4. English language—Social
aspects—History 5. English language—History. I. Title.
PE3724.S85.M65   2013
417'.2—dc23   2012034513

To John Harington and Samuel Johnson
And to my husband

CONTENTS

The Yukon

Introduction

It was the last word my grandmother ever said to me. She was suffering from advanced Alzheimer's disease and didn't speak at all as I helped her eat her lunch or even when I showed her family photos. I'm not sure she recognized me. When I took her for a walk outside in her wheelchair, though, she found her voice. I wheeled her over a crack in the sidewalk and her chair bumped. Out it came—"Shit!" This from a woman who, even when she was feeling particularly frustrated, had rarely gone further than "Nuts!" or "Darn it!" She relapsed into silence for the rest of my visit.

In 1866, the French poet Charles Baudelaire was laid low by a stroke. He lost his ability to speak, except for one phrase he repeated so often that the nuns taking care of him threw him out of their hospital: "Cré nom!"—short for *sacré nom de Dieu*. Today, the English equivalent to this would be the mild *goddamn* or *damn*, but in 1866 "Cré nom!" so unforgivably offended the nuns that they could explain Baudelaire's outbursts only as the result of satanic possession.

Embedded deep within the brains of Baudelaire and my grandmother, remaining even when other language had been stripped away, were swearwords. Baudelaire's swearing was a violation of religious taboo, taking God's name in vain. My grandmother's violated taboos against mentioning certain body parts or bodily excretions and actions. Over the centuries these two spheres of the unsayable—the religious and the sexual/excremental, the Holy and the Shit, if you will—have given rise to all the other "four-letter words" with which we swear. A history of swearing is a history of their interaction and interplay. Sometimes the Holy has been the main source of swearwords, sometimes the Shit, and sometimes the two fields have joined in what we today would consider unusual combinations—obscene words shouted during religious rituals, for example. In the twenty-first century, we have an embarrassment of riches, and can choose words from both areas, as demonstrated by one precocious four-year-old at my son's nursery school, who responded to something his mother had said with "Well, fuck me, Jesus!"

Holy Shit is a history of swearing in English. It begins in a place where public buildings are covered with graffiti ("If you're reading this, you're a faggot"); where the most popular entertainers have the foulest mouths; where swearwords graphic enough to offend not very delicate sensibilities are heard on every street corner. This is not New York City. It is Rome, two thousand years ago. We start with ancient Latin, because the Roman idea of *obscenitas* guided the development of our own concept of obscenity—along with republicanism, the Julian calendar, and numerous literary classics, the Romans gave us a model for our use of obscene words. The Romans had a very different sexual schema than we do, however, which led to some fascinating differences between their obscene words and ours, as we'll see in Chapter 1. The Bible, in turn, gave us the Holy, and a model for our oath swearing. Such swearing is very important to God, who demands again and again that believers swear by him and him alone. In the Old Testament, God is fighting a war for supremacy with other Near Eastern gods, and he wields oath swearing as one of his most powerful weapons.

The Middle Ages (a huge span of time, roughly 470–1500) was firmly under the sway of the Holy. Despite using plenty of words that we today would consider to be shocking and offensive, medieval English people were unconcerned about the Shit. Oath swearing instead was the most highly charged language—the truly obscene—thought to be able to injure God's reputation and even assault Christ physically. In the Renaissance (c. 1500–1660), the Holy and the Shit were more in balance. The rise of Protestantism and its changing definition of people's relationship to God, as well as the growing importance of "civility," created conditions for the development of obscenity, one of the things that proper, polite behavior is defined against. The eighteenth and nineteenth centuries saw the ascendancy of the Shit, what we today would recognize as fully developed obscenity. Obscenities possessed perhaps their greatest power to shock and offend during this age of euphemism, when even words such as *leg* and *trousers* were deemed too scandalous and vulgar for the public sphere. Today, all bets are off, and both obscenities and oaths are flourishing in public discourse, as any look at television, the Internet, or political debate will demonstrate.

For more than two thousand years, swearing has alternated between the twin poles of oaths and obscenities, between the Holy and the Shit. What makes a word a swearword, though? What distinguishes *fuck* from *bonk* or *sleep with*, "Jesus Christ!" from "Heavens above!"? These questions can be approached from several different angles: physiological, linguistic, and historical.

Physiologically, swearwords have different effects on people than do other, superficially similar words. They induce greater skin conductance responses than do other words, even emotionally evocative words such as *death* or *cancer*. (The skin conductance response indicates the extent of a person's emotional arousal by measuring the degree to which his or her skin conducts electricity.) Swearwords help us deal with physical pain. In a recent experiment, subjects were able to keep their hands immersed in very cold water longer when they repeated a swearword such as *shit* than when they repeated a neutral word such as *shoot*. Speaking swearwords increases your heart rate. It is also easier to remember taboo words than non-taboo ones in a word recall test. If you are given a list that includes a mix of obscenities and neutral words, you can bet that the ones that stick in your mind will be *fuck* and *nigger*, not *kiss* and *angry*.

Scientists today believe that swearwords even occupy a different part of our brain. Most speech is a "higher-brain" function, the province of the cerebral cortex, which also controls voluntary actions and rational thought. Swearwords are stored in the "lower brain," the limbic system, which, broadly, is responsible for emotion, the fight-or-flight response, and the autonomic nervous system, which regulates heart rate and blood pressure. This is why my grandmother and Charles Baudelaire could still come up with "Shit!" and "Cré nom!" even though their ability to speak had otherwise been eroded by disease.

Linguistically, a swearword is one that "kidnaps our attention and forces us to consider its unpleasant connotations," as Steven Pinker puts it. *Connotation* is a word's baggage, the emotional associations that go along with it, as opposed to its *denotation*, its dictionary definition. Cognitive psychologist Timothy Jay saw this distinction summed up in an exchange of graffiti on a bathroom wall. "You are all a bunch of fucking nymphomaniacs," one line read. Someone had circled "fucking" and added below, "There ain't no other kind." The second writer chose to interpret "fucking" as a denotative use, not a connotative one. The literal definition is, according to the *Oxford English Dictionary*, "that engages in or is engaged in sexual intercourse." It can have many connotations, however, from "really bad" to "extraordinarily good." "Fucking nymphomaniacs" could be either, really—it is difficult to tell whether the tone is one of admiration or exasperation. Swearwords are almost *all* connotation—they carry an emotional charge that exceeds the taboo status of their referents.

To put it another way, as some linguists do, swearwords are often employed in a *nonliteral* sense. "He fucked her" is a literal or denotative use—they had sex. "The fuck you are!" is a nonliteral use—nobody is having any kind of sex here, or referring to it; it is simply a vigorous denial. The *f*-word here serves as an intensifier, important for the connotation it carries and not for its literal meaning. Our strongest offensive words can almost always be used nonliterally (except, as we will see, the racial epithets).

Historically, swearwords have been thought to possess a deeper, more intimate connection to the things they represent than do other words. *Shit*, to put it another way, is more closely connected to the thing itself in all its smelly, sticky yuckiness than is *poop* or *excrement*. These words vividly reveal taboo body parts, actions, and excretions that culture demands we conceal, whether by covering with clothing, shrouding in privacy, or flushing down the toilet. A version of this theory was given legal sanction by the United States Supreme Court in 2009, when it heard a case on "fleeting expletives," including that of the musician Bono, who accepted an award at the Golden Globes ceremony with "This is really, really fucking brilliant." The Court agreed with the Federal Communications Commission that the use of the *f*-word "invariably invokes a coarse sexual image." Even when a happy rock star uses the word to describe his surprise, it "inherently has a sexual connotation." The idea is that when Bono says "fucking," you cannot help picturing people (who?) getting it on. Some language experts have criticized the FCC's and the Court's argument, and it would seem that this case pretty obviously involves a nonliteral use, employed for its connotation. It has nothing to do with sex and everything to do with expressing how happy and surprised the singer feels. But this does not change the point that *fucking* acquired its intense emotional power and its status as one of the worst words in the English language from its ability to access one of our deepest taboos and bring it to light in a way that no other word could or can.

It is fairly easy for us today to see how obscenities fit the physiological, linguistic, and historical criteria that we've laid out. But what about oaths, which were the most highly charged, most offensive language in English for centuries? Swearing an oath can mean two different things, one positive and one negative. In the "good" sense, an oath means promising before God to tell the truth—this is sincere oath swearing. Such oaths are an important part of society today: witnesses swear to tell the truth and nothing but the truth, public officials swear oaths of office, businessmen swear to their wives that they are not shtupping (Yiddish for "to push, shove") their secretaries. In the past, such oaths could be a matter of life and death. People were imprisoned and even executed because they refused to swear before God, or swore in some wrong way. In the "bad" sense, an oath means blasphemous or vain swearing, words or phrases that take God's name in vain, mention his body parts, or otherwise detract from his honor. This includes everything from making God witness a lie—swearing that you are not shtupping when you are—to exclaiming "Jesus Christ!" when you are upset.

Oaths have come a long way from the days of the Middle Ages, when *by God's bones* would have been more shocking than *cunt*. Today, *God* and *damn it* are probably too mild to increase the heart rate of many people, but, I would argue, they would have in the past. Empirical evidence for this is hard to come by—there was obviously no medieval skin conductance testing, and though the Victorians discovered the galvanic skin response in the late nineteenth century, they did not use it to investigate swearing. Anecdotal evidence suggests, however, that oaths were carriers of and triggers for great emotion, like obscenities today, and were stored in the same "lower" regions of the brain. We have already encountered Baudelaire and his "cré nom"; other evidence comes from early reports of people suffering from Tourette's syndrome. Tourette's syndrome is characterized by a variety of motor and vocal tics including, most famously, *coprolalia*, the apparently uncontrollable utterance of obscene words. The patient with the first reported case of Tourette's syndrome (1825) compulsively called out oaths as well as obscenities. She was a French aristocrat, the Marquise de Dampierre, who apparently shocked society with periodic outbursts of *sacré nom de Dieu* as well as *merde* ("shit") and *foutu cochon* (best translated as "fucking pig"). This balance is exactly what we would expect in the nineteenth century. Her brain had stored a mix of oaths and obscenities with which to offend when the irresistible urge came on.

Linguistically, vain oaths were used in the same ways and for the same reasons that we employ obscenities today. A fourteenth-century tailor who pricked himself with his needle would have shouted "By God's bones!" (or nails, blood, eyes, etc.), not "Shit!" Oaths in the past offered the catharsis we now seek in obscene language. Medieval insults too were often prefaced with an oath—"By God ... thy drasty rhyming is not worth a turd," the Host of Chaucer's *Canterbury Tales*

(1386) tells another pilgrim when he wants him to shut up. The Host uses his oath for emphasis, to make clear how much he hates the other pilgrim's poetry. Just like *fuck* or *cunt*, here "by God" has an offensive power in excess of its literal meaning. It is used for its connotation, not its denotation.

Lastly, we have the historical idea that swearwords possess a closer connection to the things they represent than do other words, and this is also true for oaths. In the Middle Ages and the Renaissance, oaths were thought to have direct and automatic effects on God—this is what gave them their power. An oath forced God to look down from heaven and witness that a person's words were true. And as surprising as it sounds, oaths in certain forms—those by God's bones and other such body parts—were thought to rip apart Christ's body as it sat in heaven. They had an extremely close connection to what they represented—they could in certain respects control God and even injure him.

English has many other terms with which to define and describe swearing. Racial slurs and epithets are the most important of these. (An *epithet* indicates a quality that is supposed to be characteristic of the person or thing being described, or is simply an abusive term.) To many people, words such as *nigger* and *paki* are now the most offensive words in the English language. Certainly for me, the sections on racial slurs in Chapter 6 and in the epilogue were the hardest to write. I found surprisingly little problem in writing *fuck* over and over and over, but I balked at thinking about and discussing the *n*-word. In 1970, the editor in chief of *Webster's New World Dictionary* was likewise more uncomfortable with epithets than with the old sexual vocabulary, referring to "terms of racial or ethnic opprobrium" as "those true obscenities."

In what sense are racial slurs obscenities? *Obscene* is the term we use to describe our worst, most offensive words, which up until the recent past have been the sexual obscenities. Racial slurs access a taboo that is now as strong as or stronger than those against mentioning or revealing certain body parts, and so we call them obscene

Britain to fend for itself around AD 400, in contrast, all traces of Latin quickly disappeared, replaced by the languages of the invading Germanic tribes. There is no record of *cunt* in English until the twelfth or thirteenth century, in Gropecuntelane, the name of a London street in the red-light district. (Some other proper names from these years have also come down to us. We have Gunoka Cuntles [1219] and Bele Wydecunthe [1328], suitable partners for Godwin Clawcuncte [1066] and Robert Clevecunt [1302]. If the Millers' ancestors ground grain, and the Taylors' sewed cloth, what did Godwin's and Robert's do—and whatever happened to some poor relative of cuntless Gunoka's?) So, though *cunnus* and *cunt* look related, it is more probable that they are not. Whether *cunt* comes from Latin or from Old English, centuries elapsed between its supposed origin and its first appearance in English. Both words, however, fulfill the same role in their respective languages.

Cunnus was frequently used as the *vox propria*—the most direct, most basic word for what it represents—and appears this way in graffiti from the city of Pompeii, which was preserved to an extraordinary degree when Mt. Vesuvius erupted in AD 79. "Corus licks cunt" (*Corus cunnum lingit*) and "Jucundus licks the cunt of Rustica" (*Iucundus cunum lingit Rusticae*), for example, appear on Pompeian apartment buildings. You can find accusations (boasts?) like these on walls, stadium bleachers, and playground equipment across America today. Another graffito is more effusive: "It is much better to fuck a hairy cunt than one which is smooth; it holds in the steam and stimulates the cock" (*Futuitur cunnus pilossus multo melius quam glaber / eadem continet vaporem et eadem verrit mentulam*). You might find something along these lines today too, except that it would probably be extolling the opposite, singing the praises of Brazilian waxes. In these examples, *cunt* is obscene—it would be shocking to see it scrawled on the walls of a building—but not insulting or derogatory. It is just the most direct word to use when talking about a most immodest subject.

The Romans also harnessed the word's power in the service of insult and degradation. Martial, a master of abusive quips, wrote a poem about an old woman who plucks her pubic hair. (The Romans appear to have been of two minds about depilation. On the one hand, "it is better to fuck a hairy cunt," but on the other, women often plucked their pubic hair or singed it with an oil lamp. The very rich and very decadent might even employ a *picatrix*, a young female slave whose job was to arrange her mistress's pubic hair.) Martial asks rhetorically:

> Why do you pluck your aged cunt, Ligeia? Why stir up the ashes in your tomb? Such elegances befit girls; but you cannot even be reckoned an old woman anymore. Believe me, Ligeia, that is a pretty thing for Hector's wife to do, not his mother. You are mistaken if you think this is a cunt when it no longer has anything to do with a cock. So, Ligeia, for very shame don't pluck the beard of a dead lion.

The poet is mocking elderly women who don't act their age, who still feel sexual urges and act on them. The Romans felt that excessive sexual desire revealed a lack of self-control, even a lack of moral fitness. A woman Ligeia's age should no longer feel desire, or, if she is still under the sway of passions she should have conquered years ago, she should certainly never act on them. She needs to stop fixing herself up for sex—to stop thinking about it entirely. In using *cunt* instead of some more delicate euphemism such as *female parts* (*partes muliebres*), genitals (*genitalia*), or even *parts of shame* (*pudenda*), Martial stresses the indignity, even the disgustingness, of Ligeia's practice.

And, like today, sometimes people two thousand years ago just had to let loose. On the wall of a Pompeian inn, someone has scratched:

> Here I bugger Rufus, dear to . . . :
> despair, you girls.
> Arrogant cunt, farewell!

The writer has been turned off the female sex—he'll sleep with boys or men from now on, to the great sadness of women everywhere. The last line implies that one woman in particular was responsible for his disillusionment, and he takes his leave of her by calling her a cunt. (He might also, of course, be renouncing the Platonic idea of Cunt, but I like to think that some particular woman has driven him into the arms of Rufus and quasi-immortality.) He uses *cunnus* as an insult, as a fighting word. His reaction—that he will go off and sleep with boys from now on—would be a bit unusual in our culture, but we'll get to that later.

caco = to goe to the stoole
meio = to pisse, to make water or urine

—Thomas Thomas, *Dictionarium*, 1587

Words for excretion are very similar in Latin and in English. *Caco* (to shit) was the standard obscene term for defecation, and, like *shit*, was a little less taboo than the sexual obscenities. As an agrarian society, Rome had lots of nouns for different kinds of shit, most of which were vulgar but not obscene—the kind of thing farmers could talk about, but which you wouldn't mention in front of the emperor. *Merda* is the most vulgar, the closest Latin equivalent to the noun *shit*. If you wanted to say "This food is crap!" you would use *merda*, as Martial does in an epigram. He describes a beautiful tart passed around at a dinner, but after a certain Sabidius blows on it, "no one could touch it—it was shit" (*nemo potuit tangere: merda fuit*). *Stercus* was more like our *excrement*, while *fimus* referred specifically to cow dung. And *laetamen* was a specialized word for manure, excrement used as fertilizer.

Caco was not as bad as words such as *cunnus* or *futuo* partly because Roman taboos against defecation were not as strong as those against sexual behavior. *Cacare* was thought to be an act best done in private, but necessity meant that most Romans, even highborn citizens, shat in quasi-public places at least some of the time. The houses of the wealthy might have had private privies, but most apartment blocks had a single latrine for multiple dwellings, with several seats but no walls, curtains, or other dividers between them. (*Privy* and *private* share the same root, the Latin *privatus*. The etymology implies that what happens there is something that should be concealed, like one's "privy member," one's penis.) There were also gigantic public latrines, called *foricae*, with up to a hundred seats. As the Roman Empire expanded, public latrines were seen as a mark of civilization, bringing sanitation to the masses. They were usually connected to a system of sewers that would carry the waste out of the city, solving the problem (in theory) of people tossing excrement into the streets. Latrines could be very grand, with marble seats, paintings on the walls, and a channel of running water near people's feet to catch any urine that wasn't aimed quite properly. The channel also served as a place to rinse out the little sponges on sticks that Romans used instead of toilet paper. Some *foricae* were a bit more like the public restrooms of today—small, dark, and stinky. Whether grand or less so, a multiseat latrine would not provide much physical privacy, but a modicum of it was created in other ways. For example, it was considered rude to talk too much to people nearby—Martial makes fun of a man who chats people up in the latrines all day, trying to finagle a dinner invitation. The seats themselves were hidden from public view, so that passers-by on the street couldn't look in through doors or windows. It must have been much like modern urinals, where, I am informed, certain codes of behavior protect men's modesty—don't talk, don't linger, and, most especially, don't look at another man's penis—except that in the *foricae*, men and women might occupy the seats together, and they were defecating.

Latin had two words for urine, *lotium* and *urina*. *Urina* was a polite, medical term in Latin, and, of course, becomes our equally polite *urine*. *Lotium* was originally a metaphor, meaning "liquid for washing." That's because the Romans washed their clothes in it. People called fullers (*fullones*) left jars around the city for people to pee into, and collected them. They poured diluted urine into big vats, dropped the clothes in, and stomped on them to get the dirt out and whiten them. Clothes had to undergo quite a bit of rinsing to get rid of the smell. Anyone with experience in these matters today—parents of young children, pet owners—might wonder, though, whether the great Roman orators didn't always smell faintly of piss.

The basic Latin terms for urination, *meio* and *mingo*, were not really bad words at all. They were not polite, but they were by no means obscene. The Roman taboo against peeing in public was very weak—men would piss anywhere and everywhere, and even women probably squatted down outside over the fullers' pots. Even more so than with *caco*, it is hard to get upset about someone saying *piss* when you see people doing it all the time.

In these words we feel our kinship with the Romans. They bring to the fore that we have similar ideas about the best ways to insult people, about what's satisfying to scrawl on a bathroom wall, about what is and isn't taboo. (Despite the fact that all-temperature Piss is no longer an option when we shop for laundry detergent.) The Roman model of bad language is like ours, based on taboos about body parts, their excretions, and certain of their acts.

Other swearwords commonly heard on the streets of ancient Rome, however, reveal bigger differences.

futuo = to doe the act of generation

—John Rider, *Riders Dictionarie*, 1626

At first glance, *futuo* is quite similar to its English equivalent, *fuck*. On the walls of the *lupanar*—the brothel—in Pompeii, a number of men have recorded "Here I have fucked many girls" (*Hic ego puellas multas futui*) or "I came here and fucked, then went home" (*Hic ego cum veni futui / deinde redei domi*). It is not generally used aggressively, though, as it so often is in English. Latin had other words that were more insulting in themselves. It was much stronger abuse to threaten *irrumatio*, call someone a *cinaedus* (a faggot or pansy, the passive partner in male-male sex), or accuse someone of *cunnum lingere*, so perhaps Romans didn't really need *futuo* as a term of aggression.

When *fututor* is used in Latin, it does not always have the negative connotation it carries in English. It simply means "one who fucks." Sometimes it is even a word of high praise, as this graffito, written outside the entrance of a Pompeian house, suggests: "Fortunatus, you sweet soul, you total fucker. Written by one who knows" (*Fortunate, animula dulcis, perfututor. / Scribit qui novit*). Did Fortunatus live there, and was he happy to have his prowess announced to passers-by?

As the most direct and shocking Latin word for sexual intercourse, however, *futuo* could, like *cunnus*, be useful in insults and abuse. Octavian, also known as Augustus, the first emperor of Rome, wrote an epigram that employs it to denigrate his enemies:

> Because Antony fucks Glaphyra, Fulvia decided to punish *me* by making me fuck her in turn. I should fuck Fulvia? What if Manius begged me to bugger him? Would I do it? I think not, if I had any sense. "Either fuck or fight," she says. Ah, but my cock is dearer to me than life itself. Let the trumpets sound.

Augustus wrote this poem to justify his conduct in the Perusine War (41–40 BC), a brief conflict he fought against rebel soldiers led by Fulvia, Mark Antony's wife. It is a masterly epigram, accomplishing many things at once. It blames Fulvia for starting the war, eliding the rebels' real complaints—lack of pay and land

Augustus had promised them. Instead, he portrays Fulvia as an irrational woman, angry that her husband is sleeping with the prostitute Glaphyra, and seeking to punish him by committing adultery herself. She demands that Augustus offer his services, threatening him, and the rest of Rome, if he refuses. He completes his poetic character assassination by explaining that he *can't* oblige Fulvia—she is too repellent, or perhaps diseased, to fuck. To preserve the health and dignity of his *mentula* (penis), Augustus is forced to fight. Martial, who was certainly a qualified judge of obscene, abusive epigrams, praises how Augustus is not afraid "to speak with Roman plainness" (*Romana simplicitate loqui*). Politicians today only wish they could "go negative" like this.

This epigram highlights the connection between sex and violence so often found in obscene words and slang. In Latin, and to a smaller extent in English, the penis is a weapon—*telum* (spear), *hasta* (javelin)—and sex is depicted as brutal, in slang such as *caedo* (to cut), *battuo* (to beat), or the English *banging, drilling, nailing*, and so on. The Latin word *vagina*, in fact, originally referred to the sheath of a sword. This connection between sex and violence was quite literal in the Perusine War. The opposing sides lobbed sling bullets at one another engraved with messages such as "Fulvia's clitoris" and "Octavian sucks cock."

A final difference between *futuo* and the English *f*-word is that in Latin, women couldn't fuck. *Futuo* referred only to the man's participation in the act. Women could be fucked, as one likely prostitute wrote on the walls of the Pompeian brothel: *Fututa sum hic* (I have been fucked here). Though the woman's part of *fututio* is referred to in the passive voice, that doesn't mean that Roman women just lay there. Latin has a unique verb for what women do—*criso*, which might be translated as "wriggling." It is also obscene, though not as much so as *futuo*, and far less common. The Romans preferred to talk and joke about the male role in the action.

landica = an andiron*

—Thomas Holyoake, *A Large Dictionary in Three Parts*, 1676

Some Roman women *were* capable of *fututio*, though not "normal" ones. They were the lesbians, called *tribades*, who were thought to have a massively overdeveloped clitoris that they used like a penis. (*Lesbian* comes from the Greek word *lesbiazein*, "to do it Lesbos style." In ancient times, however, the inhabitants of Lesbos were known not for girl-on-girl action but for fellatio.) *Lesbian* as we know it today came into use in English only around the turn of the twentieth century. Before then, *tribade* was still the ordinary word for a woman who "practices unnatural vice," as the *Oxford English Dictionary* put it until 1989. Martial attacks one such *tribas*, Bassa, recounting how he had thought that she was a woman of great moral probity because she was never in the company of men, only other women. To his horror, he discovers that she is indeed unchaste, and in a way he hadn't expected:

> So I confess I thought you a Lucretia; but Bassa, for shame, you were a fucker [*fututor*]. You dare to join two cunts and your monstrous organ feigns masculinity.†

Martial describes what she does by using the active form of *futuo*—she is a *fututor*, just like a man, her clitoris substituting for a penis.

The Latin word for the clitoris is, as we have seen, *landica*, and it was one of the worst in the language—almost too bad even for epigrams. We know it mostly from graffiti such as "Eupl[i]a, loose,

---

*An andiron is one of a pair of metal supports used to hold up logs in a fireplace. This is not a bizarre mistranslation, but an attempt to avoid obscenity through metaphor. In Latin, the female genitalia were often depicted through baking metaphors: the vagina as the oven, the labia as the hearth.

† Lucretia was a Roman paragon of chastity. When she was raped by Tarquinus, she committed suicide rather than bear the shame.

of large clitoris" (*Eupla laxa landicosa*). This is not praise of said Euplia. A *cunnus laxus* was sexually undesirable, and might even hint at character flaws—loose *cunnus*, loose morals. And "of large clitoris" links her with the lesbians. *Landica* was such a bad word in part because of its primacy in the perverted (according to the Romans) relations of the *tribades*. Martial's epigram shares this ancient disgust—Bassa "dares" to join cunts, as if this is in violation of the natural order, and her clitoris is "monstrous," not simply "big." It is horrific that women have sex like men. (It is also, as various scholars of Roman sexuality note, most likely a misrepresentation of what Roman lesbians actually did with each other.)

But there are other reasons *landica* is so obscene, ones that, to modern eyes, reflect more positively on the ancient Romans. People swear about what they care about, and the Romans cared about the clitoris. They thought that both male and female partners in intercourse had to achieve orgasm for conception to occur, a wrong, but gallant, idea. Medical writings show that they knew where the clitoris was, and what it did—that stimulating it would help bring about those orgasms thought to be necessary for the creation of sons, soldiers, empire.

In English, we don't really have a swearword for the clitoris. There's *clit*, but it's just not that offensive, and it is rarely used. If you call someone a *clit*, you'll probably get puzzled laughter, or even a pitying look. Perhaps English-speaking women should be insulted that *clitface* and *clit for brains* are more funny than shocking, that the clitoris doesn't register high enough in the cultural consciousness to deserve its own swearword.

I don't mean to portray the Romans either as medical experts or as proto-Casanovas who devoted their time to unlocking the sexual secrets of the female body. They were plenty misinformed about sex and about women. They believed, for example, that women provided the "matter" during conception, and men the "form." Women were the "dirt," according to the Greek authority on everything, Aristotle; men planted the "seed." And bodies were regulated by a balance of four humors. Men were hot and dry; women were cold and wet. This theory of humors is critical to understanding Roman views of sexuality. The boundary between male and female was not as fixed as it is today. If a woman "heated up," she could become a man; if a man "cooled down," he could become a woman. *Tribades*, then, were women who had gotten hotter, drying their "natural" moisture, and causing their clitoris to grow until it became like a penis. Today, people can change sex completely through surgery, or partly through hormones or cross-dressing. But it is hard, requiring money and determination. In ancient Rome, it was easy—too easy, it was feared. Hang around females too long, spend time playing the lyre instead of performing the military exercises that burned off moisture and kept your temperature up, and you just might find yourself turning into a woman.

Landica and *futuo* are words that on one level are very similar to their English counterparts. The Latin *f*-word means the same thing and is of the same register as the English one, and it is possible at least to imagine an English in which *clit* is a swearword like *cock* and *dick*, since it too is a direct word for a body part in a taboo zone. But the words also reveal some differences, particularly in the way Romans thought about the role of women during sex, and about the physiology that helped to determine that role.

Now we come to the really strange words, ones we don't have in English, or ones that are so different from their English equivalents that they are hardly recognizable. These words reveal fundamental differences in the way Romans thought about sexuality, masculinity, power, and the concept of obscenity itself.

irrumo = to suck in
pedico = ?
—Thomas Thomas, *Dictionarium*, 1587

The Latin word for man is *vir*, but in Rome this was not merely an indication of biological sex. *Vir* carried with it a set of cultural expectations of what "real men" should be. *Viri* were freeborn citizens, exercised strong self-control, and tried to dominate others, particularly through sexual penetration. (Think twice if ever someone should praise you as "*vir*tuous.") Men who didn't fulfill these social criteria were called *homines* (a neutral word, without the glory of *vir*) or, especially in the case of slaves, *pueri* (which literally means "boys").

What a man did sexually played a large role in whether he was a *vir*, but *whom* he did it with didn't matter at all. Our categories of "heterosexual" and "homosexual" were meaningless in Rome. It was assumed that "normal" men would want to sleep with women, boys, and sometimes adult men, and that each type of partner provided different pleasures and problems. What a man did with these various partners was the key thing. He must always be the active, penetrating one. He must never allow someone else to penetrate him—that would make him soft (*molles*), effeminate, less than a man.

The Latin vocabulary that developed around this sexual schema is all about the penetration of orifices. *Futuo* could be translated more literally as "to penetrate a vagina." *Pedicare* means "to penetrate an anus." Nothing in the verb specifies whether the anus belongs to a male or to a female—both possibilities were open to a *vir*, though the anuses of boys were generally considered more desirable. An epigram of Martial makes this vividly clear:

> Catching me with a boy, wife, you upbraid me harshly and point out that you too have an arse [*culum*]. How often did Juno say the same to her wanton Thunderer! Nonetheless he lies with strapping Ganymede. The Tirynthian used to lay aside his bow and bend Hylas over: do you think Megara had no buttocks? Fugitive Daphne tormented Phoebus: but the Oebalian boy bade those flames vanish. Though Briseis often lay with her back to Aeacus's son, his smooth friend was closer to him. So kindly don't give masculine names to your belongings, wife, and think of yourself as having two cunts [*cunnos*].

The wife is upset that her husband is unfaithful, not that he is what we today would call "gay." He is *not* gay—the category "gay" did not exist in ancient Rome, in which there were no "gay" men as we know them. Berate him though his wife does for going outside the marriage, the husband's desires are perfectly normal—*most* men wanted to sleep with both women and boys. She tells her husband that if he wants *pedicare*, he can do *her*, but he refuses, citing the examples of gods and heroes (Jupiter, Hercules, Apollo, and Achilles—not such shabby company) who have preferred their boy lovers to their wives in this respect. The poem ends with a cutting rebuke—the wife should not even use the word *culus* (ass) when referring to herself. Her ass is so different from, and inferior to, a boy's that she should instead say she has two cunts.

The verb *irrumare* involves pretty much the only other orifice available—it means "to penetrate the mouth." *Irrumo* is a bit different from the other verbs because, as we've seen, it usually carries a threat of violence. You might do it for pleasure, but part of that pleasure would be in humiliating the man you are forcing into fellatio. (You might also irrumate a woman or a boy, but in written records, adult men are usually the target.) Where we today would very likely use some form of *fuck* to threaten or insult someone, Romans would have used *irrumare*. (We do have the option of *suck my dick*, but in English this lacks the connotations of violence and domination carried by the Latin word. It is more of an obnoxious invitation, less of a threat.) There's a graffito in Ostia, a port town near Rome, that uses *irrumo* this way. It appears in a room that scholars think was a *taberna* (a small shop that sold drinks and food) in ancient times, whose owners made the interesting aesthetic choice to decorate with a bathroom theme: on the walls were paintings of people on latrines, accompanied by slogans such as "Push hard, you'll be finished more quickly." One of these slogans is *Bene caca et irrumo medicos*—"Shit well and fuck [irrumate] the doctors."

The poet Catullus assails some of his critics with *irrumo* too. Catullus was accused of effeminacy because he wrote about dalliances

Two of the "Seven Sages" who decorated a tavern in Ostia and entertained drinkers with their advice about excretion: "Solon rubbed his belly to shit well" (on left) and "Thales recommends that if you have a hard time shitting you should strain" (on right).

with women, the delights of long afternoons spent in bed, rather than about war or farming like the more manly Virgil. He asserts his impugned masculinity with a verbal attack, beginning one poem: *Pedicabo ego vos et irrumabo*, "I will bugger you and make you suck me." Threatening to stick his penis into the assholes and mouths of other men is supposed to prove that he is a *real* man. Displaying too much interest in sex with women, in contrast, is what got him accused of effeminacy in the first place.

Decimus Valerius Asiaticus provides a similar defense of his masculinity. This distinguished nobleman was falsely accused of a litany of crimes and moral failings by Publius Suillius Rufus, a crony of the empress Messalina, in AD 47. Asiaticus refused to answer any of the false charges until his honor was stained with an allegation of "softness of body"—effeminacy. Then he scornfully replied, "Suillius, cross-examine your sons: they will testify that I am a man" (*interroga, Suilli, filios tuos: virum esse me fatebuntur*). The proof that he is *not* effeminate, not perverted—that he is a *real* man—is that he has sodomized the sons of his accuser.

Scholars refer to the model of masculinity embodied in these verbs (*futuo, pedico,* and *irrumo*) as "priapic," after the garden god Priapus. Priapus was happy to use his giant, always erect penis to penetrate women, boys, or men, for pleasure, certainly, but also to establish who was boss. Integral to this priapic model of sexuality is the idea of sex as domination, as a means of exercising control. This is not to say that individuals didn't have tender, loving sexual relations, but that in the wider cultural paradigm, sex was about power. Many epigrams from the *Priapea,* the collection of poetry dedicated to the god, show this fusion of sex and domination. One poem has Priapus addressing potential thieves: "I warn you, boy, you will be buggered; girl, you will be fucked; a third penalty awaits the bearded thief" (*Percidere, puer, moneo; futuere, puella; barbatum furem tertia poena manet*). *Percido* literally means "to hit"—this was vulgar slang for *pedicatio* (anal sex). The third penalty refers to *irrumatio,* the proper way to have sex with adult men. On one level, this epigram is a joke— it is supposed to be spoken by an effigy of the god as he stands in a garden to protect it, and there is little he can actually do to effect his threats. On another, though, it is a very serious illustration of a very Roman idea about sexuality: that sex and aggression, sex and domination, sex and power are joined and cannot be put asunder.

Not all men, of course, enjoyed subjugating all these partners equally, as Priapus does. Virgil, whose virile verse was the model for generations of poets, was more inclined to boys (*libidinis in pueros pronioris*); Ovid preferred women. In his *Ars Amatoria* (*The Art of Love*), Ovid reveals that "I hate those embraces in which both partners do not consummate; that is why boys please me but little." But these are just *preferences*, not exclusive sexual orientations. Virgil and Ovid slept both with men and with women; they just preferred one sex over another. You might say that they were on different ends of the Roman sexual spectrum, but still within the "normal" range. Sometimes, though, someone comes along whose inclinations are so strange that Latin lacks words for them. The emperor Claudius was, as the historian Suetonius writes, "of an extreme lust towards women, completely lacking in experience of males" (*libidinis in feminas profusissimae, marum omnino expers*). Suetonius is flummoxed by what we today would call a heterosexual—he has no vocabulary to describe a man who is attracted sexually only to women. He does not see this as a good thing, incidentally. His description of Claudius's habits comes in a long list of his faults, from gluttony—he would eat so much that he would pass out, and his attendants would make him vomit with a feather—and a gambling addiction to a "cruel and bloodthirsty disposition."

If a *vir*'s desires were as catholic as those of Priapus, he could sleep with a large proportion of Roman society. Not everyone, however, was fair game. It was immoral, and illegal, to sleep with freeborn women (except one's wife), freeborn boys, or freeborn men. They possessed what was called *pudicitia*, roughly translated as "modesty," which meant, in practice, the right not to be penetrated. Having sex with them was *stuprum*, punishable by banishment, loss of property, and loss of certain legal rights. Only slaves, freedmen and women, and prostitutes (who might have once been free but had fallen on hard times) could be solicited without censure. "Only," though, was a large proportion of the population—25 to 40 percent of people were slaves in the Roman Empire, and probably an equal percentage were the freed slaves known as *liberti*.

Romans were especially concerned that no one should commit *stuprum* with freeborn boys. Boys of this class wore special clothing, the *toga praetexta* (a white toga with a purple border), to mark them out as future *viri*. When they were in the public baths, they wore a necklace called a *bulla*, which often featured one or two of those phallus-shaped *fascini*, to signify their status while naked. This is in direct contrast to the Greeks, whose attitude to sexuality was generally quite similar to the Romans', except where pederasty was concerned. The Greeks saw pederasty as a rite of passage, the way a boy became a man. An older man (the *erastes*, "lover") would choose a boy between twelve and seventeen as his *eromenos* (beloved). He acted as mentor, teaching the boy about *arete*, the Greek manly virtues, including courage, strength, fairness, and honesty. The Greeks appear to have been a bit conflicted about this, both idealizing the pederastic bond and also trying to regulate just what lovers were allowed to do with each other. No penetration was supposed to occur, for example. The *erastes* was supposed to limit himself to intercrural (between the thighs) intercourse, as shown on any number of Greek vases.

The Romans saw no dilemma. They were sure that pederasty with slaves was right and with freeborn boys was wrong. Penetration would destroy a boy's *pudicitia*, making it impossible for him to develop into a *vir*, into a useful citizen of Rome.

cinaedus = one abused against nature, past all shame, a wanton dancer, also a fish
catamitus = a boy hired to bee abused contrarie to nature, a Ganymede*

—John Rider, *Riders Dictionarie*, 1626

Romans had nothing but derogatory words for men or boys who allowed themselves to be penetrated, and two of the worst were

---

* *Cinaedus* was used for a fish that wriggles its tail—suggestively, the Romans thought. Ganymede is Zeus's/Jupiter's cupbearer, the archetype for a boy lover.

catamitus and *cinaedus*. These are Greek loanwords, suggesting that penetrated men were thought to be not just less manly but less than fully Roman, practicing what the culture would have preferred to see as "foreign" vices.

As with stereotypes of gay men today, *cinaedi* were supposed to have distinctive, feminine mannerisms. They took too much care over their appearance, depilating their legs, chests, and other parts of their bodies, anointing themselves with sweet-smelling lotions, and applying makeup. They sometimes wore women's clothing, and performed female activities such as spinning wool. Scipio Aemilianus, a famous general of the Republic who presided over the destruction of Carthage (a "real" man, in other words), described what he saw as the disgusting habits of *cinaedi*: "a man who daily is adorned before his mirror, covered with perfumes, whose eyebrows are shaven, who walks around with his beard plucked out and his thighs depilated . . . who wore a long-sleeved tunic." The long-sleeved tunic was a Greek fashion and would have prevented the wearer from being scratched by the rough hairshirt-esque wool of his toga. Manly Roman men toughed it out with only a short-sleeved tunic under their togas, or better yet, nothing.

The most surefire way to identify a *cinaedus*, however, was that he "scratched his head with one finger." It seems to me that scholars have enjoyed themselves mightily figuring out what this means. Some believe that the finger in question must have been the middle one, the *digitus impudicus*, already known as a sign of aggression and disrespect, from its resemblance to the erect penis. The *cinaedus* scratched his head with it to broadcast his desires to others in the know. Other scholars argue that the gesture is simply effeminate, that the *cinaedus* was so concerned about his coiffure that he wouldn't risk disturbing it by scratching with more than one digit. The finger aside, Romans had a stereotype of the effeminate man that in many ways resembles the one we have today.

The *cinaedus* or *catamitus* is not "gay," though, however much he may look it. He is *passive*. He does not penetrate, the only "normal" thing for a man to do, so now all bets are off. Romans thought him likely to indulge in all sorts of head-scratchingly deviant behavior, with men and with women alike.

fello = to suck
lingo cunnum = ?

—Thomas Thomas, *Dictionarium*, 1587

Now we come finally to the worst of the worst, the most obscene, most offensive things you could say in Latin. The worst insult you could throw at a Roman was that he practiced *cunnum lingere*. This was deemed the most twisted of all deviant behaviors, the very height of abnormality. Following close upon it on the list of things virtuous Romans didn't do was *fellatio*, and to be called a *fellator* was almost as bad as to be accused of *cunnilingus*.* What was so wrong with performing oral sex in the Roman Empire that it gave rise to the worst of Latin insults? Rome had a strong taboo against oral-genital contact (unless you were on the receiving end). Oral sex befouled the mouth, the "most sacred part of the body." A mouth that has performed oral sex was dirtier than the genitals themselves, more shameful even than those parts perverted by penetration. An epigram by Martial sums up this attitude, prevalent in Roman discourse: "Zoilus, you spoil the bathtub washing your arse. To make it filthier, Zoilus, stick your head in it."

---

*It is bad to be called a cocksucker (our equivalent to *fellator*) in English too, but this is mostly because of our culture's negative views of homosexuality. A Roman woman could be attacked as a *fellatrix*, but it doesn't make sense in English to insult a woman as a cocksucker. As Lenny Bruce reportedly said, "You call a guy a cocksucker, that's an insult. You call a lady a cocksucker—hey, that's a nice lady." On the flip side, women can take heart that though *clit* is not a swearword, neither is *cunt licker*.

Both performing fellatio and being anally penetrated were deviant (passive) sexual behaviors, but it was worse to fellate someone. Martial makes this point too:

> You sleep with well-endowed boys, Phoebus, and what stands on them doesn't stand for you. Phoebus, I ask you, what do you wish me to suspect? I wanted to believe you a soft man, but rumor denies that you are a *cinaedus*.

Phoebus is soft (*mollis*)—effeminate, passive—and his penis is not erect, so he can't be a *fututor*, *pedico*, or *irrumator* (a penetrator of vaginas, anuses, or mouths, respectively). Nor is he a *cinaedus* ("pansy," also a fish). There is only one thing left—he must be a *fellator*, even lower on what we might call the scale of humiliation.

A man who performs fellatio is not "gay"—he is just as likely to *lingere cunnum*. These acts are two sides of the same coin: "They are twin brothers, but they lick different groins. Say, are they more like or unlike?" These are both passive sexual activities—neither the *fellator* nor the *cunnilingus* is penetrating anyone. As we've seen, a normal, "active" man will desire to penetrate women, boys, and men; a man who enjoys a "passive" activity such as fellatio will be passive with respect to women too, and to be passive with respect to women means to perform cunnilingus.

The flip side of fellatio is *irrumatio*—that is what the *fellator*'s active partner is doing. But what is the flip side of *cunnilingus*? What is the woman doing? In Roman culture, women were supposed to be sexually passive by nature. They don't have penises and so can't penetrate anyone (except the *tribades*, of course). With *cunnilingus*, the man is taking the passive role, so the woman must in some sense be taking the active role, performing the female equivalent of *irrumatio*. She is fucking the man in his mouth. This was horrifying to ancient Romans for two reasons. It was "unnatural"—women were not supposed to be the active partners, even by implication. And it was completely emasculating. It was bad enough for a

Roman man to be penetrated by another man, but by a woman—
that was shame almost not to be borne, and too powerful an insult
to pass up.

mentula = a mans yarde, his pricke, his privities
verpa = a mans yard

—Thomas Thomas, *Dictionarium*, 1596

Walking around in ancient Rome, one saw a lot of penises.
There were erect penises sculpted, painted, and scratched over door
frames, on chariot wheels, in gardens, on the borders of fields, in

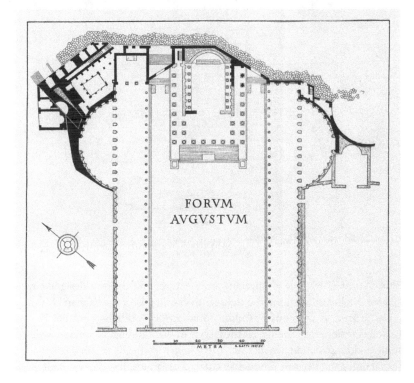

The Forum of Augustus, completed ca. AD 40. Can you find the phallus?

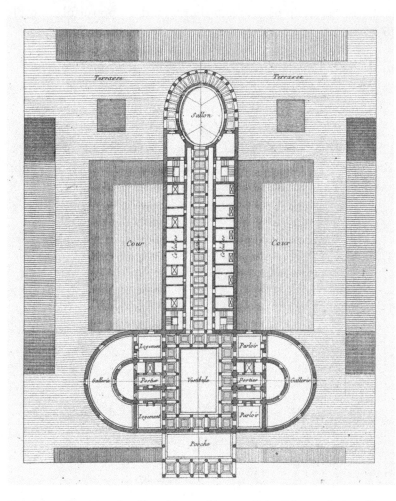

This is another example of "speaking architecture," the Oikema, designed by Claude-Nicholas Ledoux in the eighteenth century. Like the Roman Forum, it was to serve as a place of masculine initiation—it was to be a brothel. In Ledoux's vision, the calming, classical style of the building, combined with some good instruction, would teach the young men inside to subjugate their sexual urges and become productive citizens of France. It was never built.

elaborate murals in reception rooms of fancy villas, hung around the necks of prepubescent boys. Even the Forum of Augustus, the center of Roman political and military life, was designed in the shape of an erection. Some scholars argue that it is an example of *architecture parlante*—a building whose form speaks to its purpose. The forum was where military triumphs were celebrated, where law cases were argued, where boys came to put aside their childish clothing and assume the *toga virilis*, the garment that marked them out as full Roman citizens, as men. Something that today we see only in private was displayed prominently in public in ancient Rome.

Most cultures—including ancient Rome's and our own—dictate that whatever parts of the body should be concealed in clothing must also be concealed in language. Obscenities arise from the body parts and actions that a culture deems unacceptable for public display. Latin captures this link between the body and language by referring to obscene words as *nuda verba*—"naked words." These words represent the thing itself, without the linguistic drapery of euphemism or circumlocution.

Given the prevalence of the public penis, and the link between concealment and obscenity, one would expect that Latin words for the penis would *not* be obscene. If you can *see* penises everywhere in public, you should be able to *say* the word for them in public. But actually, Latin words for the penis *are* obscene. *Mentula* (penis) was quite obscene, and *verpa*—a penis with its foreskin pulled back, hence erect or circumcised—was even worse. Even the word *penis* itself was offensive in Latin, though not as shocking as the two primary obscenities, *mentula* and *verpa*.

This dichotomy between what was seen and what could be said developed because in Rome, obscenity also had religious aspects. According to Freud, taboos have two contradictory directions, at least in the "traditional" societies popular with anthropologists of the early twentieth century. Taboo things are unclean and forbidden, but they are also sacred and consecrated. In ancient Rome, the genitalia were *verecunda* (parts of modesty) and *pudenda* (parts of shame), but they were also *verenda* (parts of respect) and *veretrum* (parts of awe, with a healthy dose of fear). Modern English-speaking societies have lost the latter side of the binary—for us the genitals are shameful, but they inspire no religious respect.

As we've seen, one meaning of the Latin *obscenus* was "of ill omen," signifying things that would taint a religious rite and make it fail. This category mostly included sexual acts and language—a vestal virgin not being quite virgin enough, a priest not abstaining from sex for long enough before a ceremony, insulting the gods with bad words. But this held true for only certain kinds of religious rites. Other kinds actually relied on obscenity for their success. The obscene had its own gods and goddesses, its own place in the smooth running of nature and the Roman state. We've already met the garden god Priapus, with his huge, perpetually erect phallus; Pan was the god of woodland groves and shepherds, with the hindquarters of a goat and his own large, often erect penis. There was also the mysterious Mutunus Tutunus, who may have been nothing *but* a giant erect penis, statues of whom brides had to sit on as part of the wedding ceremony. The erect penis symbolized, and in some sense was supposed to guarantee, fertility.

Obscene language, which represents the genitalia and sex so directly, was likewise used in ceremonies to promote fertility. Uttering these ordinarily taboo words at a wedding, for example, was thought to channel the procreative power of the things to which they referred, ensuring the fertility of the marriage. Wedding guests would sing fescennine songs, full of ribaldry and teasing. Unfortunately, no examples of these survive, but you can get a flavor from an epithalamium, a poem written in honor of a wedding, by Catullus, in which the poet urges the groom to give up his smooth boys now that he is about to be married, and advises the bride to deny her husband nothing (a common euphemism for oral sex in Latin) lest he start to seek his pleasures elsewhere. Obscenity was also an important part of festivals such as the *ludi florales*, the games of Flora, the goddess of spring. At the end of these games, prostitutes danced naked while the crowd shouted obscenities to ensure the fertility of the coming season. Obscene words were thought to be magical, with the power to affect the world. If you wanted a marriage to produce children, or spring to come with healthy crops and young animals, *nuda verba* could help to bring it about.

Rome did not just associate the genitalia with fertility, however. The penis was also a symbol of threatening power. As we have seen, Roman culture thought of sex in terms of domination—the active male penetrates "lesser" creatures, whether women, boys, or passive men, defining himself as a "real man" and as a citizen. This power of the penis could be transferred to different areas. *Bullae*, the necklaces containing phallus-shaped *fascini*, were thought to shield their wearers from the evil eye—they had what is called apotropaic (from the Greek meaning "to ward off") power. Songs containing obscenities could, in the right context, also protect people from evil forces. They were sung when someone's good fortune was likely to attract *invidia*, envy or ill will. They offered protection in two ways—the obscenities themselves contained the power to ward off evil, and the songs' mockery took their subjects down a peg or two, to a level where they no longer invited *invidia*. Victorious generals were serenaded with fescennine songs—their moment of triumph was also a moment of great weakness. When Julius Caesar returned to Rome in 46 BC, for example, he was publicly celebrated for vanquishing the Gauls and publicly mocked for being the *cinaedus* of Nicomedes, king of Bithynia, many years earlier. One verse ran:

> All the Gauls did Caesar vanquish, Nicomedes vanquished him;
> Lo! now Caesar rides in triumph, victor over all the Gauls,
> Nicomedes does not triumph, who subdued the conqueror.

Some verses were even more specific, calling Nicomedes Caesar's *pedicator* (butt fucker). The obscenity and mockery of these verses were thought to protect Caesar at this vulnerable moment when hundreds, even thousands of people might be watching him with envy.

Obscene words were also involved in Roman cursing. Today *cursing* is often used to mean obscene language (does the government still have "good reason to regulate cursing and nudity on broadcast television?" the *New York Times* asked recently). But *curse* originally had a much narrower definition, referring to language that wished ill on someone and called on a deity to make it happen. In English, our most familiar curses are of the form "(May) God damn you!" and "Go to hell!" Words such as *fuck* are curses in the loose sense of the term, but "Fuck you!" might be considered a curse according to its narrower meaning as well. As Lenny Bruce supposedly noted, it makes little sense to tell someone off in this way: "What's the worst thing you can say to anybody? 'Fuck you, Mister.' It's really weird, because if I really wanted to hurt you I should say 'Unfuck you, Mister.' Because 'Fuck you' is really *nice*!" Why wish something pleasurable on the person you are trying verbally to abuse? Some theories hold that "Fuck you!" is equivalent to "Go fuck yourself!" and that the impossibility furnishes the insult. It takes two to have sex, masturbation isn't as fun—so there! Other theories hold that the phrase is a threat: "(I'll) fuck you," our equivalent to *irrumabo vos*. The phrase makes the most sense, however, when considered as a curse formula, with *fuck* simply replacing the *damn* in "Damn you!" A powerfully taboo body-related word substitutes for the weakly taboo religious one so that the curse can retain its impact.

Roman curses were much more elaborate and ritualistic. They were scratched on thin pieces of lead and tin, tightly folded up, pierced with a nail, and cast into wells or tombs so that they could reach the gods of the underworld, whose aid they invoked. They were called *defixiones*—binding spells—because they were supposed to restrain or bind the person mentioned in the curse. A typical example comes from a tablet near Rome:

> Malchio son/slave of Nikon: his eyes, hands, fingers, arms, nails, hair, head, feet, thigh, belly, buttocks, navel, chest, nipples, neck,

mouth, cheeks, teeth, lips, chin, eyes, forehead, eyebrows, shoulder-blades, shoulders, sinews, guts, marrow [?], belly, cock [*mentula*], leg, trade, income, health, I do curse ["bind," *deficio*] in this tablet.

Whatever Malchio had done, it made somebody really angry. *Bind* at first might seem an ineffectual verb with which to curse, but the idea is that such restraint renders powerless the things bound. Gladiators and charioteers, thieves, and unfaithful partners of both sexes were common targets of *defixiones*. On the back of Malchio's tablet there is a curse directed at Rufa Publica (Rufa the "public woman," the prostitute) that binds her body parts in a similar fashion, including her nipples (*mamillae*) and *cunnus*. Perhaps Rufa and Malchio had gotten a thing going and her cuckolded lover cursed them both. Or perhaps the curser simply wanted to save some money, gratifying two unrelated grudges with one curse tablet. In any case, the use of obscene words in *defixiones* seems to have had no particular significance for the working of the curse. A word such as *mentula* was employed simply as the *vox propria*, the most direct word for a thing, on a par with *dentes* (teeth) or *pedes* (feet). The concept of cursing, though, is closely connected to obscenity. The *defixiones* were, like some Roman *obscenitas*, a religious language—they called on the gods to effect the curser's wishes. In modern English, *cursing* has mostly lost its religious implications, and its meaning has changed to indicate the taboo words for body parts and actions that were a feature of Latin cursing but were not of its essence.

How We Recognize Latin Obscenity

How can we be sure that the words we've been talking about are actually obscene? Latin is a dead language. No one has a firsthand sense of what was sayable and what wasn't. How do scholars know, for example, that *cunnus* was a very, very bad word, while *meio* was not obscene at all?

The first tool linguists use is the hierarchy of genres. Latin literature observes a strict linguistic decorum, with certain kinds of words considered appropriate for particular genres. From most salacious to least, the scale goes:

1. Graffito and epigram
2. Satire
3. Oratory and elegy
4. Epic

The most taboo words are found in the graffiti that were scratched everywhere in the Roman Empire—inside and outside houses, on columns in the Forum, in the public latrines, on gravestones, on sling bullets fired at enemies. If Pompeii is representative, and scholars generally agree that it is, most Roman cities would have been covered in scrawl. Occasionally the graffiti "artists" themselves took notice of this abundance, as one did in the amphitheater in Rome: "Oh wall, I am amazed that you have not fallen down since you support the loathsome scribblings of so many writers." Walls were often the most convenient place to put any "loathsome scribblings" you might want to get off your chest. Romans didn't have paper; vellum, made of animal skin, was extremely expensive; and wax tablets were neither permanent nor always very handy. Merchants wrote their prices on the walls of their shop and figured sums there. Advertisements for goods and services—including those offered by prostitutes—were inscribed on buildings across Pompeii. Election notices can also still be seen there, in which various groups of tradesmen recommended various candidates for office: "The goldsmiths unanimously urge the election of Gaius Cuspius Pansa as aedile."* Such notices were so ubiquitous that they attracted their share of parody: "Dickhead recommends Lollius" (*Lollius . . . verpus rogat*).

---

* An aedile was an official responsible for public festivals and for the care of the city—making sure temples, sewers, and so forth were in good repair.

Most graffiti are more personal, from the sweet and touching—marriage and birth announcements—to the shocking, some of which we've already seen. (And sometimes it's both, as in this wish for a happy marriage: "Eulale, may you enjoy good health with your wife Vera and good fucking.") Since the surviving graffiti are so florid in their obscenity, scholars have generally assumed that they were written by schoolboys and "the lower classes," reasoning that only the immature or the vulgar would descend to the level of "Crescens's member is hard—and enormous." But scholars who study ancient literacy argue that only about 20 percent of the population could read and write, with a somewhat larger percentage possessing rudimentary reading ability. In reality, it must have been the pretty well-educated bragging that "I fucked here."

Epigrams are on a par with graffiti in terms of the language they use. These are short, witty poems that express a single thought or observation. Catullus wrote some, and many were collected into the *Priapea*, but Martial is the acknowledged Roman master of the genre. Martial's twelve books of epigrams depict Roman society, high and low, in all its variety—what happened at dinner parties, in fancy villas, in the public latrines, between husbands and wives, or between prostitutes and clients.

Although he was a Roman citizen, Martial was born in the provinces, in Spain, far from the centers of literary life and political power. His poems were his entrée into Roman high society—he had emperors for his patrons and was made an *eques*, a knight, part of the aristocracy. But using poetry as a means of personal advancement could have unintended, unpleasant consequences, especially for someone as attuned to the nuances of social hierarchy as Martial. Poets couldn't support themselves by the stylus alone. Booksellers took most of the profits from their works, so they relied on patrons to survive.

The patron-client relationship was widespread and quite formalized in ancient Rome. Most Roman citizens were either patrons or clients, and some were both, to different people. Every morning clients went to their patron's house for *salutatio*, the calling hour. The patron would distribute money (*sportula*, "the dole"), give legal advice, and inquire about any problems his clients were having—whether they needed money for a dowry, were having trouble selling their grain, had a sick mother, and so on. In return, clients owed their patrons *obsequium*, submission. (This gives us our word *obsequious*, referring to an overly fawning servility, which goes to the root of the problem with clientship.) They had to support their patrons politically, accompany them on walks around town, and generally be at their beck and call.

This subservient status rankled Martial. Being a client was a passive position, and in a society that equated manliness with action, self-assertion, and domination of others, no man wanted to be passive. It also affected Martial's writing, setting up a dichotomy between his poetry and his personal life. Martial knew well that his epigrams "can't please without a cock" (*non possunt sine mentula placere*)—that people liked them because they were racy, daring, and used obscene language. But as a client, he had to present at least a plausible fiction of being an honest, virtuous man, hence his continual protestations that "my little book doesn't have my morals" (*mores non habet hic meos libellus*) or "my page is wanton, but my life is virtuous" (*lasciva est nobis pagina, vita proba*).

Writers had a license to use bad language in epigrams, which were meant to reveal the often unlovely truth about people and things and so needed to employ the plainest words possible. As Martial says: "A lascivious truth of words, *that* is the language of epigram" (*lascivam verborum veritatem, id est epigrammaton linguam*). It is hard to translate this properly—the Latin implies something like "the truth found in lascivious words," alluding to their ability to expose what people most try to hide.

A poem from the *Priapea* makes it even clearer what kind of language is appropriate for epigrams:

May I die, Priapus, if I am not ashamed to use obscene [*obscenis*]
and improper [*improbis*] words. But when you, a god without
shame, display your balls to me in all openness, I must call a cunt a
"cunt" and a cock a "cock."

Epigrams can also be fun, frivolous poems, full of dirty jokes and
mock insults. Whether their purpose is recreation or moral improvement, their language is *bad*. If a word is found in epigrams and graffiti and nowhere else, we can be pretty sure that it was considered
obscene by the Romans.

If a word appears in satires, it might be bad, but it is most likely
not one of the primary obscenities.* Satires too had a mandate to
reveal the truth about the world (which is, usually, that the vast majority of the population is corrupt, sexually perverse, or neglectful of
the gods—never that people are good, law-abiding, and ready to
help one another). Satires were supposed to use more decorous
language than epigrams, however. We can assume, then, that a word
such as *criso* (what a woman does during sex), which appears in the
works of the satirists Juvenal and Persius, was bad but not deeply
offensive, or the authors would have chosen something more befit-
ting the dignity of their genre.

Going up a step on the ladder, Latin elegies often were sexually
suggestive—Ovid was supposedly banished for his *Ars Amatoria*
(*The Art of Love*)—but their vocabulary was clean. Ovid's *Elegy* 1.5
gives a typical example of this mix of lascivious subject matter and
chaste language (this is Christopher Marlowe's translation, done
while he was a student at Cambridge and published posthumously
in 1603):

---

* The great exception is the first volume of Horace's *Sermones*, where the language is as salty
as that of any epigram. (*Salty* came to mean "racy, piquant, earthy" from two different directions. It describes the language of sailors, "old salts," whose vocabulary is sprinkled with
obscene and vulgar words. In the seventeenth century, however, *salt* was used, as the *Oxford
English Dictionary* puts it, "of bitches: In heat." It came to be applied to people as well,
meaning "lecherous, salacious.")

Then came Corinna in a long loose gown
Her white neck hid with tresses hanging down . . .
I snatched her gown: being thin, the harm was small,
Yet strived she to be covered therewithall,
And striving thus as one that would be cast,
Betrayed herself, and yielded at the last.
Stark naked as she stood before mine eye,
Not one wen in her body could I spy,
What arms and shoulders did I touch and see,
How apt her breasts were to be pressed by me,
How smooth a belly, under her waist saw I,
How large a leg, and what a lusty thigh?
To leave the rest, all liked me passing well,
I clinged her naked body, down she fell,
Judge you the rest, being tired she bade me kiss.
Jove send me more such afternoons as this.

Marlowe's language offers a good approximation of Ovid's—it is racy and suggestive without being obscene.

Roman culture mandated that the language of oratory too should be above reproach, and that its themes should contain nothing titillating, even when recounted in the most restrained of terms. The rhetorician Seneca instructs that when publicly pleading a case for someone, "one must stay far away from every obscenity in both words and thoughts. It is better to be quiet, even if it damages your case, than to speak if it damages your sense of shame." Any words in these genres would not be obscene, even if they were used in a vicious attack on an opponent in a debate, or in a plea for one's mistress to get back into bed. *Crepo*, for instance, must be a polite way to say "to fart"—along the lines of "to break wind"—since the orator Cato uses it in a speech, while *pedo* (also "to fart") is a less polite version, found only in satire and epigram. And we can tell that Romans did not consider *meio* an obscenity, despite its best translation as "to piss," because it too is found in oratory. If not for the hierarchy of genres, our prejudices as English-speakers would lead us to class it as obscene.

Epics are at the top of the list because they deal with such lofty subjects as the Olympian gods, battles, and the founding of nations. The language must be equally elevated. Here, for example, is how Virgil describes Dido and Aeneas getting it on for the first time: "Dido and the Trojan leader make their way / To the same cave. Earth herself and bridal Juno / Give the signal. Fires flash in the Sky / Witness to their nuptials, and the Nymphs / Wail high on the mountaintop." Here is no place for a *cunnus*, or even a little *criso*; if Martial were telling this story, it would have sounded a bit different.

This hierarchy of genres is the most useful tool we have for gauging the relative obscenity of Latin words. If a term is found in graffiti or epigrams and nowhere else, we can be pretty sure that it's a *very* bad word. If it appears in satire, graffiti, and epigrams, it's *pretty* bad, but not one of the worst, and so on, up the ladder. Occasionally, however, Roman authors themselves comment on appropriate language, providing direct evidence for a scale of obscenity. Cicero's letter about the word *mentula* is the most famous example. In this response to his loose-tongued friend Paetus, who mentioned *mentula* in a letter, Cicero discusses the Stoic idea that nothing is obscene, in word or in deed—that "breaking wind should be as free as a hiccough" (*crepitus aiunt aeque liberos ac ructus esse oportere*). Note his use of *crepitus*, the more polite word for "fart." Cicero himself is on the side of modesty—he doesn't agree with the Stoic proverb that "the wise man tells it like it is." But his letter is a lengthy investigation into which words should be avoided, and why. *Penis* is *obscenus*, but it is not as offensive as *mentula*, for which it was originally a euphemism meaning "tail." Cicero will actually write out *penis*, but he only alludes to *mentula*. He appears to consider *landica* and *cunnus* extremely obscene, and *pedo*, *colei* (balls), and *testes* (testicles) less so. *Battuo* (to beat) is merely vulgar slang for *futuo*; the synonymous slang *depso* (to knead) is outright obscene. Authors such as Cicero, who were self-conscious about their language and recorded their thoughts, provide another way for modern linguists to get a feel for swearing in a language long dead.

From Profanity to *Politesse*

If *penis* was obscene to the Romans, why has it become the most proper English term for the male organ of generation? It is not the only Latin word to make this transition. *Vulva*, a polite English word for the external genital organs of the female, was in Latin a vulgar word for the womb. And *vagina* (literally "a sheath," "a scabbard," as we have seen) was originally a crude metaphor for the anus. *Fellatio* and *cunnilingus* aren't as common in English, since they refer to acts that are even more taboo than the body parts they involve. If we ever need to talk about these things, however, they are again our most proper words. How did all these obscene Latin words become our most polite sexual terms in English?

During its long tenure as the language of the Roman Empire, Latin gradually split into two different languages, according to levels of discourse—a literary language that was used by the educated elite and which remained fairly stable over the centuries, and a "vulgar" language that over the years evolved into the Romance vernaculars: French, Italian, Spanish, Portuguese, Romanian, et cetera. In England, there was no vernacular Latin, only the elite language used by the Catholic Church, and later (beginning in the fourteenth century) by humanists, a new class of civil servants cum philosophers who wanted to revitalize ancient Roman and Greek texts and virtues. Latin was the lingua franca through which educated people of various countries could communicate with each other, and it was used this way into the eighteenth century. (John Milton, for example, was appointed Latin secretary to Cromwell's republic in 1649. His job was to compose the government's foreign correspondence in Latin. The poet Andrew Marvell was his assistant.)

Latin was, at this time, what historian and linguist Nicholas Ostler calls "a language for male initiates." These languages are not learned naturally but transmitted through an artificial procedure—school. Latin was handed down from teacher to student unchanged, since no one was using it in daily life, and almost the only people who could speak and write it were well-off and well-educated men. Ordinary people didn't know Latin; women didn't know Latin (with few exceptions, including Queen Elizabeth I); children didn't know Latin. This made the language particularly suitable for talking about things you didn't want the majority of people to understand—dangerous things such as sex. In the Renaissance, when many obscene Latin terms were being rehabilitated, there was great value placed on sexual continence, on staying in control of one's base bodily urges (an ideal in ancient Rome as well, as we've seen). People of weak will and poor judgment—pretty much anyone *not* part of the Latin language community, that is, women, children, and uneducated men—would lose control of themselves if they read or listened to descriptions of sexual activity or even overheard obscene words. Women's passions would be inflamed, and they would become sexually insatiable. Children would be corrupted, their early promise blasted. Latin became the appropriate language in which to talk about sexual parts and actions since it was understood only by the few who wouldn't get carried away reading about, say, penises. And so it remains today. If you are teaching a junior-high sex ed class, you had better say *penis* and *vagina* instead of *cock* and *cunt*—the former are almost abstractions, going as far as words can to desexualize the things they represent.

Though Latin lived on after the fall of the Roman Empire, it never again achieved the same grandeur of obscenity it boasted under the Republic and the Caesars. As it retired into its Renaissance role as the source for polite and technical English vocabulary, however, it left behind the model of obscenity that we still employ today, based on sexually and excrementally taboo body parts and actions. Today we have lost the religious aspects that *obscenitas* possessed—the Shit stands alone, if you will. But, as we will see, the Holy-Shit connection returned in English too, in a slightly different form, in the Middle Ages.

Chapter 2

On Earth as It Is in Heaven

The Bible

Latin showed us how consistent some broad categories of obscenity have been across time and culture, while revealing some interesting differences in the details. But there is another kind of swearing, which was once more powerful than even *landica* could ever hope to be— the oath. Swearing an oath means calling on God to witness that a person is telling the truth or intending to fulfill a promise. I've mentioned that such swearing is still important today in courts of law, oaths of office, and personal relations. In the past, oaths were even more important. Sincere oath swearing was seen as the glue that held society together, and when done falsely or badly—when oaths were blasphemous or vain—it threatened to tear the fabric of civil life apart.

For the origins of oaths as we know and use them, we look of course to religion. Or perhaps we should say that for the origins of religion, we look to the oath. In the Bible, swearing is the foundational act of the Jewish and Christian faiths. The covenants that God makes with Abraham are oaths, pledged by both Abraham and God. For Jews, these oaths establish God's special relationship with the Jewish people; for Christians, they create the conditions for Christ's eventual arrival. Either way, in the beginning was the Word, and the word was an Oath.

Divine Swearing

Almost the first thing we learn about Abram (as Abraham, founder of the three "Abrahamic" monotheistic religions, is originally called) is that God will bless him. God says to him, "Go from your country and your kindred and your father's house to the land that I will show you. I will make of you a great nation, and I will bless you, and make your name great, so that you will be a blessing" (Gen. 12:1–2). It takes a while for God to make good on his pledge, though, and Abram doesn't have much time to waste—he is already seventy-five years old when he gets the call. He leaves his homeland as ordered with his wife, Sarai (later renamed Sarah), spends some time in Egypt, and gets Pharaoh into trouble by claiming that Sarai is his sister, not his wife. The unsuspecting Egyptian marries the still sexy sexagenarian Sarai, and "for her sake" gives Abram "sheep, oxen, male donkeys, male and female slaves, female donkeys, and camels" (Gen. 12:16). In return for Pharaoh's generosity, God afflicts him with plagues until he finally realizes his mistake—"Why did you say, 'She is my sister,' so that I took her for my wife?"—and kicks Abram and his entourage out. Abram then wanders into Canaan, and God repeats his promise of numerous offspring, specifying that Canaan is the land he will give him: "I will make your offspring like the dust of the earth; so that if one can count the dust of the earth, your off-spring also can be counted. Rise up, walk through the length and the breadth of the land, for I will give it to you" (Gen. 13:16–17). Thus begins a long period of wandering, during which Abram begins to doubt that God will—or is able to—fulfill his promises. How can his descendants be like the dust on the ground if he doesn't have any children? Who exactly is going to inherit this land he's living in?

God decides he needs to assuage Abram's doubts and to bind himself to his words even more strongly than he has done so far. He instructs Abram to collect a three-year-old heifer, she-goat, and ram, as well as a turtledove and a pigeon, and then to cut the bigger animals in half. Abram falls into a deep sleep and sees God, in the form of a smoking firepot and a flaming torch, pass between the pieces of the animal carcasses (Gen. 15:7–21). This is God's first covenant with Abraham, in which he formalizes the promises he has been making to give the land of Canaan to Abraham's descendants.

God here enters what amounts to a traditional Hittite covenant, which would have been sworn between enemies at the end of hostilities, between rulers and vassals to set up the terms of their relationship, or by a person committing himself to some weighty action.* A covenant is "a solemn promise made binding by an oath, which may be either a verbal formula or a symbolic action. Such an action or formula is recognized by both parties as the formal act which binds the actor to fulfill his promise." In Hebrew, covenants were said to be "cut," not "made," because the ritual killing and slicing of animals was an important part of the ceremony. The sacrifice sealed the deal—anyone who broke the covenant was supposed to end up as dead as the doves, heifers, or sheep that were killed. The covenant God cuts here is unilateral—it binds God to do what he has promised, but it doesn't require Abram to do anything in return. In walking through the animal sacrifices, God is implicitly swearing an oath that if he breaks his word, he will end up like those slaughtered ruminants.

This is the only place in the Bible where God utters what scholars call a self-curse. Usually he is on the administering end, and it's humans swearing, "So may God do to me"—what will be done is often unexpressed and always assumed to be awful—"if I break my word." (King David swears this way, as do Ruth, Solomon, Saul, and many other figures.) In these oaths, God is expected to carry out whatever horrible punishment the speaker has invited upon him- or herself. But in his first covenant with Abraham, God is putting *himself*

---

*From 1600 to 1200 BC, the Hittites ruled a wide-ranging empire in what is now Turkey, Syria, and possibly Israel. They left fairly extensive written records, including a collection of laws quite similar to those laid down in the early books of the Bible. These differ in some of the details, however. Exodus forbids bestiality on pain of death (Ex. 22:19), for example, while the Hittites had a more complicated view: "If any have intercourse with a pig or a dog, he shall die. If a man have intercourse with a horse or a mule, there is no punishment. But he shall not approach the king, and shall not become a priest. If an ox spring upon a man for intercourse, the ox shall die but the man shall not die. One sheep shall be fetched as a substitute for the man, and they shall kill it. If a pig spring upon a man for intercourse, there is no punishment. If any man have intercourse with a foreign woman and pick up this one, now that one, there is no punishment." The more things change . . .

under a curse. Who will punish *him* if he breaks his word? Who will
ensure that he ends up like the sacrificial animals? (And in what
sense would that be possible?) These questions are analogous to the
"paradox of the stone," a staple of college philosophy classes: can
God, who is omnipotent and thus can do anything, create a stone too
heavy for him to lift? The philosopher Harry Frankfurt, perhaps best
known for his *On Bullshit*, offers a succinct reply, which boils down
to "He can, and then he lifts it." God "can handle situations which he
cannot handle." Likewise, God could destroy himself if he breaks his
oath. God would never need to, however, because he is Truth itself
and would never go back on his word. This early in the Bible, though,
there are some other possible solutions, which we will get to later. In
any case, God has not just made promises to Abram; in cutting the
covenant with him, he has pledged himself even more strongly. He
has sworn.

When Abram is ninety-nine years old—getting on in years even
by biblical standards—God confirms the covenant with him. This
time, though, God requires Abram to do something—this new version is a mutual covenant, with responsibilities on both sides. God
will make Abram the father of a multitude of nations and give his
descendants the land of Canaan, per above; he will also "be God to
you and your offspring after you" (Gen. 17:7) and start calling him
Abraham ("ancestor of a multitude"). For his part, Abraham promises to "be blameless" (Gen. 17:1) and agrees to circumcise the males
of his household, as a sign of the covenant: "So shall my covenant be
in your flesh an everlasting covenant. Any uncircumcised male who
is not circumcised in the flesh of his foreskin shall be cut off from his
people; he has broken my covenant" (Gen. 17:13–14). This appears
to be divine humor, by the way. Anyone who breaks the covenant of
circumcision will be "cut off." (This joke actually occurs twice in the
Bible, making it the most popular joke in a book not known for its
humor. When in the New Testament Paul argues that Christ has ab-
rogated the need for circumcision, he declares of those still in favor
of it: "I would they were even cut off" (i.e., castrated; KJV Gal. 5:12).

God reaffirms the covenant one more time, after Abraham obeys God's command to sacrifice his only son, Isaac, born to him at the age of one hundred. When the boy is weaned, God orders Abraham to "take your son, your only son Isaac, whom you love, and go to the land of Moriah, and offer him there as a burnt offering" (Gen. 22:2). Abraham sets off the next day, without hesitation or complaint. He builds an altar, binds Isaac and lays him on top, and is about to plunge a knife into him when an angel tells him to stop; he has proved that he fears God. Abraham looks up and sees a ram caught in a thicket, and sacrifices it instead.

Because Abraham has "been blameless" and obeyed God even in something so heart-wrenching and terrible, God once again reaffirms the covenant. An angel calls down from heaven and tells Abraham, "By myself I have sworn, says the Lord: Because you have done this, and have not withheld your son, your only son, I will indeed bless you, and I will make your offspring as numerous as the stars of heaven and as the sand that is on the seashore" (Gen. 22:16–17). God has now committed himself to Abraham in several, increasingly serious ways. He has promised him, made and renewed a covenant with him, and sworn an oath by himself that he will bless Abraham and look after his descendants.

Why does God swear? It seems an odd thing for him to do—perhaps not as odd as when he puts himself under a self-curse by passing through the slaughtered bodies of three-year-old animals, but still. Every word that God says is true, so why does he need the extra security an oath provides? That he swears is both a mark of favor to Abraham and his descendants and a recognition of their frailty. In binding himself here with an oath, and earlier with his self-curse, God is reassuring Abraham that he will fulfill his promises, in language that people can readily understand. This doesn't increase the probability that he will do what he says, as it is supposed to when people swear; God knows that there is never a difference between his word and his deed. It acknowledges instead that even faithful believers have moments of doubt, that human hearts and minds are fallible. As the Hellenistic Jewish philosopher Philo wrote around AD 30, God "is said to swear, because of our weakness. . . . And since He is blessed and gracious and propitious, He does not judge created beings in accordance with His greatness but in accordance with theirs." God loves his creation so much that he is willing to assume the restrictions and obligations of an oath to assuage our insecurities.

Why God Wants Us to Swear

God also swears to give people a model for the use of this powerful language. He swears a lot in the Bible, almost always by himself or by a part of himself: "By myself I have sworn" that I will be everybody's God (Isa. 45:23); "As I live, . . . I will do to you the very things I heard you say: your dead bodies shall fall in this very wilderness" (Num. 14:28–29); "Once and for all I have sworn by my holiness; I will not lie to David" (Ps. 89:35); "The Lord has sworn by his right hand and by his mighty arm: I will not again give your grain to be food for your enemies" (Isa. 62:8); "For I lift up my hand to heaven and swear: As I live forever, when I whet my flashing sword, and my hand takes hold on judgment; I will take vengeance on my adversaries, and will repay those who hate me. I will make my arrows drunk with blood, and my sword shall devour flesh" (Deut. 32:40).

We can infer some rules about swearing from these divine examples. You must swear by God, or by some synecdoche for him, in which an attribute or a part of God stands for God himself—his name, his holiness, or his arm. You must swear seriously and only in weighty matters, and you must never use an oath as expletive or insult. Most of all, you must swear sincerely, as God does—if you are swearing to the truth of something, it had better be true; if you are swearing that you will do something, you had better do it.

The Bible is full of explicit rules about swearing as well, the most famous of which is of course the third commandment: "Thou shalt not take the name of the Lord thy God in vain: for the Lord will not hold him guiltless that taketh his name in vain" (KJV Ex. 20:7).* What does it mean to take God's name "in vain," or "wrongfully," "idly," or "for no good," as this phrase can also be translated? This commandment is usually understood to prohibit the making of false oaths, picking up on God's earlier instruction that "you shall not swear falsely by my name, profaning the name of your God" (Lev. 19:12). False oaths invoke God as a witness to a statement that isn't true, or to a promise you don't intend to fulfill. When you swear by God, you ask him to guarantee your words, and to punish you if you have not spoken the truth. If you swear falsely, you are asking God to give his imprimatur to a lie, implicating him in your dishonesty and dishonoring him in turn. As the catechism of the Catholic Church puts it in its explanation of this commandment: "Promises made to others in God's name engage the divine honor, fidelity, truthfulness, and authority. They must be respected in justice. To be unfaithful to them is to misuse God's name and in some way to make God out to be a liar."

The commandment also prohibits what scholars call "vain" oaths, which means oaths sworn to no purpose. Vain oaths were seen as a major problem in the Middle Ages, when the swearwords of choice, as I've suggested, were "by God" and "by God's bones [hands, nails, feet, blood, etc.]." These expressions had the form of an oath but the force and register of an expletive. "Telle us a fable anon, for cokkes bones!" (Tell us a fable now, for God's bones!) the Host of Chaucer's *Canterbury Tales* swears again, this time at the Parson on the pilgrimage. The Host is not swearing to the truth of his statement, not intentionally asking God to witness his words. He is instead using the oath as an intensifier, to convey how much he wants the Parson to tell a story, and to show his frustration because the holy man is obviously reluctant to oblige. Paraphrased

---

*Different religious groups have different ways of numbering the Decalogue. To Jews and Protestants, this is the third commandment; to Catholics, it is the second.

in modern English, the Host is saying something along the lines of "For God's sake, tell us a story!" or perhaps rather "Tell us a fuckin' story already!"

The third commandment doesn't just forbid false or vain oaths, however—it prohibits any abuse of God's name, any reference to him that is not respectful, that doesn't acknowledge his majesty. People use the divine name today in imprecations like "God damn it, he took my parking space!" or a simple "Jesus Christ!" upon, say, surveying the wreckage of a living room after four toddlers have passed through. And nearly everyone uses "Oh my God" (helpfully shortened in text-speak to OMG). These are not oaths per se, but they still misuse God's name, calling on God for trivial purposes or in demeaning circumstances. As with the Host's oath, these words have been more or less emptied of content, of what linguists call "referential meaning"—they are nonliteral uses. It doesn't matter, though, that most people who use these phrases don't intend to dishonor God. When God's name passes your lips, according to the third commandment, it must be reverently and in full knowledge of what you are saying—anything more or less than this is blasphemy.

The Bible doesn't just define and forbid bad swearing, however; it actively encourages, indeed commands, believers to swear properly: "The Lord your God you shall fear; him shall you serve, and by his name alone you shall swear" (Deut. 6:13; also 10:20). When the Israelites are having one of their periodic flirtations with idolatry, God tells them that he will welcome them back if they get rid of their idols and "if you swear, 'As the Lord lives!' in truth, in justice, and in uprightness" (Jer. 4:2). God even swears by himself that "to me every knee shall bow, every tongue shall swear" (Isa. 45:23).

God wants people to swear by him because oaths are crucial to the smooth running of human society, and as always, he has our best interests at heart. But there is also something in it for God. At the beginning of the Bible, God is waging a war for supremacy with the other gods of the Near East, and swearing is a powerful weapon.

Top God

God was one of hundreds of gods a person could worship in the ancient Near East. It is no wonder that the Israelites were constantly going off and committing adultery or fornication, the Bible's metaphors of choice for idolatry, with foreign gods. A list in the Book of Judges helps to define the scope of his competition: "The Israelites again did what was evil in the sight of the Lord, worshiping the Baals and the Astartes, the gods of Aram, the gods of Sidon, the gods of Moab, the gods of the Ammonites, and the gods of the Philistines. Thus they abandoned the Lord, and did not worship him" (Judg. 10:6). Baal is the Canaanite god of storms and war, and Astarte is another name for his consort Anat, goddess of war and fertility—the rest of the names indicate city-states or ethnic groups, each with an entire pantheon of gods. A list of just a few of God's rivals includes El, ruler of the Canaanite pantheon; Asherah, his consort; the aforementioned Baal and Anat/Astarte; Haddad, a storm god; Sin, god of the moon; Yamm, Canaanite god of the sea; Mot, god of death; Yarih, another moon god; Eshmun, a god of healing; Deber and Resheph, gods of pestilence and plague; Marduk, chief Babylonian deity; Chemosh, chief god of Moab; Milcom/Moloch, who demanded child sacrifice as part of his worship; Dagon, a fertility and crop god; Derceto, a half-fish fertility goddess; Shapash, goddess of the sun; and Athtar, god of irrigation.

The ancient Israelites had a surfeit of choice. Luckily, most of these gods didn't mind if people worshipped more than one of them—hailing from polytheistic cultures, they had polytheistic worldviews. It was fine with Eshmun if you were a partisan of Baal too, since the two were supposed to work together to protect the Sidonians. If you sacrificed to El, it made sense to slit a few doves' throats for Asherah as well—they were a couple. The Judeo-Christian God alone is a jealous god; it was his great innovation to demand exclusive worship.

There is a surprising tension in the Bible as to whether these other gods are real, like God, or merely what Jeremiah calls "no-gods"

(Jer. 2:11) and Ezekiel "turd-gods" (Ezek. 22:3–4)—nothing but idols that can lure the Israelites into sin but have no power to help their worshippers or otherwise affect the world. Many of the prophets are in the turd-god camp. Isaiah, for example, rails against the stupidity of worshipping mere pieces of wood or iron: "Half of it I burned in the fire; I also baked bread on its coals, I roasted meat and have eaten. Now shall I make the rest an abomination? Shall I fall down before a block of wood?" (Is. 44:19). But some parts of the Bible reveal traces of other gods who do exercise real power. The Bible is like a palimpsest. Before paper, books were written on parchment, specially treated animal skin, which was expensive and hard to produce. When a scribe wanted to copy a new text, he sometimes scraped the old ink off parchment he already had and started over. Traces of the old writing remained under the new text, still faintly visible in places. In 1998, for example, scientists used multispectral imaging (taking photographs of the text at different wavelengths of light) to reconstruct two works of the Greek mathematician Archimedes, which had been erased and covered over in the thirteenth century with a Greek religious text. Likewise, traces of the Israelites' polytheistic past can be still be seen, dimly, in the Bible. If we use our own, rather more low-tech, version of multispectral imaging, we can reconstruct how some of these other gods related to God, working with him and competing against him. Some of them, it turns out, even helped with the creation of the world.

God goes by several different names in the Bible. His personal name—his "real name"—is the Tetragrammaton, Yhwh, usually written *Yahweh* in English. In the original Hebrew of Genesis 1, though, creation is attributed to Elohim. The noun *elohim* is plural in form, like *Hasidim* (Hasidic Jews) or *kibbutzim* (more than one kibbutz), and means "gods." *Elohim* is usually paired with a singular verb, however, indicating that the plural title has been adopted by a single god: "In the beginning when God [*Elohim*; plural] created [*bara'*; singular] the heavens and earth..." We can see a similar transition from plural to singular in *United States* before and after the

Civil War—from "the United States are" to "the United States is."
America's gradual evolution from a fairly loose collection of former
colonies to a tightly knit federal nation is encoded in the transition
from plural to singular. Likewise, the word *Elohim* is a reminder of a
time when Yahweh was not alone in the formless void and darkness
but had other gods for company.

We can see the traces of these other gods even more clearly when
humankind is created: "Then God said, 'Let us make humankind in
our image, according to our likeness'" (Gen. 1:26). Here, "God said"
uses the combination of a plural noun and singular verb, but "Let us
make" is a plural verb, and "our" is a plural pronoun. There is no disputing (or rather, there is very little disputing—you can never say
never) the plurality of entities involved here. Scholars who are
invested in the immediate and complete monotheism of the Bible
see the plural here as referring to God and his heavenly court of
angels, or to the Trinity; scholars who see monotheism as developing slowly throughout the Bible cite these lines as evidence that
Yahweh once had co-creators.

The early Yahweh doesn't always work together with these other
gods. Sometimes he appears as just one of many, with his own,
limited, sphere of influence. In Deuteronomy's Song of Moses, he is
depicted as a rather junior member of the council of gods:

> When the Most High [*Elyon*] apportioned the nations, when he
> divided humankind, he fixed the boundaries of the peoples accord-
> ing to the number of the gods;
>   the LORD's [*Hashem's*] portion was his people, Jacob his al-
> lotted share. (Deut. 32:8–9)

Hashem ("the Name") is one of Yahweh's standard titles in the
Hebrew Bible, used by Jews to avoid pronouncing his sacred personal name. So here we have a puzzling account of the Most High
assigning responsibility for the tribe of Israel (Jacob) to Yahweh,
just as, the verse suggests, he might have given the Ammonites to

Milcom, the Sidonians to Eshmun, the Babylonians to Marduk, and so forth. Who is Elyon, the Most High? Scholars committed to the Bible's monotheism tend to see the name *Elyon* as another title of Yahweh, and so interpret these verses as a description of Yahweh dividing the peoples of the world and taking the Israelites for himself. The *New Oxford Annotated Bible* even adds the word *own* ("the LORD's *own* portion") in order, as the editors explain, "to identify Yahweh with Elyon and avoid the impression that Yahweh is merely a member of the pantheon." Scholars of a less determinedly monotheistic bent identify Elyon with El, the chief god of the Canaanite pantheon, and see in these verses remnants of a time when Yahweh was a minor war and storm god in Canaan and El ruled the roost. El, then, would have divided the people and given the Israelites to Yahweh.

Even one of the most famous Mosaic declarations of monotheism actually, upon closer inspection, reveals hints of the existence of other gods. When the Israelites are about to cross the Jordan River into the Promised Land, Moses exhorts them to remember all that God has done for them. Has "any god ever attempted to go and take a nation for himself from the midst of another nation, by trials, by signs and wonders, by war, by a mighty hand and an outstretched arm, and by terrifying displays of power, as the Lord your God did for you in Egypt before your very eyes?" Moses ends his speech by asking the Israelites to "acknowledge" that "the Lord is God in heaven above and on the earth beneath; there is no other" (Deut. 4:32–39). This assertion of monotheism seems to be implying, though, not that God is the only god, but that he is the *best* god. If there aren't any other "real" gods, Moses's speech is a bit silly—it falls victim to Isaiah's mockery of people who worship idols. Where is the glory in taking a nation from the midst of another nation if there is no one around who could make the least attempt to stop you? What is the point in boasting that "God has done more signs and wonders than a lump of wood"?

All this puts God's first covenant with Abraham in a different light. When God puts himself under a self-curse, he does it knowing that there is a plethora of other gods who could cut him into pieces just as Abraham slaughtered the sacrificial animals. Looked at this way, there is no worry about God handling a situation that he cannot handle—El, the ruler of the Canaanite pantheon, or Baal, the fierce war god, could handle it for him very capably. It also becomes clearer why in the second version of the covenant God insists that Abraham swear loyalty to him (and circumcise the males of his family as a sign of it): the possibility that Abraham will worship other gods too, and perhaps eventually abandon him. He wants to lock Abraham into an exclusive relationship with him, just as he has thrown his lot in with the tribe of Israel, to the exclusion of everybody else.

Swearing is a key weapon in God's campaign to become the one true God. When you swear by God, you make an appeal to him—you ask him to listen to your words, assess their truth, and punish you if they are false or if you don't perform what you have promised. An oath by God, then, implicitly acknowledges that he is omnipresent, able to hear you whatever you say and whenever you say it; that he is omniscient, able to judge the truth of your words; and that he is omnipotent, able to punish you no matter how far you run. If you swear by Baal, Yahweh's rival war god, though, you acknowledge *his* omnipotence instead. God seems very worried about this possibility in the Bible. In Jeremiah, we have seen, God tells the apostate Israelites to return to him and swear "as the Lord lives!"—to swear by *him*, not by those other gods they've been worshipping on "the multitude of mountains" (3:23).*

---

* Or with "orgies on the mountains," depending on your translation. This is a good example of the difficulties involved in translating the Bible from Hebrew. The Hebrew word *hamon* means anything from "a sound, murmur, roar, tumult" to "abundance, wealth" to "many, multitude, hordes, population." In choosing "the multitude of mountains," the translators of the King James, Webster, and Darby versions are linking the phrase to the worship of idols that often takes place in "high places"—as when God warns any Israelites thinking about backsliding that he will "destroy your high places and cut down your incense altars; I will heap your carcasses on the carcasses of your idols" (Lev. 27:30). In choosing "orgies on the mountains," translators of the NRSV fit the verse into the biblical narrative that describes idolatry in terms of sexual deviance—"this people [those Israelites, again] will begin to prostitute themselves to the foreign gods in their midst" (Deut. 31:16). Both translations have something to recommend them, though perhaps getting *orgies* from *crowd* and *tumult* is a bit more of a stretch. Which one is "correct"? God knows.

God makes this connection between swearing by him and worshipping him again and again. We have already come across the Deuteronomic command to fear God, to serve God, and to swear only by his name. In the Book of Joshua, God urges his people to keep the laws of Moses so they do not mix with the Canaanite tribes, "or make mention of the names of their gods, or swear by them, or serve them, or bow yourselves down to them, but hold fast to the Lord your God" (Josh. 23:7). He seems to be warning against a chain reaction in which first you simply mention that you heard about Moloch at the marketplace, then you're swearing by him, and pretty soon you are sacrificing your firstborn son to him on a giant fiery bier. In Jeremiah, he charges that the Israelites, false again, "have forsaken me, and have sworn by those who are no gods" (Jer. 5:7)—swearing by other gods means abandoning Yahweh.

Vows are another important way that Yahweh gains influence over the Israelites and power over his rival gods. We use the term *vow* fairly loosely today, and mostly during weddings. In the Bible, a vow establishes a reciprocal economic relationship between God and the person vowing—it is an exchange. If God does something for me, I will do something for God. A farmer might vow that if God helps him have a successful crop, he will sacrifice a heifer to him at the end of the harvest. Hannah, an infertile woman, vows that if God gives her a son, she will make her son a Nazarite, a person specially dedicated to the service of the Lord. If God comes through and does what you have asked, you must "pay" your vow, fulfilling your side of the bargain. If you do not pay your vow, "the Lord your God will surely require it of you, and you would incur guilt" (Deut. 23:21). Vowing means going into debt, and payback is always involved.

Vowing is a very useful practice for a deity such as Yahweh, interested in increasing his influence. If a person's wish comes true, God gets the credit since it is obvious that he has fulfilled his side of the bargain. If the wish isn't granted, it is probably because you did something wrong, or because Yahweh is angry with you; such failures can always be explained away. Psychologically, when you "pay" something to God in return for his help, you feel invested in the relationship—there are sound economic principles acting here to strengthen faith. So the Bible includes quite a long and intricate series of laws abut vowing, detailing what kinds of animals are acceptable as payment to God (none with "bruised or crushed or torn or cut" testicles [Lev. 22:24]) and who can be held legally responsible for making vows (not women, unless their fathers or husbands give their okay [Num. 30: 1–16]).

Despite the Israelites' occasional backsliding into idolatry, Yahweh's trusty weapons, oaths and vows, stand him in good stead, and in the end he wins his war against the other gods. Partly by encouraging swearing and vowing, Yahweh goes from being a fairly minor god among many to being the best god among many and then to being the only God who exists.

Fallen Idols and God's Wife

What happens to the other gods, Yahweh's competition? Historically, they fell into obscurity as the peoples, cities, or empires they were supposed to protect were conquered or collapsed into ruin. In the Bible, they are disposed of in two ways. On the text's surface, narrative level, Yahweh has several face-offs with other gods, which he wins handily. He triumphs, for example, over Baal. His prophet Elijah arranges a contest in which the first god to set a pile of wood on fire wins (1 Kings 18:20–40). The 450 priests of Baal try everything to get their god to start a fire, but nothing happens. When Elijah, the Lord's lone prophet, asks Yahweh to light his pile, it goes up spectacularly, even though Elijah has drenched his wood with water. The people watching feel that this settles the matter—they declare, "The Lord indeed is God," and capture the priests of Baal so that Elijah can kill them, all 450.

On a deeper level, Yahweh subsumes Baal. He takes over many of his rival storm god's most famous mythological deeds. Baal battles

Lotan, a seven-headed dragon; Yahweh defeats Leviathan, a great sea beast (and, as it happens, *Leviathan* is the Hebrew name for Lotan). Baal fights with Yamm, a sea god, and Mot, god of death; Yahweh conquers sea and death (Ps. 74:12–17; Isa. 25:8). These battles were major parts of Baal's mythology, but in the Bible they are mentioned only in passing, and only in generalized form. Yahweh can fight "sea" or even "Sea," as some translations put it, but he can't fight Yamm. If he did battle directly with another god, that would be an outright acknowledgment that other deities existed, and Yahweh is now too powerful and dignified to acknowledge the existence of rivals.

Yahweh also takes on many attributes of El, the most important Canaanite god, including his name. Yahweh is called El—"I am God [El], and there is no other" (Is. 45:22)—and also El Elyon (El most high), El Shaddai (God of the uncultivated fields, God almighty), Elohim (God, gods), and El Elohe Israel (El, the god of Israel), among others. There is an interesting passage where Yahweh seems to acknowledge this syncretism, the melding of religious beliefs or concepts. In Exodus, he declares that he is changing his name—it used to be El, but from now on it's going to be Yahweh. God tells Moses: "I am the Lord [Yahweh]. I appeared to Abraham, Isaac, and Jacob as God Almighty [El Shaddai], but by my name 'The Lord' [Yahweh] I did not make myself known to them" (Ex. 6:2–3). Anybody who used to pray to El should now worship Yahweh—Yahweh is the new and improved El.

Yahweh had perhaps the hardest time displacing the rival who was closest to him, his consort, Asherah. Many scholars believe that Yahweh adopted not just El's name and titles but also those of his partner, at least in what is called popular or folk religion, as opposed to the priestly, orthodox religion of Deuteronomy and Leviticus. In the Near East, we have seen, gods often came paired with goddesses— El and Asherah, Baal and Anat/Astarte, Horus and Hathor (Egyptian deities)—and it would be highly unusual for a god *not* to have a consort or to show any interest in sexual relations, whether with other deities, humans, animals, humans in the shape of animals, or what have you. Archaeologists have found some evidence that Yahweh was not entirely out of the normal Near Eastern way in these matters, in the form of inscriptions linking his name and Asherah's. Several come from a complex of buildings called Kuntillet Ajrud in the eastern Sinai Desert. Kuntillet Ajrud was a caravanserai—a stop-over along a route between the Red Sea and the Mediterranean that served as a defensive fort and inn for travelers, as well as a shrine. "To [Y]ahweh [of] Teiman [Yemen] and to his Ashera[h]" is written on a wall in the shrine, while two storage jars are inscribed "I [b]lessed you by [or 'to'] Yahweh of Samaria and by his Asherah" and "Yahweh of Teiman and his Asherah." The pictures below were found on the former jar, and many scholars interpret them as an illustration of the inscription, which would yield a rare portrait not only of the fa-mously image-averse Yahweh but also of his consort. But which image depicts Yahweh and Asherah? Yahweh might be the calf and

Pictures from the *pithos* inscribed "I [b]lessed you by [or 'to'] Yahweh of Samaria and by his Asherah."

Asherah the cow. Or Yahweh might be the obviously male figure and
Asherah the also pretty obviously male figure next to him (this figure
has breasts, too). Or Asherah is the lyre player in the background, Yahweh is the male figure, and the one with a penis and breasts is . . . who
knows? The picture below, from the same jar, is easier to interpret—
it is Asherah as the tree of life, upon whom the standing goats are
feeding.

Asherah is originally included in Elijah's wood-burning
challenge—her four hundred prophets are supposed to light a fire
too. (She also has a royal supporter, the wicked queen Jezebel.) We

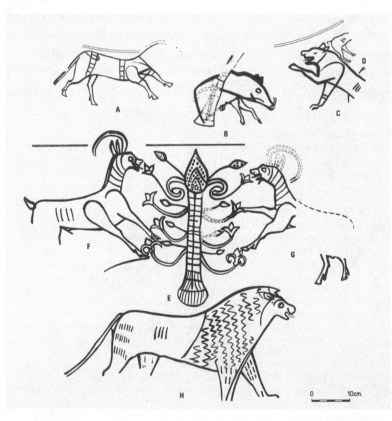

Asherah, from the same *pithos*.

hear all about Yahweh's subsequent victory over Baal and the slaughter of his prophets, as archaeologist William Dever notes, but nothing more is reported about Asherah. Did she manage to light a fire too?

Asherah was worshipped by erecting sacred poles or planting trees, as her symbol was the tree of life—she was a goddess of fertility. On pots, pendants, seals, and offering stands, she was often depicted as a tree or bush flanked by two animals standing on their hind legs, who are nibbling her leaves—she gives nourishment. Sometimes the bush they are nibbling is pretty explicitly her pubic hair.

In the Bible, there is only one moment of happy union for Yahweh and Asherah, involving an oath. It occurs after Abram cuts a covenant with the Philistine king Abimelech, resolving a dispute they had been having. Abraham claims that Abimelech's servants have seized a well that belongs to him. Wary of antagonizing someone so obviously under the protection of a powerful god, Abimelech immediately cedes the well to Abraham, and "the two men made a covenant. . . . Therefore that place was called Beer-sheba [Heb.: "well of the oath"]; because there both of them swore an oath" (Gen. 21:27–31). Abimelech goes on his way, while Abraham "planted a tamarisk tree in Beer-sheba, and called there on the name of the Lord, the Everlasting God" (Gen. 21:33). In the Hebrew, Abraham calls on "El Olam," "El the everlasting" or "El the eternal"—this is one of the places in the Bible where we can see evidence of the convergence of Yahweh and El. Then he invokes Asherah, El/Yahweh's consort, by planting one of her sacred trees. It seems that he would like both gods to witness his covenant with Abimelech, Yahweh and his Asherah.

(Though he is the founder of the Jewish nation, Abraham is not a good role model when it comes to swearing. He not only plants a tree for Asherah, he makes his servant swear an oath on his genitals. He wants his servant to travel back to his homeland to find a wife for his son, Isaac, and engages him to do it with an oath: "put your hand under my thigh," he tells the servant, "and I will make you swear by

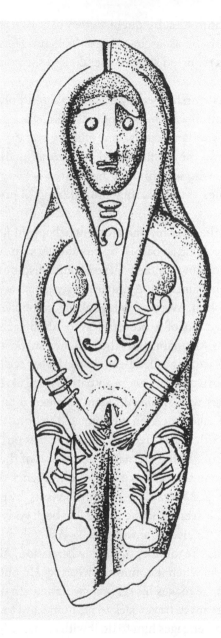

Goats nibbling Asherah's, ahem, bush.

the Lord, the God of heaven and earth" [Gen. 24:2–4]. In the Bible *thigh* sometimes means what it appears to, but more often it refers to the penis and/or balls [and occasionally to the female genitals]. This is a very old form of swearing, an oath not by God but by Abraham's powerful reproductive organs, which founded the tribe of Israel. Of course the servant has to swear by God as well—Abraham is hedging his bets. This oath is used once more in Genesis, when Jacob makes Joseph put his hand under his thigh and swear to bury him with his ancestors [Gen. 47:29], but then it falls into disuse. God wants people to swear by him, not by their own procreative powers.)*

While ordinary Israelites who practiced folk religion and even the first patriarch, Abraham, paired Yahweh with Asherah, the priestly authors of Leviticus and Deuteronomy rejected her. "You shall not plant any tree as a sacred pole beside the altar that you make for the Lord your God; nor shall you set up a stone pillar— things that the Lord your God hates," Deuteronomy 16:21 instructs believers. In Exodus 34:13–14, God warns the Israelites not to make covenants with the inhabitants of Canaan—instead they should "tear down their altars, break their pillars, and cut down their sacred poles (for you shall worship no other god, because the Lord, whose name is Jealous, is a jealous God)." In both cases, what gets translated as "sacred pole" is the word *asherah*—these poles or trees are sacred to Yahweh's (former) partner but must now be destroyed as relics of idol worship, along with stone pillars used in the worship of Baal and other Canaanite gods.

Eventually Yahweh won out over Asherah as well, and mono-theism was born. These traces of other gods, which we've made so much of, are just that, traces. The Bible on the whole did a much more thorough job of erasing evidence of Yahweh's battles than

---

*A similar connection between genitals and swearing is present in the English word *testify*, which comes from the Latin word for "witness," *testis*. In Latin, *testis* was also a "risqué and jocose" (as J. N. Adams put it) word for "testicle," perhaps because the testicles "bear witness" to a man's virility. The English *testify* thus isn't derived from a Latin term for "balls," but the words share a common ancestor in *testis*.

The famous "Ram in a Thicket," formerly known as the "ram eating the tree that grows out of Asherah's vagina."

did those monks when they wrote over Archimedes. There is a famous statue (actually a pair of them) of a black and gold goat, standing on its hind legs and supported by a stylized tree, that was unearthed in Ur, in modern-day Iraq. It probably represents Asherah, or at any rate is very much in line with her iconography—the goddess as sacred tree, flanked by goats standing on their hind legs and nibbling. The figure is known as the "Ram in a Thicket," though. The archaeologist who discovered it named it after the scapegoat God provides when Abraham is about to sacrifice his son: "And Abraham looked up and saw a ram, caught in a thicket by its horns" (Gen. 22:13). Poor Asherah has no claim anymore even on her most famous symbol. Yahweh's victory over the other gods, even his nearest and dearest, was so complete that the memory of them was practically erased. God's covenants (which are themselves oaths) with the Jews, his commands to swear by him, and his prohibition of oaths on other gods were key factors in his victory.

Out with the Old, In with the New

In the New Testament, Christ changes the rules. In contrast to what his Father commands over and over in the Old Testament, Jesus appears to tell his followers not to swear, ever. In the Sermon on the Mount, he preaches:

> Again, you have heard that it was said to those of ancient times, "You shall not swear falsely, but carry out the vows you have made to the Lord." But I say to you, Do not swear at all, either by heaven, for it is the throne of God, or by the earth, for it is his footstool, or by Jerusalem, for it is the city of the great King. And do not swear by your head, for you cannot make one hair white or black. Let your word be "Yes, yes" or "No, no"; anything more than this comes from the evil one. (Matt. 5:33–37)

Scholars have argued about this passage almost since it was written (around AD 80 or 90). Is Christ contradicting earlier scripture and really telling his audience not to swear at all? Is he in effect urging people to abandon the very means by which God established his dominion? Or is he asserting something less revolutionary, something like "Swear only when you really *have* to, as required in legal cases or by certain authorities"?

The argument starts within the New Testament itself, with James asserting that it is not allowable to swear in any case: "Above all, my beloved, do not swear, either by heaven or by earth or *by any other oath*" (5:12; italics mine). Other almost equally venerable authorities contend that Christ would never ban all oaths, because they are so crucial for the functioning of society. St. Augustine (fourth century) and Thomas Aquinas (thirteenth century) claim that Christ forbade only false or vain swearing; oaths are too important to dispense with entirely. Philipp Melanchthon, the German reformer who collaborated with Martin Luther, provides a concise summary of this view: to prohibit swearing is "a destruction of secular government and justice, for government and justice are based on oaths."

These were not abstract academic arguments. In the early fifteenth century, proto-Protestants called Lollards were persecuted because they would not swear oaths on the Bible, though they would swear by God alone.* Many were imprisoned and some were executed because of their belief in the lawfulness of one form of swearing but not another. The Quakers, in contrast, believed (and still believe) that all forms of swearing were forbidden. The movement's founder, George Fox, argued in the late seventeenth century that Christ means exactly what he says when he tells people not to swear: "plainer words than these, cannot be in the scriptures." This refusal

---

* Like later Protestants, Lollards denied the physical presence of God's body in the Eucharist, translated the Bible and encouraged individual reading of it, and protested against what they saw as the material excesses of the Catholic Church. (We'll talk more about the Lollards in the following chapter.)

led to endless problems for the Quakers. They could not take the oath of allegiance to the king, or the oath of supremacy acknowledging that the king was head of the English Church, which made them liable to a sliding scale of punishments that increased with each repeated offense, from a five-pound fine to transportation to America. They also couldn't give testimony in court, whether as a witness in a criminal trial or in their own defense. A good technique for getting rid of a Quaker you didn't like was to accuse him of doing something illegal. Whether or not he was guilty, when he refused to take an oath his property would be confiscated and he would be thrown in jail for contempt of court.

So who is right here? The Quakers whose lives were ruined because they insisted that Christ forbade people to swear? The Lollards who would swear in some ways, but not on a Bible? The many theologians who, through the years, have argued that it is perfectly fine to swear under any circumstances? George Fox had a point when he said that nothing in the scriptures could be clearer than Christ's command not to swear at all. But God is no less clear when he has Moses tell the Israelites that they should swear by his name—and Christ declares that he has "come not to abolish but to fulfill" the law (Matt. 5:17). Other parts of the Gospels support both the anti-oath and pro-oath positions. We have seen that the letter of James restates even more clearly the command not to swear. But the other time Christ himself talks about oaths, he condemns the scribes and Pharisees only for chopping logic about which oaths are binding and which are not (Matt. 23:16–22). He tells them not that they shouldn't be swearing but that they should be swearing *properly*.

There is no right answer, at least for us wandering in the wilderness of error. But in a sense the debate doesn't matter. History has resolved that swearing is permitted. In fact, it is more than permitted, it is necessary—our government and legal system would have a hard time functioning without it. The indications are that for Christ, swearing wasn't very important—it certainly wasn't as much of an issue for him as it was for his Father. When Yahweh was insisting that people swear by him and only him, there were, as we've seen, hundreds of other gods competing for the affections of the polytheistic Israelites. More than a thousand years later, when Christ arrived on the scene, these other gods were no longer so much of a concern—the Jews were monotheistic. Yahweh had won his battle to be the only God of the Israelites, and Christ could lay down his father's arms.

Thou Shalt Not Piss on the Wall: Obscenity in the Bible

The Hebrew Bible has its share of obscenity as well as oaths. When the Assyrian king Sennacherib is planning to besiege Jerusalem, he sends an emissary to the city to ask its people to surrender. This official paints the horrors of the coming siege as vividly as possible, telling the Jewish leaders and the ordinary people of the town, "the men which sit on the wall," that they "may eat their own dung, and drink their own piss" (KJV 2 Kings 18:27). They will starve, the Assyrian warns, until they are so hungry and thirsty that they eat and drink their own waste in desperation. It is a powerful image, helped by the forthright, vulgar language, but it doesn't do the job. The Jews don't surrender, and Yahweh ends up killing 185,000 Assyrians, forcing Sennacherib to withdraw to his capital, Nineveh, where he is murdered by two of his sons while worshipping his (obviously powerless) god Nisroch.

To the ancient Israelites, excrement and bodily effusions such as semen and menstrual blood were defiling. The Bible details an elaborate code of purification for various emissions so that people do not dishonor God's tabernacle by approaching it in an unclean state. Here is a small sampling of the rules:

> When any man has a discharge from his member [actually *flesh*, in Hebrew], his discharge makes him ceremonially unclean. The uncleanness of his discharge is this: whether his member flows with

his discharge, or his member is stopped from discharging, it is uncleanness for him. . . . If a man has an emission of semen, he shall bathe his whole body in water, and be unclean until the evening. . . . When a woman has a discharge of blood that is her regular discharge from her body, she shall be in her impurity for seven days, and whoever touches her shall be unclean until the evening. (NRSV Lev. 15:2–19)

God also tells the Israelites how and where they can relieve themselves—they must go outside the camp, dig a hole with a trowel each must carry among his tools, and cover it up. Depositing excrement inside the camp would be defiling, obscene in the second Roman sense of the word. The Lord is with the Israelites, and "therefore your camp must be holy, so that he may not see anything indecent among you" (NRSV Deut. 23:14). Yahweh is not only a jealous god but a fastidious one. Cleanliness is next to godliness.

Many versions of the Bible shy away from rendering all this excrement in its full glory. With a passage like "eat their own dung and drink their own piss," translators usually keep the slightly vulgar *dung* but go for the more decorous "drink their own urine" (NRSV, NIV, ESV, NASB, Douay-Rheims; the Vulgate uses *stercora*, "excrement," and *urinam*). Some go more formal and have the Israelites eating "excrement" and drinking their own "water" (Young's Literal, Word English, ERV). And some just do their own thing: one version has the Israelites devouring their "vilest excretions" (Webster's), while another leaps from the toilet into the crib without a look back: "they'll be eating their own turds and drinking their own pee" (The Message).

If eating dung and drinking urine make translators hesitate, another famous crux stops them short. Several times God makes dire threats like the following: "Therefore, behold, I will bring evil upon the house of Jeroboam, and will cut off from Jeroboam *him that pisseth against the wall*" (KJV 1 Kings 14:10).

What does this phrase mean? Some scholars argue that "him that pisseth against the wall" is simply a vivid way of saying "all men." In biblical times (and right up to the Victorian era), it was socially acceptable, indeed the normal practice, for men to urinate in public. *All* men would pee on walls, trees, or whatever was handy when the urge struck. God is not using bad language, in this view. The translators of the King James Bible used *pisseth* to render the Hebrew *shathan*, "to make water, to urinate," because that was their usual, though still slightly vulgar, word for it. Englishmen of 1611 shared the ancient Israelite disregard for micturational modesty, and they had no problems saying what they were not embarrassed to do.

Other scholars insist that "him that pisseth" is derogatory, that God *is* in a sense using obscene language about these men who have displeased him. By defining them through a low bodily function, God's language makes members of the house of Jeroboam seem like dogs, marking their territory the only way they know how.

In any case, two things are clear. The phrase does not pertain to women, to whom stricter standards of modesty were applied (and who probably would have trouble pissing against a wall). And the translators of the King James Version had a different sense of the register of *piss*, or perhaps simply a greater toleration for vulgarity, than we do today. Modern translations of the Bible uniformly reject the richness of "him that pisseth," replacing it with "every last male" (New International), "every male person" (New American Standard), or "every male" (English Standard).

As these various translations show, many people today would prefer to ignore the bad language in the Bible. But how shocking was this language to the ancient Hebrews? Would words such as *gelel* and *shathan* have been obscene, and thus best translated as *shit* and *piss*, respectively, or would they have been polite words for indelicate subjects, more like our *defecate* and *urinate*? It is almost impossible to tell. Hebrew is like Latin, in that it was a vernacular language that became frozen in time as a religious, scholarly one. For hundreds of years it was read and studied, not spoken, until it was resurrected as the lingua franca of Jews in Palestine in the nineteenth century. Huge numbers of Latin texts have come down to us, from the basest graffiti to the most high-flown oratory, allowing us, as we saw in the last chapter, to reconstruct the hierarchy of genres and assess the registers of words. But unlike Latin, there is no such record for ancient Hebrew—it comes to us from the Bible and from the Mishnah (c. AD 200), the first part of the Talmud, itself a commentary on the Bible. These texts are too similar in purpose and vocabulary to reveal anything about the register of words when they were written.

Most of the Bible's obscenity is in deed, not in word, though. The language is often quite chaste, even when the acts being described feature the most flagrant "whoredoms," as the King James Version likes to call them. As translated in the New Revised Standard Version, Ezekiel 23:20 depicts things that would fit right into a pornographic movie, but in language that is G-rated (okay, maybe PG): "Yet she increased her whorings, remembering the days of her youth, when she played the whore in the land of Egypt and lusted after her paramours there, whose members were like those of donkeys, and whose emission was like that of stallions" (Ezek. 23:19–20). Biblical Hebrew is extremely euphemistic—it often substitutes an indirect and inoffensive term for one thought to be blunt or offensive. It never refers to the *genitals* when *hand*, or *foot*, or *side*, or *heel*, or *shame*, or *leg*, or *thigh* will do. It never says *have sex with* when a man can *know* a woman, or *go into* her, or *approach* her, or *touch* her, or *lie with* her, or just *go up to the bed*, or when, sexiest of all, the two can *eat bread* together. For defecation, the euphemism of choice is *covering the feet*. Here *feet* means feet, not genitals—when you defecate, you've got your trousers, skirt, or robe around your ankles, covering up your feet.

Some of these euphemisms are obvious, as in the Song of Songs.

> My beloved thrust his hand into the opening,
> and my inmost being yearned for him.
> I arose to open to my beloved,
> and my fingers dripped with myrrh,
> my fingers with liquid myrrh,
> upon the handles of the bolt. (Song 5:4–5)

If *hand* = "genitals," and *fingers* = "genitals," and *dripped* = . . . well, you get the idea. It is almost painful to watch scholars insist that this passage has nothing at all to do with sex. No, it is truly and only about God's love for Israel, Christ's love for the Church, or the soul's spiritual union with God. The esteemed eighteenth-century commentator Matthew Henry explains, for example, "In this chapter we have . . . Christ's gracious acceptance of the invitation which his church had given him, and the kind visit which he made to her."

The Hebrew Bible's penchant for euphemism can lead to surprising reinterpretations of familiar passages. Everyone knows that Eve was created from Adam's rib, right? But ribs aren't mentioned anywhere in the Hebrew—that is a translation made by the Septuagint, the early Greek version of the Hebrew Bible. The word actually used is *side* (*tsela*), and, as we've seen, *side* can be used as a euphemism for the genitals (Gen. 2:20–23). Scholar Ziony Zevit takes this euphemism and runs with it, arguing that in the Genesis narrative Eve is actually made from Adam's penis, in particular from his penis bone. Most mammals have a baculum, a bone in their penis, which helps with erections. Only humans, spider monkeys, whales, horses, and a few other species lack it, achieving erections through blood pressure alone. Zevit thinks that the ancient Israelites would have been quite knowledgeable about comparative anatomy, given that they probably encountered lots of skeletons—of animals in fields, and of humans in caves where bodies were entombed. They would have known that men and women have the same number of ribs, another mark against the rib theory, and would have seen that the bone men were in fact missing was the baculum. It makes a certain kind of sense, then, to have God create Eve from Adam's baculum. This explains the bone's disappearance in humans and gives new richness to Adam's famous welcome of Eve: "This at last is bone of my bones and flesh of my flesh"—*flesh*, of course, being one more euphemism for the penis.

There is sometimes a certain difficulty in deciding when the Bible is using a word in its ordinary sense and when euphemistically. One biblical law is a case in point: "If men get into a fight with one another, and the wife of one intervenes to rescue her husband from the grip of his opponent by reaching out and seizing his genitals, you shall cut off her hand; show no pity" (Deut. 25:11–12). You can imagine a rash of these fights breaking out, men struggling with each other, dust flying, women darting in and making mad grabs for the, ahem, feet. Or perhaps something like this once happened to the author of the passage and he wants to make sure that no man should ever again have to suffer such an indignity. In any case, there is one obvious euphemism here. The Hebrew doesn't actually say "genitals" in this passage; it uses "that which excites shame."

But what about *hand*? Sometimes this is also a euphemism for the genitals, but does it function that way here? Most scholars take it at face value—the law stipulates that the woman's hand should be cut off, an eye for an eye, and a hand for a handful. Biblical scholar Jerome T. Walsh takes a different view, arguing that *hand* is indeed a euphemism for the genitals here. The law is not mandating clitoridectomies for the women who transgress, however. Walsh thinks that the Hebrew that is usually translated as *cut off* is actually closer in meaning to the English *shave*, and he translates the punishment as "You shall shave the hair of her groin." The woman has shamed the man by touching his genitals; she will be shamed in turn by having her pubic hair removed. We have no historical evidence about how the ancient Israelites actually handled situations like these (if, indeed, they ever came up), so we can't know for sure what the law stipulates. But the debate raises interesting questions about how to read a book translated from a language in which it sometimes seems that every other word can be a euphemism for something else.

Let Not Fornication Be Named Among You

The New Testament is even stricter than the Hebrew Bible when it comes to obscene language. It issues guidelines for speech that would seem to restrict even euphemistic uses. The Letter to the

Ephesians, which was possibly written by Paul, instructs: "But fornication and impurity of any kind, or greed, must not even be mentioned among you, as is proper among saints. Entirely out of place is
obscene, silly, and vulgar talk; but instead, let there be thanksgiving"
(Eph. 5:3). The letter doesn't simply command Christians not to do
various bad things; it tells them not to speak of them. It is not enough
to avoid fornication—you also have to avoid talking about it. This is
not so much because the words involved are themselves foul—*greed*,
for instance, is not a bad word—but because saying the word leads
to thinking about what the word represents, which can all too easily
lead to action. Just as when God forbids people even to mention the
names of other gods, lest they be inspired to worship them, the
author of Ephesians seems to fear a chain reaction in which you
mention fornication, then you begin thinking about fornicating, and
pretty soon you're "fucking like any furious fornicator," in the immortal words of sixteenth-century Scottish poet Sir David Lyndsay.
The theory of language that motivates this fear is the same one that
linguists and other scholars often use to understand swearing.
Swearwords are thought to have a deeper connection to the things
they represent than do other words; implicit in the Letter to the
Ephesians is a similar claim about all words. In Ephesians, the link
between word and referent is almost magical, so strong that merely
saying a word seems almost inevitably to lead to the doing of the
thing to which it refers.

The passage goes on to forbid "obscene, silly, and vulgar talk."
These are the kinds of talk that are most likely to contain words that
might lead their speakers or listeners to sin. Obscene and vulgar
language is made up almost entirely of words for various kinds of
impurities, whether sexual or scatological—it is fairly obvious why
the author of Ephesians would want to discourage their use. "Silly
talk" is less obvious, but exegetes explain it as coarse jesting and
jokes that bring up dangerous topics. But this passage is also entirely
in line with the New Testament's strict demands for the language of
"saints," which refers to *all* Christians, not just to particularly holy

people, as it does today. Christ tells his followers that "on the day of judgment you will have to give an account for every careless word you utter; for by your words you will be justified, and by your words you will be condemned" (Matt. 12:36–37). *Careless* is often translated as *idle*—Christ wants every word a person speaks to be useful. It is not enough to abstain from obscene language, hurtful speech, or lies. If what you are saying doesn't improve or edify you or your hearers, you shouldn't say it. This is how St. Jerome interprets the passage: "An idle word is one that is spoken without benefit to both the speaker and the hearer, for example, when we speak about frivolous things to the neglect of serious matters, or when we tell old wives' tales." This is the standard against which *all* language is judged in the New Testament. Christ and his apostles are not so concerned with obscene language per se as with any speech that is not serious and improving, whether it's a silly knock-knock joke or the most lewd description of some sexual act. Nevertheless, some words are worse than others. Language that is not just distracting but actually spurs people to do bad things is especially to be avoided, whether those words are obscene words such as *fuck* or polite terms for the same things, such as *fornication*.

The New Testament's stance on language had a profound influence in the Middle Ages, in preference to the Roman—and contemporary—one that privileges words for taboo topics as worse and thus more powerful than other words. It goes some way toward explaining why medieval medical texts used words that the *Lancet* or the *New England Journal of Medicine* would never employ, and why the Canterbury pilgrims very likely would have wended their way wearing little pins in the shape of erect penises and vaginas with wings, as we'll see in the next chapter. The Old Testament's stance on language determined what kind of words actually were shocking, offensive, and thought to be dangerous in the Middle Ages: oaths.

Chapter 3

Swearing God to Pieces

The Middle Ages

In the year 715 a monk named Eadfrith began a wonderful and ambitious labor of love. In a cold, damp, windswept priory on the coast of northeast England, he poured all his energy and artistic skill into a gift to honor God, producing the Lindisfarne Gospels, one of the most beautiful illuminated manuscripts in the world. This exquisite manuscript contains Vulgate (Latin) versions of Matthew, Mark, Luke, and John, illustrated in the insular fashion, a combination of Celtic and Anglo-Saxon styles. Some 250 years later a priest of the same community named Aldred added an English gloss to the Latin text, producing the oldest surviving English version of the Gospels. "Liber generationis Iesu Christi filii David Φilii Abraham," Matthew begins, and Aldred translates: "Bóc cneurise haelendes cristes dauides sunu abrahames sunu."

This is Old English, almost incomprehensible to modern speakers of the language. (The line means, as the King James Version puts it: "The book of the generation of Jesus Christ, the son of David, the son of Abraham.") And so Aldred goes on, glossing the Latin quite literally, until he comes to Matthew 5:27: "Audistis quia dictum est antiquis non moechaberis"—in the KJV, "Ye have heard that it was said by them of old time, Thou shalt not commit adultery." Aldred, however, translates this rather differently, as "Geherde ge forðon acueden is to ðæm aldum ne gesynnge ðu [vel] ne serð ðu oðres mones wif"—"You have heard that it was said to them of old, don't sin, and don't sard another man's wife."

Much later, during the English Renaissance, *sard* was seen as only slightly more acceptable than *fuck* is today. In a 1530 English-French dictionary, for example, it is defined with *foutre*, French for *fuck*: "I sarde a queene [a prostitute]. Je fous, nos foutons, je foutis, jay foutu, je fouteray, que je foute, foutre . . ." (I fuck, we fuck, etc.). The question is, what is a word like *sard* doing in the Bible? In this sacred book, so beautifully crafted for the honor of God, why did the priest translate the Latin as, in essence, "Thou shalt not fuck thy neighbor's wife"?

Aldred was not the only one to include obscene words in a translation of the Bible. In fact, his use of *sard* is more the rule than the exception. In the 1370s, four centuries later, John Wyclif and his associates started work on an English version of the Bible, so that ordinary people who didn't know Latin could understand God's word directly, without the intercession—what they saw as the interference—of a priest. And what these ordinary people learned couldn't be said out loud in church today: "A geldynge, þe ballogys brusyd or kut off, & þe ȝarde kut awey, shal not goon yn to þe chirche" (Deut. 23:1) (a gelding [eunuch], the bollocks bruised or cut off, and the yard [penis] cut away, shall not go into the church). The same constraint went for sacrificial animals: "Ye shall not offer to the Lord any beast whose bollocks/balls [*ballokes*] are broken" (Lev. 22:24). In American English, *balls* is not a polite word, but it is not a particularly bad one. In Britain, however, *bollocks* was and is quite obscene. In a 2000 ranking of the top-ten swearwords by members of the British public, *bollocks* came in eighth.

Readers of Wyclif's Bible also learned what God promised to do to anyone who didn't obey and honor him: "The Lord will smite you with the boils of Egypt [on] the part of the body by which turds are shat out" (Deut. 28:27). This is a close translation of the Latin, which accounts for the odd circumlocution that avoids one vulgar word by using two more. It's not that the Wycliffites couldn't bring themselves to use *arse*. They could. We later find out that "the Lord . . . smote [the people of] Azothe [Ashdod] and its coasts in the more private/secret part of the arses" (1 Sam. 5:6).

This is only a sampling of the obscene words that Wyclif and his associates put into their vernacular Bible. Their version is much more obscene, by our standards, than the usually euphemistic Hebrew Bible or the Latin Vulgate (the latter served as their source text). Deuteronomy 28:27's "Parte corporis per quam stercora digeruntur" means, in modern English, "the part of the body by which dung is spread." *Stercora*, we saw in Chapter 1, is a fairly polite Latin word, and *spreading* is vastly more polite than *shitting*. Here Wyclif et alia took what in Latin is a highly euphemistic and quite vague description and turned it into something specific and dysphemistic. They did this over and over, sticking *arses* and *bollocks* where there had never been any before.

The naked truth is that words such as *bollocks*, *sard*, and even *cunt* were not obscene in the Middle Ages. Generally, people of medieval England did not share our modern concept of obscenity, in which words for certain taboo functions possess a power in excess of their literal meaning and must be fenced off from polite conversation. A word such as *cunt*, which today "kidnaps our attention and forces us to consider its unpleasant connotations," as we've seen Stephen Pinker define a swearword, was an ordinary word in the Middle Ages—direct, to be sure, but not wielding any special power to raise hackles or offend. Medieval people were, to us, strikingly unconcerned with the Shit.

This is not to say that medieval people had no concept of bad language. They adopted the New Testament's stance on the immorality of idle speech. They were especially concerned with what were called "foule wordes" or "wordes of vyleny" (villainy), but these were not coextensive with our obscene words. "Foule wordes" were any words that could lead people into sin—they had bad moral effects, such as we saw in the previous chapter. Any word could be a foul word if its use enticed its speaker or hearer into doing some sort of evil, whether that would be lechery, theft, murder, gaming, or what have you.

The worst, most dangerous kind of language in the Middle Ages, however, was swearing. *Swearing* at the time had a very particular meaning, the biblical meaning—it referred only to oaths by God. Sincerely done, swearing was one of the bases of stable government and social order. Badly or frivolously—that is, vainly—done, it threatened to wreak havoc with the smooth running of society and even to injure God himself. The Holy provided the strongest taboos and most highly charged language.

Before we go on, we need to clarify what we mean by the Middle Ages, and what the linguistic situation in England was during this period. For hundreds of years, English was only one of three languages spoken in England, and not the most important one. England was triglossic—its three languages were used by different social classes and imbued with varying amounts of prestige. Latin was the language of learning, the international lingua franca, used by monks, clerks, doctors, philosophers, and many literary authors in England and across the rest of Europe. Anglo-Saxon—the Old English of Aldred's Bible translation—was the primary language of everybody else from the sixth century to 1066, when the Normans conquered England. After the Conquest, Norman French became the language of power, *parlée par* the nobility, employed in the courts of law, and prized as an expressive literary language. English became in turn the language of the downtrodden, the dispossessed. King Richard the Lionheart, portrayed in tales and movies as the savior of the brave and oppressed Saxons in Sherwood Forest, actually wouldn't have been able to talk to them—he never bothered to learn English.

By the late thirteenth century, the situation was changing. French remained the language of government, but it was no longer always the first language acquired by the nobility. Some nobles were growing up speaking English and learning French, which they still needed to walk the corridors of power, from tutors later. At this point too, English started to look much more like modern English. An influx of French words transformed it from the Old English we saw earlier, "Bóc cneurise haelendes cristes dauides sunu abrahames sunu" (950), to this: "The book of the generacioun of Jhesu Crist, the sone of Dauid, the sone of Abraham" (1370s–1380s). This is Middle English, still somewhat of a challenge to read but certainly recognizable as the ancestor of the language we speak today.

This startling transformation brings to the fore that what I have been calling "the Middle Ages" comprises a thousand years, give or take, and large cultural and linguistic variations. Aldred belongs to the end of the Early Middle Ages, the period traditionally dated from the fall of the Roman Empire in 476 to the year 1000. The High Middle Ages ran from 1000 to approximately 1300, followed by the Late Middle Ages, the time of Chaucer, from 1300 to around 1500.

In this chapter, we are talking about broad cultural trends. A thousand years is obviously a long time, and sources are scarce, especially at the beginning of the period. Most of the texts discussed in this chapter come from the Late Middle Ages, and sometimes I argue backward from Renaissance (approximately 1500–1660) sources. There simply is more material that has come down to us from these later periods. What we learn from the texts that we do have is that words we consider to be obscene today were not obscene to medieval English people. Within the thousand years of the Middle Ages, however, there were already signs that this attitude was changing and becoming more like contemporary ones. What historian Norbert Elias called the "civilizing process"—an increased concern with etiquette and decorum, coupled with tighter control over and stronger taboos around the body and its functions—began, very roughly, in the fourteenth century. Combined with the rise of Protestantism, and with it a strain of Puritanism, this civilizing process slowly transformed formerly innocuous words into what modern observers would recognize as obscenities. But I'll leave these changes for the following chapter.

A Pride of Lions, a Murder of Crows, and a Heap of Shitrows: Obscenity in the Middle Ages

Words that to modern eyes would be obscene appeared everywhere in medieval English, from the names of common plants and animals to grammar-school textbooks, medical manuals, and literature.

Now let us pause, to reflect on nature's rich store. What a wondrous bounty of plants and animals exists to gratify our eye and sense. In the single, humble ecosystem of a pond, to narrow our attention to a single example, there are stilt-legged herons that stalk the waters for finny prey; kestrels that soar above, seeming to hover in the air; smartweed and fumitory, with their delicate pink flowers beautifying the boundaries of the sylvan pool, and the lowly dandelion, that delights Youth with its bright flowers and plumaceous seeds.*

All these are literary expressions of a later sort, however. A medieval pond would have looked the same but sounded different. There would've been a *shiterow* in there fishing, a *windfucker* flying above, *arse-smart* and *cuntehoare* hugging the edges of the pond, and *pissabed* amongst the grass. If you'd have brought a picnic, perhaps to eat under an *open-arse* (medlar) tree, *pisse-mires*—ants—probably would have started to crawl on your food. These are not obscene or otherwise bad words—*shiterow* was the common, ordinary name for *heron*, *pissabed* that for *dandelion*, and so on. (*Heron* comes from the French. The *Nominale sive Verbale*, a poem from the early 1300s that translates words and phrases from Anglo-Norman into English, renders "un beuee de herouns" [a bevy of herons] as "a hep of schiterowys" [a heap of shitrows]. The translation goes some way toward explaining the centuries-long British sense of cultural inferiority.)

Medieval street and personal names also featured words that we would consider to be obscene today. In the thirteenth century, London and Oxford both boasted a Gropecuntelane, in Warwickshire there was a Schetewellwey (Shitwell Way), and several towns had Pissing Alleys. These were descriptive, not derogatory—Gropecuntelane in Oxford was the haunt of prostitutes, and the others need even less

---

*Blame Alexander Pope, at least for "finny prey." In his translation of Homer's *Odyssey*, we get both "finny prey" and "scaly tribe," and moving lines about how said tribe "its loss of Ocean's flood bewails" while "the sun's torrid radiance each fish / Condemns to die" (618–25). We will talk in Chapter 5 about how this kind of sensibility and idea of literary diction affects swearing.

explanation. They were also formal, official names, appearing on maps, in parish lists, and in legal documents such as wills. In Lincolnshire in 1202, a Randulfus Bla de Scitebroc (roughly, Randall Shitboast) was recorded in the court rolls, while Thomas Turd lived in Canterbury in 1357. There were Bastards all over the place as well, right up through to the Reverend Thomas Bastard, a somewhat famous Elizabethan poet. (His friend John Davies addressed a poem to him in 1611: "Bastard, thine Epigrams to sport inclines.") And we shouldn't forget those Cunts we met in Chapter 1—Gunoka Cuntles, Bele Wydecunthe, Godwin Clawcuncte, and Robert Clevecunt.

Dictionaries and *vulgaria*, books designed to teach young children how to speak Latin, were also full of such terms. The *Ortus Vocabulorum*, printed in 1500, defines the Latin *vulva* as "anglice a conte" ("in English, a cunt"), hundreds of years before *cunt* makes it into the *Oxford English Dictionary*. "Cunt," in fact, seems to have been the standard way to define *vulva* in the fifteenth century. A manuscript dictionary known as the *Pictorial Vocabulary* also defines it this way, as does a fifteenth-century *Nominale* (a dictionary that includes only nouns) that was owned by a schoolmaster and probably used in his classroom, since it was rolled up to be easily portable.

Likewise, *arse* (or *ers* or *ears*) was the standard way to refer to the buttocks. People sometimes refer to obscenities as "Anglo-Saxon" words, implying that they are earthy relics of a time when people spoke more freely. Actually only *arse, shit, fart*, and *bollock* really date from the Anglo-Saxon, or early medieval, era—our other obscenities are all of more recent descent. The abbot Ælfric's tenth-century collection of Latin-English vocabulary calls *nates* "ears-lyre" (arse-muscle) and *anus* "ears-þerl" (arse-hole). (He identifies *verpus*, which, we saw in Chapter 1, means "erect or circumcised penis," as the arse-hole too. Perhaps the holy man was outside his area of expertise.) Another early vocabulary defines *anus* and *culus* as "a ners." The *Catholicon Anglicum* of 1483 even includes entries for both *arse* and *erse*, in case a reader encounters a variant spelling. Several dictionaries also include the word *erse wyspe* (arse-wisp). An arse-wisp is a bunch of straw or grass used to wipe one's behind. The dictionaries have trouble translating this concept into Latin, since the Romans didn't for the most part use straw, but wiped themselves with those little sponges on sticks. They are forced to make up Latin words to define it—the *Promptorium Parvulorum* (1440) gives *memperium* and *anitergium*, "a bundle, an anus-cleaner."* This is the medieval equivalent of deciding on a word for *computer* in Hebrew. (A late fourteenth-century vocabulary gives an example of how one might use the word in a sentence: *Dum paro menpirium, sub gumpho murmurat anus*, "While I prepare the wiper, my arse roars beneath the seat of the privy.")

Despite their name, *vulgaria* were not supposed to be collections of bad language—they are vulgar in the old sense of the word, meaning "common" or "vernacular." These lists of English words and phrases with their Latin translations were used in medieval and Renaissance grammar schools by boys seven to twelve years of age. Though not obscene at the time, many of these words have come to be vulgar in the modern sense of the word too. The vulgaria compiled by Oxford don John Stanbridge around 1509 begins by going through the parts of the body, including "Hic podex . . . for an arse hole; hec urina . . . for piss; hic penis . . . for a man's yard." These terms are apparently the polite words to refer to these parts—the ones you would use if you were forced to talk about them and didn't want to give offense.

Stanbridge's text continues with a variety of phrases a schoolboy needs to know, presented in seemingly random order: "I am weary of study. I am weary of my life. . . . I am almost beshitten. You stink. . . . Turd in your teeth. . . . I will kill you with my own knife. He is the biggest coward that ever pissed." Clearly Stanbridge chose topics that would interest young boys, but he is not trying to pique their

---

* Led, by a creative but false definition in the 1976 Robertson Davies novel *The Manticore*, to believe that *anitergium* meant "trifle," choreographer Phoebe Neville inadvertently entitled a 1988 performance "Anitergium II Hohodowndownho," otherwise known as "Ass-wiper 2, the Hoedown."

interest by using bad words. Schooling in this period focused on moral development—one of the primary purposes for learning Latin was to be able to read the ancient authorities and absorb their virtues—so textbooks would have been unlikely to include language that would threaten a student's growing love of virtue.

"Courtesie" was another important part of schooling—an understanding of what kinds of language and behavior were appropriate to various circumstances. A curriculum devoted partly to instilling a sense of courtesy in students would hardly utilize a textbook that violated its dictates by including offensive language. Schools often expressly opposed themselves to bad language as well, as did the Dronfield Grammar School in Derby, which drafted a statute that mandated beatings or expulsion for "lying, swearing, and filthy speaking." Medieval schoolmasters were concerned with "bad language," but Stanbridge's *Vulgaria* makes clear that words such as *beshitten, turd, piss, yard,* and *arse hole* were not it. The vocabulary that Stanbridge used in his *Vulgaria* was not obscene. Indeed, it was appropriate to young boys whose moral development was at a delicate stage and who were learning the rudiments of courtesy.*

Medical texts likewise often used terms we might find obscene but which were then considered direct but unremarkable. As a translation of Lanfranc's *Science of Cirurgie* (c. 1400) reveals, "In women the neck of the bladder is short and is made fast to the cunt." It explains many other medical mysteries as well—how a man's "yard" has two holes, one for urine and one for sperm; how the "bollocks" collect blood to make sperm; and what to do if a man's penis gets accidentally cut off (in such a case, you should anoint him with oil of roses "about his ass and the region of the yard" and then burn him with a hot iron to stop the bleeding; the rose oil is for pain relief).

And of course medieval literature is famously obscene. Chaucer's *Canterbury Tales* (1386) is bawdy and scatological—we've already

---

* Stanbridge *does* avoid oaths. Phrases such as "by God's bones" are what schoolboys should avoid, not "turd in your teeth."

seen the Host informing someone that his rhyming is "not worth a turd," and *shitten, arse,* and *coillons* (another word for "balls"), among others, make appearances. Chaucer was also liberal with *swive,* which, along with *sard,* was the direct word for copulation until *fuck* came along in the 1500s. "For on thy bed thy wife I saw him swive," one character in the Manciple's Tale informs another. The moral of his tale, the Manciple later explains, is: "Never tell any man in your life / How another man has dight his wife," *dight* being a slightly more polite way to say the same thing, akin to today's *screw.*

The so-called mystery plays, which were performed on religious holidays and which dramatized events from biblical history, were also fairly earthy by our standards, filled with lines such as this one, spoken by the venerable patriarch Noah to his wife: "We! hold thy tongue, ramskyt, or I shall thee still" ("Shut your mouth, ram's diarrhea, or I'll shut it for you"), and this one, spoken by a shepherd: "Take out that southern tooth [stop speaking like a southerner] and put a turd in its place!" All this is evidence that these words were not "obscene" in any traditional sense. They occur in too many places in which we would never find them today, and seem to be used simply as the ordinary words for what they represent, not in deliberate attempts to shock or offend.

Obsolete "Obscenities"

Many of the words we have been discussing are in frequent use today, but medieval English had words for similar subjects with which we are less familiar. If these words were still in use today, they would probably be obscene—they are vernacular words for taboo parts of the body and bodily functions. In the Middle Ages, though, they were simply direct words for things that medieval people had less trouble talking about.

We've already encountered *sard* and *swive.* (*Swive* is not, strictly speaking, obsolete—it is undergoing something of an ironic revival today, especially in printed media, where it is employed as a jocular alternative to the *f*-word). *Kekir* and *bobrelle* are forgotten words for the clitoris, probably. The word *bobrelle* is recorded only once, in the *Pictorial Vocabulary* of the fifteenth century, where it is given as the English for *hec caturda*. In fifteenth-century Latin, *caturda* was used to indicate the labia majora or labia minora (the outer or inner lips, respectively, of the vagina), as well as the clitoris, so it is difficult to know exactly to which part of the female genitalia *bobrelle* refers.

Kekir is more clearly identifiable as the clitoris. The *Pictorial Vocabulary* (which despite its vocabulary doesn't have any good pictures) defines it as "hic tentigo." A 1425 treatise on uroscopy also gives *kykyre* as the vernacular word for *tentigo*: "lewd folk [call it] the kykyre in the cont" (the kekir in the cunt). Note that *lewd* doesn't mean "unprincipled" but rather "uneducated"—learned people would have used the Latin word itself, presumably. In Latin, *tentigo* connotes stiffness and was used for both the clitoris and an erect penis. There is some evidence that *kekir* could also be used for "erect penis" in the period—there is a Latin-English vocabulary list from 1450 that defines *kekyr* as "extensio vel arrectio virilis membri"—"an extension or erection of the membrum virile." The word embodies those Aristotelian fears about women who use their monstrous clitorises for penetration, while also gesturing toward a real biological homology—a *kekir* is what gets erect in both men and women.

Pintel, *tarse*, and *ʒerde* are all medieval English words for the penis. *Tarse* or *ters* is the oldest word, appearing first in Anglo-Saxon. *Ʒerde* (or *yard*) was originally a euphemism—it also meant "staff" or "rod"—that became a direct word for the thing it had been employed to avoid, like *penis* in Latin. An early fifteenth-century anatomy text informs its readers that "the yard is an official member (one that performs a service for the rest of the body, such as a finger or foot) . . . which men call a ters but for courtesy women call it a yard . . . a ters was principally ordained to enable the piss and spermatic matter to be cast out." *Pintel* appears to have come into general use, for the most part replacing *ters*, in the mid-fourteenth century, although it appears in names—Robertus Pintel, Johannes Swetpintel—two hundred years earlier.

One mid-fifteenth-century poem, *A Talk of Ten Wives on Their Husbands Ware*, manages to fit in both *pintel* and *tarse*, as well as several metaphors for the penis. None of the ten women in the poem has found a satisfactory penis, and each complains bitterly. One says her husband's "meat" is the size of a snail, another that his "ware" is the size of three beans, while the third complains: "I have one of those, that is worthless when it's needed. When 'our sire's' pants are torn, his penis peeps out of the hole like a maggot." The fifth wife thinks she has it even worse: "'Our sire' breeds like a deer. He pisses his tarse [ejaculates]—once a year, just like a buck." These lines are certainly insulting—"Your penis is like a maggot"?—but again the vocabulary would not have been considered obscene. *Pintel* and *tarse* are direct—these tavern-going women do not mince words— but the poem gives no sense that they carry more charge than *meat* or *ware*, which other women use as metaphors for their husbands' penises. *Pintel*, as we have seen, was employed in medical texts as well as tirades—you could cast aspersions at the thing it represented, but the word itself was beyond reproach.

Medieval Fighting Words

Given that so much of what we would define as obscenity was in this period simply bracing and direct, how did people insult each other in medieval England? To learn what people said to abuse and offend each other seven hundred years ago, one can look at court records for charges of defamation or slander, assault with contumelious words (words that are "reproachful and tending to convey disgrace and humiliation," according to the *Oxford English Dictionary*), scolding, and barratry (bringing false lawsuits; more generally, obstreperous public behavior). These are crimes of the spoken word, consisting of insults to authority or to someone's personal reputation; libel is the written equivalent. Often court records were kept in French or Latin, and often they state simply that Alicia Garlek scolded William Wipetail, or that Rogerus Prikeproud is a "common barrator." (These are all actual medieval names: Alicia Garlic, William Wipe-Dick—though *tail* could refer to both the penis and the vagina—and Roger Proud-of-His-Prick.) Occasionally, however, scribes wrote down the precise English words at issue, so we know that when medieval English people traded insults, they were usually accusations of sexual immorality, such as *whore,* when directed at women, and accusations of dishonesty, such as *false, thief, robber,* or *knave,* when directed at men. The Victorian legal scholar Frederic William Maitland published a number of thirteenth-century cases from manorial courts (run by feudal lords) and translated them from the Latin in which they were recorded. Of the slander cases included, which were brought from 1249 to 1294, six involved accusations against men of stealing or other dishonesty, one involved a woman being called a meretrix (a prostitute), and in one the slanderous accusation was not recorded.

Late medieval accounts provide a more vivid record of invective, as cases began to be transcribed in English instead of Latin or law French. In London in 1497, as just one example, Joan Rokker was charged with defamation of Joan Sebar for saying publicly, "Thou strong whore and strong harlot . . . Go home thou strong whore and bid thy dame ordain the clouts [cloths to use as diapers or swaddling]; an ever I had child in my belly thou hast one. Here wert thou dight [screwed], and here lay thy legs and here thy feet." Likewise in 1496, Elizabeth Whyns was fighting over some property with her neighbor Edward Harrison and verbally assaulted him: "Thou art a false man and false harlot to me." (*Harlot* originally meant "beggar or vagabond," as in these lines from a circa 1360 version of the *Morte Arthure*: "For harlots and servants shall help but little— / They will hie them hence." Around 1400, it acquired the additional meaning of "a professional male entertainer; buffoon, jester; story-teller"—in both cases it was a term that indicated low social status and applied to men only. Through a process that literary critic and author C. S. Lewis called "the moralisation of status words," "words which originally referred to a person's rank—to legal, social, or economic status and the qualifications which have often been attached to these—have a tendency to become words which assign a type of character and behavior. Those implying superior status can become terms of praise; those implying inferior status, terms of disapproval." As Lewis points out, words that in the past denoted high social status, such as *noble* and *gentle*, now indicate good moral character. Others, such as *villein* [an unfree tenant], *churl* [any person not nobility or clergy], *knave* [a boy child], *caitiff* [a captive or slave], and *wretch* [an exile], went in the other direction. These pejorated, as philologists say, becoming terms of abuse or opprobrium. Likewise, *harlot* acquired a negative meaning. In the mid-fourteenth century it began to be used for a man "of licentious habits," as the *Middle English Dictionary* puts it—and to add insult to injury, it came to be applied to women as well.)

Occasionally men were insulted with sexual terms too, including *cuckold*, *whoreson*, or *whoremonger*, as when Thomas Wybard attacked William Richardson as "whoreson and whoremonger priest." Wybard probably did not mean that Richardson was literally the child of a loose woman or that he kept a stable of prostitutes. Wybard is simply searching for the most effective way to abase the man, and in a society that valued lineage, female chastity, and (at least in theory) male sexual continence, the concept of whoredom proved a promiscuous source of abusive terms. Today we could scarcely conceive of an assault with contumelious words that doesn't contain at least a few obscenities. But the court records from 1200 to 1500 indicate that for medieval people, a simple "you false whoremaster son of a whore" sufficed.

Privacy and the Privy Members

The image on the next page shows a pilgrimage badge from the end of the fourteenth century. Badges like this were purchased by pilgrims at the shrines they visited and worn on hats or clothing as

Three phalluses carrying a crowned vulva on a litter.

souvenirs of their travels. Some of the badges feature motifs we
would consider to be more appropriate for a holy journey: images
of saints, religious mottos, crucifixes. But many resemble the one
above: winged phalluses; vulvas hunting on horseback or climb-
ing ladders; a crowned vulva and a phallus, both with legs, over the
inscription "pintel in." Despite all appearances to the contrary, these
are Christian religious objects. Such badges were thought to have

apotropaic power to protect against envy and the evil eye, like the *fascini* worn by young Roman boys. And like fescennine songs, some of the badges used mockery to protect pilgrims and the sacred relics that inspired their travels. The badge pictured above, for example, parodies processions in which icons of the Virgin Mary were carried. Similar figures can be found in churches beginning around the twelfth century: the sheela-na-gigs, "stone carvings of naked women exposing their genitals," and ithyphallic men, with large erect penises. This is obscenity in its second Roman sense, the Shit married to the Holy, obscenity with religious functions.

Unlike Roman religious obscenity, such pilgrimage badges were not officially sanctioned. The chancellor of the University of Paris, for example, decried the "shameless and naked images displayed for sale in churches and during church festivals" in the late fourteenth century. They were expressions of popular as opposed to "orthodox" religion, like the Israelite worship of Asherah. And they were far from the only place in medieval English society where "private" parts of the body were on display.

In previous chapters we've talked about the connection between what is "shameful to perform in public" and what is "shameful to name," as the great Renaissance humanist Erasmus put it. So what actually was shameful to perform or to show in public in the Middle Ages?

The short answer is, not much. There was almost no such thing as privacy as we know it, even for the very rich. The earliest houses consisted of a large, central great hall and a few outbuildings. Most of the business of life was conducted in the hall—visitors were entertained, meals were cooked (over a large open fire in the middle of the room), meals were eaten, justice was dispensed for the manor court, and so on. The hall was also, apparently, where one might openly perform some bodily functions we would most definitely conceal today. In his *De civilitate morum puerilium* (*On Civility in Boys*), Erasmus announces that "it is impolite to greet someone who is urinating or defecating," implying that even as late as 1530—when

Henry VIII was king—it was normal to run into people thus occupied and engage them in conversation. Two sets of court regulations from the sixteenth century specify where these voluble voiders might be encountered: "One should not, like rustics who have not been to court or lived among refined and honourable people, relieve oneself without shame or reserve in front of ladies, or before the doors or windows of court chambers or other rooms." Also, "Let no one, whoever he may be, before, at, or after meals, early or late, foul the staircases, corridors or closets with urine or other filth, but go to suitable, prescribed, places for such relief." These rules are from the 1500s, when, evidently, people were *still* making use of the floor and corners, and it was beginning to be seen as a problem. Before then, it was unremarkable.

We can reconstruct what a dinner party in the Great Hall during the High Middle Ages—1100 to 1300—might have been like by reading between the lines of medieval conduct books. First of all, most food would have been eaten with the fingers and a knife. Forks were either unknown or thought to be an eastern affectation. Dishes were passed, and each person helped himself with his fingers, placing his food on his trencher, a thick piece of stale bread. Soups and drinks were passed down the table with each person taking a sip, or occasionally eaten with soup spoons. People apparently felt the urge to spit much more than we do today and did it wherever the urge took them—in the washbasin, on the table, over the table. Conduct books assert, however, that really the only polite place to spit is on the floor. The 1430 *Boke of Curtasye* warns that "if you spit over the table or upon it, you shall be held an uncourteous man," and "When you wash after you eat, don't spit in the basin or splash water around." It was thought to be unhealthy to retain "wind," so there was probably quite a lot of farting and belching—it takes until 1577 for instructions to arrive in Hugh Rhodes's *Book of Nurture*, perhaps one of the "books for good manners" Shakespeare mentions in *As You Like It*, that one should "belch near no man's face with a corrupt fumosity; / Turn from such occasion, it is a stinking ventosity." Rushes were strewn on the floors of most halls and were supposed to be changed weekly or even daily to keep them clean and fresh-smelling, but this was an ideal and not always a reality. When he traveled to England from Holland in the early 1500s, Erasmus noted that "the floors too are generally spread with clay and then with rushes from some marsh, which are renewed from time to time but so as to leave a basic layer, sometimes for twenty years, under which fester spittle, vomit, dogs' urine and men's too, dregs of beer and cast-off bits of fish, and other unspeakable kinds of filth."

In the evenings, most people in the household bedded down in the hall as well. They slept on the floor amid those sweet-smelling rushes, or on benches, as described in these lines from the Anglo-Saxon epic *Beowulf* (c. 800):

> Soon then Beowulf
> Yearning for bedrest bent to his hall-bench
> Sank gratefully to slumber in Heorot (the Hall)
> Once more a night-guest in that mighty hallroom.
> The Danes' thane-servant thoughtful of their needs
> Spread bench-covers bore final cupfuls
> Readied the meadhall for rest in the night.
> The great-hearted slept in that steep-gabled hall.

The lord and lady of the manor probably would have had a chamber to themselves at the head of the hall, at first behind a curtain, then by the thirteenth century as a solar, a separate bed-sitting room. Even then, these rooms were not private in our sense of the word. Servants, male and female, would have slept in the same room as their masters, and since most people slept naked, this meant that "the sight of total nakedness was the everyday rule up to the 16th century," as one historian puts it. Female servants would bathe their male masters, and vice versa, and they would bring drinks to their naked lords and ladies in bed. All this naked togetherness makes it sound like medieval English people witnessed other people having sex more often than we do today, and that was probably the case. Historian Ruth Mazzo Karras writes, "Medieval people would be much less likely to see representations of sex acts, but they would be much more likely than modern ones to witness the actual performance of those acts." Charges of adultery were supported by eyewitnesses; clandestine marriages were determined to be valid because someone saw the parties involved having sex; defamation suits about "whoredom" were affirmed or denied on the basis of whether witnesses had seen the defendant in flagrante delicto. In a 1366 case about a clandestine marriage between an older man and an heiress who may or may not have been of age, it was determined that the two had consummated their marriage because the girl's companion, Joan, had been lying next to them in bed when she "heard a noise from them like they were making love together, and how two or three times Alice silently complained at the force on account of John's labour as if she had been hurt then as a result of his labour." This was not some sort of kinky setup—it reflects the limited privacy available to medieval couples. The two women shared a bed, and there was probably no other place for the couple to go.

These behaviors—profuse spitting, defecating, and fornicating in public—go hand in hand with what historian Norbert Elias identifies as a low threshold of shame and repugnance. "What was lacking" in the Middle Ages, Elias writes, "was the invisible wall of affects which seems now to rise between one human body and another, repelling and separating." Medieval people lacked what we feel as "embarrassment at the mere sight of many bodily functions of others, and often at their mere mention, or as a feeling of shame when one's own functions are exposed to the gaze of others." People could freely do and say things that we tend to conceal in our actions and in our language (if we want to be considered polite). This is a major reason that words that are obscene to us today were not in the Middle Ages. The things represented by *cunt* and *sard* and *shit* were much less charged: they carried no onus of taboo. Thus the words themselves had less power.

This doesn't mean that such words were never used as insults or in jokes. Excrement, for example, was just as unpleasant seven hundred years ago as it is today, and so it offered a useful way to convey disapproval. When Chaucer wants to criticize corrupt priests, he writes that it is a shame to see "a shitten shepherd and a clean sheep." We've seen that characters in the mystery plays use excrement to insult each other, with Noah calling his wife "ram's diarrhea." A well-known comic set piece in Chaucer's "Miller's Tale" involves Nicholas and Alison tricking the clerk Absolon into kissing Alison's "naked arse." He is clued into what he is kissing by the fact that he feels a "beard." The humor runs on humiliation and comeuppance rather than on obscenity. The word *arse* itself is not the punch line of the joke, and Chaucer could have used *buttocks* or *tail* to make the same point, though he would have lost the directness of *arse*. Likewise, Chaucer's "shitten shepherd" could have just as easily been "befouled shepherd" or "filthy shepherd," and Noah's wife is lucky that he didn't call her something *really* offensive, like *false* or *whore*.

This is not to say that all words had the same register in the Middle Ages, or that medieval authors couldn't choose among a variety of synonyms with different valences depending on what they were trying to express. Part of the richness of Chaucer's work is that he could and did. There is in fact a famous crux involving a choice of register in "The Wife of Bath's Tale," where at one point the Wife refers to her womanly parts as a "queynte" (quaint). Noted Chaucer scholar Larry Benson observes that many scholars have identified *queynte* as "the forerunner of the modern cunt, and the normal, if vulgar, name for the vagina" back then. They suggest that the Wife of Bath's uses of *queynte* are blatantly obscene, referring to the vagina by its most offensive name. As we have seen, though, if she had wanted to say *cunt*, she easily could have—the word was in plentiful use when the *Canterbury Tales* was written. (One manuscript of the poem actually does have her saying *conte* instead of *queynte*.) But above all the Wife wants to sound refined, so she employs French-derived euphemisms—*queynte*, meaning "quaint," as well as *bele chose,* meaning "elegant, pleasing thing." Benson argues that despite what so many believe, *queynte* was not "the forerunner of the modern obscenity." Indeed, it was not even the normal word for *vagina.* The Wife, Benson contends, wasn't "talking dirty." She was "talking cute." Rather than uttering the *c*-word, she was coyly avoiding it.

The reason scholars would like to believe that *queynte* was obscene is that it fits nicely with the images we have of the Middle Ages, images that, we have seen, contain a large degree of truth. Writers did indeed use many words that we would consider to be obscene, in contexts we might find alternately shocking and hilarious. But they weren't always "talking dirty"—they could choose words from higher or lower registers, from *queynte* to *cunt.*

Wurdys Waste—Wasted Words

So what was "bad language" in medieval England? There were campaigns against it, conducted mainly by religious writers who railed against "foule wordes," "words of villainy," or "words of ribaldry." These "foule wordes" were not necessarily obscene; they were any and all words that might lead people to sin. Medieval English people had a New Testament attitude toward "talking dirty." As in the Letter to the Ephesians, the problem with "foul language" was not that it was shocking or offensive but that it could start people down the yellow brick road to hell.

Unsurprisingly, most explanations of what "foule wordes" were and why they were dangerous occurred in what are now called pastoral texts. These were manuals written by learned churchmen, designed to classify the multitude of ways it was possible to sin, and to pinpoint the one and only way to be redeemed. Some of these works contained high-flown philosophical arguments about, say, the nature of the Antichrist, but most were meant to be used by less learned priests as they cared for the souls of their parishioners. They discussed what was involved in making a full confession, described the joys of heaven and the terrors of hell, and mostly listed sins mortal and venial, from Adultery, Theft, and Murder to Delight in Soft Beds and Excessive Fondness for Cushiony Places to Kneel. They devote large sections to the "sins of the tongue"—the ways words themselves can be sinful, and the ways they can precipitate even worse sins when spoken.

If the authors of these texts had thought that obscenity was a particular problem, they would have found a way to make that clear. They knew and revered St. Augustine, the Roman theologian (from the tail end of the Roman Empire, AD 354–430), who in his *City of God* argued that obscenity developed as a result of the Fall. When God punished him for eating the fruit, Adam lost the ability to control his penis with his will, as he could his hands and feet. (Some people, Augustine notes, have so much control over various body parts that they can "sing" by emitting stinkless farts at will.) Instead, Adam had to submit to Lust, which sometimes gave him erections when he didn't want them, and refused to cooperate when he did. This is the origin of Shame, according to Augustine, and it is Shame that renders certain words obscene. In the Garden of Eden, he speculates, "there would not even be words that could be called obscene [*obscena*], but all our talk on this subject would be as decent as what we say in speaking about the other members of the body."

The pastoral texts ignore Augustine's wishful thinking about his disobedient member and do not discuss obscenity, though it could easily be seen as a "sin of the tongue." The early fifteenth-century *Speculum Christiani* (*The Christian's Mirror*) contains a pretty exhaustive list of the ways your tongue can get you into trouble, none of which is by speaking obscene words:

> These are the sins of the mouth: Intemperance or unlawful tasting, eating, or drinking; idle jangling [chattering]; words of harlotry speaking; God's holy name in vain taking; lies; false [promises]; vain swearing; forswearing; slandering, scorning; banning [cursing]: backbiting; discord sowing; false deeming [judging]; wrong upbraiding;

secrets or advice foolishly discovering; chiding; threatening, boasting; false witness bearing, evil counsel giving; flattering; evil deeds praising; good deeds perverting; Christ or his word or any of his servants scorning, slandering, or despising; unskillful pleading [in a court case]; vain arguing; foolishly laughing, scornful mocking; proud and presumptuous speaking; nice and jolly chanting [wanton and merry singing]; or to sing more for the praising of men than of God.

These texts are quite obsessively concerned with classifying sin and laying it out for scrutiny—*Jacob's Well* (early fifteenth century) breaks down the "wose of synne" (the ooze of sin) into several sub-oozes, including, first, the ooze of pride, which itself has eight corners, the first of which is presumption, which itself has six feet in breadth, including self-will, extravagance, litigiousness, et cetera. The fourteenth-century *Ayenbite of Inwyt* (*The Again-Biting of the Inner Wit*, or *The Remorse of Conscience*) divides sin according to the "the seven heads of the beast of hell." Pride is the first head, as it was the initial ooze, and it has seven boughs growing on it (so much for the beast metaphor)—untruth, despite, presumption, and the like. The first bough, untruth, has three twigs: foulhood, foolishness, and apostasy. Some of the sins are further divided into leaves on the twig on the bough (on the head of the beast)—a this-is-the-house-that-Jack-built of everything that people can do to alienate themselves from God or bring down his wrath. If there was a category of "obscenity," or any particular words that were commonly thought to be worse than others, there would be room for it somewhere in the ooze or on the head of the beast. If anything like the today's "Big Six" existed in the Middle Ages, they would find a perfect home in these flow charts of sin.

Instead, the pastoral texts worry about *any* words that lead to sin. *The Ayenbite of Inwit* describes a chain reaction like that implied in Ephesians, in which foul words lead to foul deeds:

The devil tempts of this sin in five manners, as Saint Gregory says. First in foul sight, then in foul words, then in foul touching, then in foul kissing, and afterward I come to the deed. For of foul sight, I come to speech. And from speech to handling, from handling to kissing, from kissing to the deed. And this subtly does the devil make [people] go from one to the other.

Foul words bring people into sin, particularly into the sin of lechery (though sometimes into gluttony—excessive indulgence in the pleasures of the body—as well). The danger of this sort of speech, "as medieval writers repeat, is that indecent words lead to indecent actions," as literary critic R. Howard Bloch puts it. Speech leads to touching, touching to kissing, and kissing to the deed. Obscene words such as *cunt* might lead people into sin, but so could an innocuous— to modern ears —poem, perhaps Andrew Marvell's "To His Coy Mistress": "Had we but world enough, and time / This coyness, Lady, were no crime." In the schema set out by the pastoral texts, these are equally bad kinds of language. In fact, "Had we but world enough" could be considered *worse*. It is the beginning of a beautiful poem that might actually be quite an effective means of seduction, whereas if you called a woman a "filthy cunt," she would not be super likely to sleep with you.

This moral judgment of bad language accounts for a difference in the way medieval writers tended to use words for sex and words for excrement. The vocabulary lists in John Stanbridge's *Vulgaria* exemplify this difference. After translating Latin names for parts of the body with their most direct English equivalents, as we've seen— *podex* for "arse hole," *urina* for "piss," and so on—Stanbridge comes to *hec vulva*. He does not translate this as "cunt"—in fact, he fails to translate it at all, chickening out with a Latin explanation: "locus ubi puer concipitur," "the place where a boy is conceived." A few decades earlier, the *Ortus Vocabulorum* and many other dictionaries had given *vulva* simply and directly as "cunt," but Stanbridge evidently thought that the vernacular version would be too much for his young charges to handle, inappropriate for a textbook or for the schoolroom.

Words for sex and for the parts of the body involved in it are inherently more dangerous in the medieval scheme of bad language. Talking about excrement will very likely entice no one into sin. But if you employ a word such as *cunt* or *pintel* or *sard*—or if you simply describe an especially fetching dress or a well-formed leg—you risk conjuring up foul thoughts, and foul thoughts lead to foul deeds.

Chaucer was aware of this possibility. He himself composed a pastoral text, "The Parson's Tale," the final tale told on the pilgrimage to Canterbury. It is entirely typical of these manuals, dealing with the importance of true penitence and the dangers of the seven deadly sins, including the sins of the tongue. It is followed by "Chaucer's Retraction," in which he begs Christ's pardon for his "worldly vanities" including the *Canterbury Tales*, because they "sownen into sin"—they tend toward, are conducive to, sin. Whether or not Chaucer was really apologizing for his secular poetry, and critics debate that, he is acknowledging that his poems about lecherous wives, angry friars, and butt-kissing students might at least be interpreted as "foul words."

By God's Bones

In the Middle Ages, the equivalent of modern obscenity was not "foul words" but oaths. Swearing, as we saw in the previous chapter, historically meant only one thing—oath swearing. Today, of course, it refers to both oaths and obscene words. But from the earliest Old English texts right to the end of the nineteenth century, the word *swearing* referred to oaths alone.

There were and are two kinds of oath swearing, as we saw with the Bible. There is *sincere* swearing, making an oath before God that what you say is true, or that you really will do what you say you intend to do. And there is *vain* swearing, which is any kind of bad swearing—swearing habitually, which trivializes God's name and power; swearing falsely, which makes God witness to a lie; or swearing wrongly in forms such as "by God's bones," which had catastrophic effects on God's body. Vain swearing *was* medieval obscenity, carrying all the power of the public utterance of taboo topics that defines obscene words. Vain swearing shocked and offended people when they heard it. It was used in order *to* shock and offend, to insult or injure someone. It was used as an intensifier, to supply extra strength to some aspect of an utterance. And it provided an inexhaustible topic for controversialists, who, then as now, looked at its efflorescence and saw the end of civil society and perhaps the world.

Sincere swearing was extremely important in medieval culture. In the early and high Middle Ages, England was a feudal society, in which oaths guaranteed key political relationships between lords and vassals. From the king on down, men swore a series of interlocking oaths of fealty to set up networks of land ownership, military support, and agricultural labor. The king granted huge estates to his nobles; they in turn granted bits of land to lesser aristocrats, who granted some to peasants. (At the bottom of the heap were the aforementioned villeins, the unfree peasants, who needed their lord's permission to marry, leave the estate, join the clergy, etc.) At each stage, the person of higher status swore to protect his vassal and to provide enough land for him to maintain his position in society. The person of lower status swore to provide military service, furnish counsel, and administer the land he had received. There were few written contracts to give these relationships force, and little recourse to be had in the legal system. God did the enforcing. If you broke your oath, God was supposed to punish you, either directly, by visiting a plague upon your children or livestock (or perhaps upon your part by which turds are shat out), or indirectly, through the strong arm of the person with whom you broke faith.

Just such a broken oath was the cause of—or at least the justification for—the Norman Conquest of England. In 1064, the Saxon

Earl of Wessex, Harold, found himself in Normandy at the court of its duke, William the Bastard (as he was known before he conquered England and made people stop calling him that). Harold had been either blown off course or sent there as a messenger by the ailing and childless King Edward the Confessor to inform William that he had been chosen as heir to the English throne. Whether he arrived by accident or by design, Harold swore an oath of fealty to William, promising to defend and further the duke's right to the English throne. Some sources have him swearing this oath on a chest full of holy relics, to give it weight. But within two years of his pledge, Harold had returned to England, King Edward had died, and Harold had acceded to the throne. William was outraged at Harold's violation of his oath of fealty and went into battle carrying the chest of relics upon which his vassal had sworn.

Harold's broken oath may have been merely an excuse for William to take the throne he so clearly wanted, but we should not underestimate how "oaths were taken with deadly seriousness in medieval Europe," as historian Simon Schama writes in his recounting of this incident. William probably *was* outraged at the violation— the whole feudal system of government depended on people like Harold being sincere in their oaths. He also probably reckoned that this would be a good time to invade, since God would be on his side. God would punish Harold to avenge his own tarnished honor—he might even make William the instrument of his vengeance. (In the Bayeux Tapestry, you can see Harold trying to pull a spear out of his eye before he is trampled to death by horses. You be the judge.)

Sincere oaths were also a fundamental part of the medieval legal system. As today, witnesses in court were usually required to swear that they were telling the truth. But it was also possible for a person's guilt or innocence to be proven by an oath alone, through a process called compurgation. If someone was accused of a crime, he could swear an oath that he was innocent. If he found a certain number of compurgators or "oath helpers" who would swear that they believed he was telling the truth about his innocence—that his oath was sincere—he would be released. In 1276 in London, for example, Christiana de Dunelmia was accused of killing her husband with poison. She swore that she hadn't, and managed to find the requisite thirty-six people to swear that she was of good character and that her oaths were credible. She was acquitted. Other, less serious crimes required fewer oath helpers—twelve was a more usual number.

If people couldn't come up with compurgators, they could sometimes undergo a trial by ordeal instead, which most often involved walking a set distance while carrying a red-hot iron, pulling something from a pot of boiling water, or being thrown into a pond to sink or float. In the first two cases, the person's injuries would be checked after three days. If they were starting to heal, the person would be judged innocent; if they were festering, he was guilty. In the pond case, an innocent person would float and a guilty one sink (the opposite valuation was assigned during the witchcraft trials of the sixteenth and seventeenth centuries—there, the innocent sank and usually drowned). In these ordeals, God was thought to be judging the guilt or innocence of the accused. If the person was innocent, God would intervene directly to make sure that he was not burned by the iron or that her skin wouldn't slough off from reaching into the boiling water.

Compurgation worked the same way. God would judge the truth or falsity of the oaths of the accused and of his oath helpers. If any of them was swearing falsely, he would inflict horrible punishments. To us, compurgation seems like a more or less ridiculous procedure. What contemporary criminal wouldn't swear before God that he was innocent, if it meant he could go free? What modern murderer would stick at a little perjury? But to medieval English people, false swearing wasn't a minor thing—it was a major sin, equivalent or almost equivalent to murder. St. Augustine held that "worse is he than an homicide, that compels a man to swear, whom he knows to forswear himself. For the homicide slays but the body, whereas he slays the soul, yea two souls rather." It was also dangerous—God would take vengeance on an oath breaker, not just for the term of a prison sentence, but perhaps for all eternity.

In the previous chapter, we mentioned the Lollards, who took a stand on Matthew 5:34–37—"I say to you, Do not swear at all"—and were persecuted for it. I will discuss them in more detail here, because their story vividly reveals just how seriously people took oaths in the Middle Ages. Lollardy began in England in the late fourteenth century. Its members are often thought of as proto-Protestants, since many of their beliefs prefigured central tenets of the Reformation. They translated the Bible into English so that everyone could read it (Wyclif's Bible, with the turds and the bollocks, is the Lollard Bible), they refused to acknowledge the Pope's authority, they spoke out against what they saw as the corruptions of the established Catholic Church, such as selling indulgences—what Martin Luther was attacking when he nailed his Ninety-Five Theses to the door of a church in Wittenberg in 1517 and started the Protestant Reformation. The most famous Lollard may be Sir John Oldcastle, who appears as Falstaff in Shakespeare's Henry the Fourth, Parts One and Two, and Henry V. (In real life, he didn't die peacefully in his bed, babbling of green fields, as Falstaff is said to have done. He was tried and convicted for heresy, but escaped from prison to lead a series of rebellions and plots against his former friend Prince Hal. He was eventually captured, hanged, and then burned, gallows and all.) Lollards were never particularly numerous or widespread, partly because their attempts to foment a revolution in religious practice occurred before the invention of moveable type. It was hard to advocate individual reading of the Bible in English when all Bibles had to be copied by hand. Without inexpensive and easily available printed books, they couldn't disseminate their ideas widely enough, and the movement failed to catch on across England or over its borders.

In the fourteenth and early fifteenth centuries, though, the Catholic authorities didn't know that Lollardy would simply peter out. They were terrified that Lollard ideas of reform would catch on, stripping them of their gold-embroidered robes and bejeweled chalices, perhaps even putting them out of a job. In 1401, Parliament enacted a new law, De Haeretico Comburendo—"of the burning of heretics"— which stipulated that anyone found to be "usurping the office of preaching," teaching or writing books about heretical doctrines, instilling doubt about the sacraments, or otherwise acting like a Lollard would be arrested and, if he or she didn't recant, punished severely, possibly even burned at the stake. Under this law, any person suspected of harboring irregular religious views would be interrogated by high-ranking churchmen, the English version of the Spanish Inquisition. Many of the questions asked in these examinations centered on what was perhaps the Lollards' most controversial belief, involving the Eucharist. Orthodox Catholic doctrine held that after the Host was consecrated by the priest, it was no longer bread but was entirely the physical body of Christ.* The "accidents" of the bread were the same, so it still looked like a wafer, but the "substance" was transformed—it *was* God. Many Lollards, in contrast, believed that there was still some bread in there, coexisting with God's body. Other Lollards, even more radical, asserted that the Host was merely bread and that the importance of the Eucharist was in spiritual communion with God. At her trial in 1429, Margery Baxter described how she knew that God was not physically present in the Host: "If every such sacrament were God, and the very body of Christ, there should be an infinite number of gods, because that a thousand priests, and more, do every day make a thousand such gods, and afterwards eat them, and void them out again in places, where, if you will seek them, you may find many such gods." The Host can't be God's body, because then thousands of Gods would be shat into privies every day.

Unless you were dealing with someone as forthright as Margery Baxter, these issues were abstruse and confusing, even in the fifteenth century. If somebody told you that "the sacrament on the

---

* By *orthodox* I mean the strand of Catholicism that upheld traditional, Church-sanctioned views, as opposed to heretical groups that questioned parts of those doctrines—not the Eastern Orthodox churches.

altar is very God's body in form of bread, but it is in another manner God's body than it is in heaven," as one Lollard stated his position on the Eucharist, would you call him a heretic and burn him, or not? Rather than wade around in the murky waters of accidents versus substance, orthodox authorities preferred a simpler test for heresy: they would ask suspected Lollards to swear on a Bible. If the person swore, okay; if not, pile up the faggots.

When threatened with punishment or death, some Lollards agreed to swear on the Bible, as did John Skylly, who in 1428 recanted his beliefs and asserted that "I abjure and forswear, and swear by these holy gospels by me bodily touched that from henceforth I shall never hold error." The authorities didn't want to give him any wiggle room—he had to swear his oath exactly as the orthodox Catholic authorities specified, "bodily touching" the Bible. In the same situation, many other Lollards refused to swear and were sentenced to death. Mostly they were burned at the stake, like William White, Hugh Pye, and John Waddon in 1428; occasionally the executions were more imaginative, as was the case with John Badby, who in 1410 was burned to death in a barrel.

The bizarre thing about using swearing as a litmus test is that, generally, Lollards had nothing against it. Lollards and orthodox Catholics both agreed that it was proper to swear, that Christ did not forbid all oaths. They agreed that oaths should not be made vainly or rashly, but according to the rules that God laid down in Jeremiah. And they agreed that you shouldn't swear by creatures, created things that reflect God's glory but are not part of him, exemplified by the list Jesus gives in the Sermon on the Mount—not by heaven, not by the earth, not by Jerusalem, not by your own head.

Where they disagreed was on whether the Bible should be considered a "creature." The orthodox Catholics thought that the Bible should be considered a part of God, since it is his Word. The Lollards argued that the Bible was a physical book made by human hands, hence earthly and forbidden to use in oaths. If the orthodox authorities had asked them to swear by God, or by God's holiness, or by God's great name, they would have, but they would not do it with their hand on the Bible, touching, as they believed, a creature. William Thorpe, for example, was all ready to swear at his trial in 1407— "Sir, since I may not now be otherwise believed, but by swearing . . . therefore I am ready, by the word of God (as the Lord commanded me by his word) to swear." But when his examiners brought out a Bible and told him to "lay then thine hand upon the book, touching the holy gospel of God," suddenly he wouldn't do it. The fate of the steadfast William Thorpe is obscure, but he was probably imprisoned for life. Orthodox authorities imprisoned or executed hundreds of people for a disagreement, in part, over an interpretation of an interpretation of Matthew 5:34–37.

Given that swearing had so central a role in medieval English society, it is no wonder that "false swearing becomes one of the most commonly (and vehemently) denounced sins of medieval times," as philologist Geoffrey Hill notes. Even if an oath is false or is sworn for sinful reasons, God looks down from heaven to witness it. He guarantees oaths that seduce young girls into ruin, that trick people out of their lawful inheritance, that basely deny responsibility for a murder. Because of the bargain he made with humanity in the Bible, God has in essence no choice but to witness these oaths that are repugnant to him. God can punish these swearers, though, and he was often thought to do so—the pastoral literature abounds with stories about false swearers who incur his wrath. In one example from 1303, a rich man and a poor man are fighting about a piece of land. The rich man declares his intent to swear that the land is his, though it actually belongs to the poor man, and he is able to find many compurgators who are themselves willing to swear that his oath will be good. It looks as if the rich man will triumph, but "when he had sworn his oath / And kissed the Book [the Bible] before them all / He never rose up again / But lay dead before them there." God knows that the rich man has forsworn himself, and strikes him dead. "See how vengeance was his reward," the story concludes, "Almighty God, who is Truth, / He would take to false witness."

Sometimes, inscrutably, God doesn't punish such swearers. False swearing then damages God's honor and reputation, denigrating the Holy Name that language should instead praise and glorify. Or, as Steven Pinker writes, "every time someone reneges on an oath and is not punished by the big guy upstairs, it casts doubt on his existence, his potency, or at the very least how carefully he's paying attention." We saw in the previous chapter how Yahweh's rise to the top of the celestial hierarchy was linked inextricably to his reputation vis-à-vis the other gods. Swearing by Yahweh confessed him to be omniscient and omnipotent—the only God you need. False swearing dares him to prove this, again and again. The more people swear falsely and escape punishment, the less reliable God's power comes to seem.

Vain swearing—swearing habitually and/or for trifles—was seen to be another problem in medieval England, for similar reasons. God had to fulfill his side of the bargain and judge the righteousness of an oath anytime someone mouthed the proper formula, whether in a matter of life or death or to express annoyance while playing cards. Reading Chaucer, or indeed almost any piece of medieval literature, it is obvious that vain swearing was widely practiced. Chaucer's characters can barely start a sentence without prefacing it with "By God's soul," "For Christ's passion," or "By God's precious heart." The Pardoner addresses this kind of language before he starts his tale, warning that God will take vengeance on these swearers: "Frequent swearing is an abominable thing." He notes that vain swearing is so important to God that he forbids it in the second commandment, before he outlaws "homicide, or many other cursed things" in later commandments.

One kind of vain swearing worried medieval commentators more than all the rest—swearing by the parts of God's body. Chaucer's Pardoner gives examples of these oaths as he rails against improper swearing: "by the blood of Christ," "by God's arms," "by God's nails," and similar phrases. In tract after tract, writers single out these oaths for prohibition, repeating with the anonymous author of "On the Twenty-Five Articles" (c. 1388) that "it is not lawful to swear by creatures, nor by God's bones, sides, nails, nor arms, or by any member of Christ's body, as most men do, for this is against holy writ, holy doctors, and common law, and great punishment is set on it." *Jacob's Well* discusses these oaths as the fifth leaf on the branch of forswearing (which is the sixth branch on the tree of evil tongue, which grows somewhere in the ooze of gluttony), and explains why they are so very dangerous. People who use such oaths "rend God limb from limb, and are worse than Jews, for they rent him only once, and such swearers rend him every day anew. And the Jews didn't break his bones, but they break his bones, and each limb from the other, and leave none whole." The problem with the body-part oaths is that they "rend" God—they tear his body apart. In Catholic doctrine, Christ ascended to heaven in his physical, human body and now sits at the right hand of God, waiting to come again in glory to judge the quick and the dead. (One Lollard has somehow acquired the information that Christ's body "in heaven . . . is seven foot in form and figure of flesh and blood"—Christ is seven feet tall.) This is the divine body that is under threat from oaths. When you swear "by God's nails," you tear the nails out of Christ's hand as he sits in heaven. The first pattern poem written in English depicts the result of such swearing. Pattern poems, in which the lines are laid out on the page to form a specific shape, were more usually made to look like eggs, wings, altars, or crosses. In Stephen Hawes's 1509 *The Conversion of Swearers*, though, the lines scattered across the page suggest Christ's bones, and printer's ornaments resemble flowers strewn over a corpse. "See me / Be kind," Christ pleads. "Tear me no more / My wounds are sore / Leave swearing therefore." (See next page.)

How could God's creatures wield such power over their Creator? Yet it is the same power that people exercise in the ceremony of the Eucharist. Swearing by God's body parts is in fact a perverse version of this sacrament. In the Eucharist, a priest speaks a "working word" to create God's body, then breaks it with his hands; in swearing, all who utter the requisite formulae can break God's body with their words alone.

See
Me ꝑ kynde
Be
¶ Agayne
My payne ꝑ in mynde
Reteyne
¶ My swete bloode
On the roode ꝑ my broder
Dyde the good ✱

¶ My face ryght red
Myn armes spred ꝑ thynke none oder
My woundes bled ✱
¶ Beholde thou my syde ✱
Wounded so ryght wyde ꝑ all for thyn owne sake
Bledynge sore that tyde ✱
¶ Thus for the I suerted ✱
Why arte þ harde herted ꝑ thy swerynge aslake
Be by me conuerted
¶ Tere me nowe no more
My woundes are sore ꝑ and come to my grace
Leue swerynge therfore
¶ I am redy ✱
To graunte mercy ꝑ for thy trespace
To the truely ✱
¶ Come nowe nere
My frende dere ꝑ before me
And appere ✱
¶ I so
In wo se se ✱ ✱
Dyde go
¶ I

The first page of the pattern poem from *The Conversion of Swearers*, 1509.

To Catholics, the Eucharist is the sacrament in which God's physical body is shown to or eaten by his people, effecting and signaling their salvation. Though worshippers appear to consume bread, they are actually eating God's physical body—the same body born of Mary, crucified on the cross, and now sitting in heaven— transubstantiated into a wafer. An Easter Sunday sermon from the late fourteenth century explains what the Host consists of and how it is the sole instrument of salvific grace: "And the same body that died on the Cross and this day rose truly God and man, the same body is on the Sacrament on the altar in form of bread . . . And whosoever eats it, he shall live forever." The mechanism of this miracle is based on Aristotelian theories of matter, as we saw with the Lollards. The wafer can look like bread but be Christ's body because after consecration the "accidents" of bread, its whiteness and roundness, remain, but its "substance" or "subject" has been changed or annihilated and replaced with the body of Christ. The priest performs this miracle by pronouncing the words of the sacring during Mass: "Hoc est enim corpus meum," "This is my body." These words literally transform the bread on the altar into Christ's body, the Real Presence.

There are many exempla from the medieval period that explain in bloody detail exactly what is going on during the Eucharist. *Handlyng Synne* tells the tale of a monk who doubts the real, physical presence of Christ in the Host since he cannot see it with his bodily eyes. It looks like bread—how could it be God's body? He and two abbots pray to God to "to show the truth / that you are the sacrament of the Mass" and are "rewarded" with a behind-the-scenes look at what really goes on when the priest speaks the magic words. After the words of consecration, a living child appears on the altar. The priest kills the child and divides him up, offering the monk a piece of bleeding human flesh instead of the wafer. The monk "thought that the priest brought on the paten / Morsels of the child newly slain, / And offered him a morsel of the flesh, / With all the blood on it, still fresh." The sacrifice of the Mass is quite literally a sacrifice. This exemplum also makes clear why Christ's body must be concealed in the "accidents" of bread, "for if we took it as flesh, we would be sick and disgusted and forsake it."

These miracle-of-the-Host stories resemble the complaints against swearers that also abound in the pastoral literature. These complaints demonstrate in equally graphic terms what swearing does to the body of God. The *Gesta Romanorum*, an early fourteenth-century monastic collection of moral fables, contains a representative tale about the consequences of vain swearing. There was once a man who swore constantly, the tale goes, his whole life long. He left no part of Christ's body untouched with his terrible oaths. His friends warned him that he should stop, but he would not, no matter what anyone said to him. One day, the most beautiful woman he had ever seen visited him. She was Mary, Christ's mother, and she came to show the man her son. "Here is my son," she told him, "lying in my lap, with his head all broken, and his eyes drawn out of his body and laid on his breast, his arms broken in two, his legs and feet also. With your great oaths you have torn him thus." Just this scene is depicted in a circa 1400 wall painting from St. Lawrence's Church, Broughton. Here, fashionable gentlemen hold parts of Christ's body, which they have ripped from him with their oaths. Christ himself lies partially dismembered in his mother's lap—note his right arm and leg, with the bones sticking out. Just as miracle-of-the-Host stories are supposed to show what really happens when the priest pronounces his "working word," these complaints against swearers show what really happens when people swear.

In these two kinds of exempla, God reveals to our physical senses truths that we must ordinarily apprehend through faith. They echo the story of Doubting Thomas, who "will not believe" Christ's resurrection until he "shall see in his hands the print of the nails, and put my finger into the print of the nails, and thrust my hand into his side" (John 20:25). Jesus makes allowances for Thomas's human frailty and exposes his body to the disciple's touch, his body proving his resurrection. Thomas deems this physical sight and touch to be satisfactory evidence, and he finally believes his God is risen.

The "Warning to Swearers" in St. Lawrence's Church, Broughton.

With their promotion of the physical senses as the most reliable means of verifying truth (for us fallen humans), these complaints also suggest why medieval swearing is portrayed as having the power to touch God's physical body. Since oaths guarantee the truth of our statements by securing God as witness, and since we prefer physical proof that things are true, oaths work best by anchoring themselves in God's body. Every oath in effect re-creates the Doubting Thomas scenario—our voice goes out from our bodies to touch God's body and the truth is secured. What better way to understand and to shore up swearing's power to make God act as witness to our words than by depicting those words as basing themselves in his body— almost as if, when we swear, we tap him on the shoulder and say, "Hey, look!"

The Eucharist was the center of complex spiritual and worldly hierarchies, constructed around God's body as present in the Host and through people's various relations to it—who got to make it, who could partake of it, and who had to admire it from afar. Historian Eamon Duffy succinctly lays out these connections between sacrament and medieval society: "The body of Christ . . . was the focus of all the hopes and aspirations of late medieval religion." As Duffy points out, it was also the means by which those in power stayed in power, "a device in the process of the establishment of community [and] the validation of power structures."

In this society, priests occupied the top of the hierarchy, they alone having the power to transform bread and wine into Christ's body and blood. Lay men and women had no part in and were not supposed to understand these mysteries to the same degree as could priests—they were forbidden "even [to] touch the sacred vessels with their bare hands." Members of the aristocracy and gentry had quite ready access to the Host, since they were able to hear Mass several times a day and to take Communion every month or more. Most of the population, however, took Communion only at Easter, and for the rest of the year were reduced to worshipping the Host at a distance during the Elevation. Even this long-distance admiration was carefully scripted, the congregation's smallest movements dictated. Before the consecration of the Host, for example, "a bell was rung to warn worshippers absorbed in their own prayers to look up." Next, "holding up of the hands and the more or less audible recitation of elevation prayers at the sacring was a gesture expected of everyone: refusal or omission was a frequent cause of the detection of Lollards." The ceremony was so tightly regulated that the smallest deviation could bring accusations of heresy—Christ's body was thought to be powerful, and it had to be handled with extreme care.

Like the Eucharist, lawful swearing was a pillar of medieval English society. It secured people's honesty by making God a witness to people's promises, without which allegiances would waver, criminal and Church trials would grind to a halt, marriages would remain unsolemnized, and baptism would be impossible—and without which, as one clergyman put it, "no state can stand." Vain swearing, however, carried with it a terrifying potential for chaos. Unlike administering or receiving Communion, swearing was not a class prerogative. It threatened to disrupt the carefully maintained Eucharistic hierarchy of power by allowing anyone and everyone access to God's body—anyone, that is, who could put together the talismanic words. Catholic pastoral literature expresses great anxiety about this democratizing potential, typically echoing the sentiments of this fifteenth-century sermon, which worries how the second commandment "is broken entirely among learned and uneducated, among young and old, among rich and poor, from a little child who can barely speak, to an old bearded man from whom age has almost taken his proper speech." Pastoral tracts such as *Jacob's Well* and *Handlyng Synne* react to swearing's disruptive potential, as we have seen, with a slew of rules to regulate proper and improper use of oaths, rules as complex and rigid as those that govern the ceremony of the Eucharist. These restrictive regulations demonstrate a strong desire for control over the language, but also a fear that control is ultimately impossible. Given this ever-present suspicion that precepts, however iron-clad, might not be able to stem the flood of oaths, complaints against swearers and some pastoral texts rely on another means of protecting God, and the society organized around his body, from damage: pity. As we saw in the *Gesta Romanorum*, these tales depict not a wrathful God, angry that people are trying to pull off his feet, but Christ as a child, bloody and helpless. His mother often begs swearers to stop, and sometimes Christ himself asks them to have mercy. These depictions stress what pastoral literature's strict prohibitions are intended to limit and tend to disguise—the extent to which swearing places God in our care, to be cherished or torn apart.

In the Middle Ages, swearing followed the biblical model, concerned with the Holy and not with the Shit. Many of the obscene words we use today were already in use by the medieval period, but they did not have the same offensive and emotive power. The period was not without Roman influences—we saw the religious sense of obscenity make an appearance in the apotropaic vulvas and penises of medieval Catholicism. But for the most part, obscenity as we understand it was in abeyance. It was in the Renaissance that the Shit started to make a comeback.

Chapter 4

The Rise of Obscenity

The Renaissance

Robert Southwell knew that he was sailing to his death when he left Calais for England on the morning of July 17. He landed on the southeast coast between Folkestone and Dover, dressed soberly but richly, like the gentleman he once had been. The secret service was informed of his impending arrival and hoped to eliminate what it saw as a dangerous threat as soon as he touched English soil. But here Southwell had a bit of luck. In England, it was still July 7—the English continued to refuse to adopt the "Popish" Gregorian calendar—and one of the feast days of St. Thomas Becket. Despite the Protestant government's abolition of the holiday, hundreds of people were on the roads, traveling to and from local fairs. Southwell was able to disappear into the crowds of revelers and elude the government informers who watched the coastline.

Southwell was not a spy, not an assassin. He came to England to say Mass, to administer the sacraments, and to offer spiritual comfort to Catholics. He was, in other words, a Catholic priest, and in 1586 this was illegal.

Though he escaped capture that morning, and indeed for six more years, Southwell was eventually arrested and executed. The 1585 Act Against Jesuits, Seminary Priests, and Other Such-Like Disobedient Persons had made it high treason for priests to enter or to stay in England. Southwell, a Jesuit, was clearly in violation of the statute. When he was put on trial, however, the primary charge against him was not that he remained in England illegally but that he taught Catholics a certain kind of swearing—equivocation. Equivocation is a way to deceive your listener without lying, through the use of double meanings or mental reservation (words thought but not spoken). If you say out loud "I did not have sexual relations with that woman" but add in your mind "So that it's any of your business," you are equivocating through mental reservation.* It's equivocation too when you say "Thank you for the book. I will waste no time reading it." The person who has given you the six-hundred-page doorstop thinks that you will dive into it right away; you mean that you will never crack it open. This kind, relying on double meanings, was called amphibology (from the Greek for "both," as in *amphibian*) during the Renaissance.

It might seem like mere wordplay to us today, but in the sixteenth and seventeenth centuries equivocation was a deadly serious matter. It allowed Catholics to escape unjust persecution without committing the terrible sins of lying or perjury. When questioned by the government, Catholics could save their souls *and* their bodies— they could deny that they heard Mass, that they harbored a priest, that they carried a rosary, without lying to God and so damning themselves. To the Protestant government, equivocation was a violation of law, a flouting of its just authority. It is ironic, perhaps, that in the fourteenth and fifteenth centuries, Catholics had persecuted proto-Protestants for their views on swearing, but by the sixteenth century, it was Protestants persecuting Catholics over what they thought about oaths.

The trial of Robert Southwell was one of the last appearances of the medieval model of swearing, since at its crux was the idea that

---

* Was Bill Clinton equivocating in the sixteenth-century sense of the word when he denied his involvement with Monica Lewinsky? While it is perennially popular to make statements that are hard to pin down, equivocation in the technical sense of the term had been out of fashion for almost four hundred years at the time of the scandal. Clinton, however, was educated at Georgetown, a Jesuit university, and was strongly influenced by the Jesuit father Tim Healy. This background raises the possibility that he added the crucial "so that it's any of your business," to make a mental reservation. More likely he employed amphibology, playing with two different meanings of *sexual relations*, e.g., oral sex isn't "sex."

oaths are so sacred, so powerful, that circuitous techniques such as equivocation are needed to avoid perjury. His trial also marked the beginning of the end for this model of swearing, however. Later in the Renaissance (usually dated 1500–1660), the strength of oaths began to decline because of the development of Protestantism and its changing definition of man's relationship with God, and because of the growth of capitalism, with its emphasis on contracts and on man's word as his bond. At the same time, there was an increase in "civility," as characterized in the previous chapter—an advancing of the threshold of shame and repugnance. Body parts and actions that in the Middle Ages had been shown in public and not considered particular loci of concern became "private" and invested with the great significance of taboo. Words for these things became taboo as well. This "rise of civility" began in the later Middle Ages and was completed by the end of the seventeenth century, but it happened gradually, with stops and starts, advances and retreats, and at different stages in different geographical areas, social classes, and genres of texts. As a result, obscenities slowly gained the power lost by oaths, and the greatest linguistic taboo became not words that could rip apart God's body but words that could reveal the human one. The balance began to swing away from the Holy and back to the Shit.

A Jesuitical Doctrine

In the 1580s, England was in religious ferment, and had been for some time. Henry VIII had halfheartedly begun the Protestant Reformation when he broke with the Catholic Church in 1534 over its refusal to grant him a divorce from his first wife. His son, Edward VI, was a staunch but very young and sickly Protestant, whose ministers tried hard to Protestantize the country during his six-year reign. When Edward's half sister Mary acceded to the throne in 1553, she brought Catholicism back with a vengeance.

Queen Elizabeth I returned the country to Protestantism once again when she was crowned in 1558, but she looked to be quite tolerant of Catholics. At this point, toleration was welcomed by a large part of the English population, who had had to adapt to four religious changes in thirty-four years, each time having to figure out whether they would or would not go to purgatory after death, whether the soul of a child who died before baptism was in limbo or with God.

When Elizabeth acceded to the throne, many Catholics were so-called schismatics who attended Protestant church despite their differences with the liturgy and doctrines. In 1564, however, Pope Pius V specifically forbade English Catholics from attending Church of England services. And in 1570 he issued the bull *Regnans in Excelsis*. This decree excommunicated Elizabeth, declared that she was not the lawful queen of England, absolved her subjects of allegiance to her, and excommunicated anyone who would "dare obey her orders, mandates, and laws." It was rumored (falsely) throughout the country that the bull also granted full remission of sins to anyone who assassinated her. After this, English penal laws against Catholics grew ever more oppressive. Statutes passed in 1571 made it treason to reconcile anyone to the Catholic Church or be oneself reconciled, to procure or publish papal bulls, and to bring into England crucifixes, rosaries, or an Agnus Dei (a small wax cake impressed with the figure of a lamb bearing a cross, blessed by the Pope and thought to possess apotropaic power—a more modest version of the flying phallus pilgrimage badge). In 1581, the government prohibited celebration of the Mass, imposing large fines and year-long imprisonment for the celebrant and hearers. This law also increased the recusancy fine—the penalty Catholics paid if they refused to attend Church of England services—to £20 per month, forty or fifty times the wage of artisans such as carpenters or tailors. The 1585 statute that made it illegal to be a priest in England, under which Southwell was tried, also made it an offense punishable by death to shelter or aid a priest in any way. And in 1587, recusants were to forfeit two-thirds of their income if they refused to pay the huge fines levied on them.

In short, it was a difficult time to be a Catholic in England. If you helped priests—necessary to your salvation because only they could provide access to the sacraments—you risked death, not just for yourself but also for members of your family. If you followed the Pope's dictates and refused to attend heretical services, you faced poverty brought on by crippling fines. If you didn't do these things, though, you were at best, as Catholics of the time believed, preparing for yourself a long, long time in purgatory. Purgatory was not to be taken lightly—it was very much like hell, but with the possibility of release after much suffering. Depending on their sins, souls in purgatory might, according to historian Eamon Duffy, be "suspended by meat-hooks driven through jaws, tongue, or sexual organs, frozen into ice, boil[ed] in vats of liquid metal or fire." At worst, you were damning yourself eternally, going straight to hell, where those souls on meat hooks writhe forever.

The crown had many methods to discover and prosecute suspected Catholics. They employed pursuivants, special Catholic-hunters who traveled through the country raiding houses to look for priests and Catholic paraphernalia such as crucifixes and rosaries. They had torture. The head pursuivant, Richard Topcliffe, even constructed a special room in his basement in which to practice his favorite form of torture, to extract confessions from priests. (A bit like crucifixion, it involved hanging a prisoner by his hands, in irons. The body cannot endure this position for more than ten minutes without terrible pain; internal injury follows shortly, and it eventually becomes very difficult and then impossible to breathe.)

But the crown's chief and most insidious weapon seems almost harmless on its face—it was the oath ex officio. The oath ex officio (meaning "by virtue of office") was put to all people arrested for heresy, whether Catholic or Puritan (Protestants more reformist than the Church of England), before their interrogation. They had to swear that they would answer all questions truthfully, before they had been given any idea of what those questions might be. This violated the principle, established in common law since at least the twelfth century, that people should not be forced to incriminate themselves (a principle enshrined in the Fifth Amendment of the U.S. Constitution). A Puritan petitioner to Parliament complained that "to a conscience that feareth God [the oath] is more violent than any rack to constrain him to utter that he knoweth, though it be against himself and to his most grievous punishment." It seems that he was not exaggerating to any great degree in describing this oath as a kind of torture in a society where to forswear oneself was to injure God and commit one's soul to the fires of hell, but to answer according to one's oath would be to condemn one's mortal body, and possibly others', to imprisonment or death.

The "Bloody Question" was another coercive oath employed frequently by the Tudor state and greatly feared by English Catholics. It was meant to divide the Catholic community, forcing Catholics to choose between loyalty to the queen and loyalty to the Pope. Arrested Catholics would be asked what they would do if the Pope sent an army into England to overthrow the queen and commanded all Catholics to support the army. Would they side with the queen or with the Pope? This was a genuinely difficult question for most Catholics. They owed loyalty and obedience to Elizabeth, their temporal sovereign, but were also bound to obey the Pope, the spiritual leader of the Church, in all his dictates. The issue was made doubly complicated by the Pope's declaration that Elizabeth was *not* the lawful queen of England and by his excommunication of her and all her "followers." A few Catholics, including Southwell himself, came down firmly on the side of the queen, but many chose the Pope, or made no answer at all to the question. These latter Catholics could then, with at least some justification, be prosecuted as traitors, giving a more plausible coloring to the 1585 statute that made it treason for priests to remain in the land and for anyone to help them.

As many Catholics saw it, equivocation was their only defense against coercive oaths that forced them to incriminate themselves. Southwell's trial gives us an idea of how this technique worked. Southwell was accused of telling Catholics that if Protestant authorities asked whether they knew the location of a priest, they could swear that the answer was no, "reserving this intention: 'Not with a purpose to tell you.'" This is the mental reservation we've mentioned before, which depends on a distinction between what is spoken out loud and what is intended silently. A Catholic could swear out loud that she had not seen a priest, as long as she added silently, "With a purpose to tell you." Though what the listeners heard was false—she had indeed seen the priest—what God heard is true, since he understood the entire speech, its spoken and unspoken components. The Catholic saw the priest, but not with the intention to tell the authorities—true. God, not the Protestant authorities, is the audience that matters here. Without equivocation, the Catholic would have been constrained to admit that she had seen the priest, a crime punishable by huge fines and even death for her and for the priest, or she would have refused the oath, an act the authorities would have seen as a confession of guilt, for why refuse to swear unless you had something to hide?

Secular authorities hated equivocation, since it allowed suspected criminals to escape incriminating themselves by oath. It would allow a man to repudiate and ruin a woman whom he had, for all intents and purposes, married; it would allow a thief to claim that stolen goods were really his own; worst of all, it would allow someone caught plotting against the queen to deny his involvement. Equivocation would give these criminals freedom to mislead their prosecutors, indeed to perjure themselves in men's eyes as long as they told the truth in God's. In effect, it would take the threat of divine punishment, upon which any kind of testimony relied, out of the equation. Lord Chief Justice Popham (who also condemned Mary, Queen of Scots to die) summed it up: "If this doctrine should be allowed, it would supplant all justice, for we are men, and no gods, and can judge but according to their outward actions and speeches, and not according to their secret and inward intentions." The legal system cannot function, civil justice cannot be done, if people are free to swear whatever they like to the authorities as long as they do not perjure themselves to God. The system needs to—and today does—define this kind of language as perjury; otherwise, "all judgments, all giving of Testimonies should be perverted." Southwell was sentenced to death.

Equivocation eventually backfired for parties on both sides of Southwell's trial. Though the Tudor authorities were appalled by equivocation, the general populace was apparently not particularly concerned about it. They were horrified, however, that the government was executing a man whose only "crime" was being a priest. The usual procedure in these executions was hanging, drawing, and quartering. A noose was put around the prisoner's neck, and he was allowed to hang for a while until he was weakened but not dead. Then he would be cut down, still alive, and his privy parts sliced off; then he would be disemboweled. His heart would be cut out, killing him, and thrown into a fire along with his intestines. Finally he would be decapitated and his body hacked into pieces to be nailed on the gatehouse of London Bridge as a warning to other would-be traitors. An early seventeenth-century account of the Babington conspiracy, a Catholic plot to replace Elizabeth with her cousin Mary, Queen of Scots, notes that this procedure is "not without some note and touch of Cruelty."

When it was Southwell's turn to suffer this not entirely uncruel punishment, the spectators prevented it from being carried out in the usual way. The hangman tried to cut the rope so that Southwell could be disemboweled alive, but the crowd stopped him with cries of "Let him hang till he be dead" and "Pull his legs." In response, the executioner pulled down on his legs to end his torment quickly. When he later held up Southwell's head with the customary announcement "Here is the head of a traitor," no one in the crowd shouted "Traitor, traitor," the standard response. People instead scrambled to dip pieces of cloth in pools of his blood, to preserve as relics. Southwell died a martyr, the authorities having failed to turn the populace against him because of his advocacy of equivocation.

Popular indifference to equivocation didn't last long, however. Advocated by Southwell, the Jesuit superior Henry Garnet, and other Jesuits of note, equivocation became known as a primarily Jesuit doctrine, and thus was tainted by English suspicion of Jesuits as traitors, Spanish agents willing to do or say anything to overthrow the queen. Its involvement in the Gunpowder Plot finished it as a respectable doctrine. In 1605, a group of Catholics attempted to blow up Parliament and with it, King James I and much of his family. Henry Garnet was one of the men arrested in connection with the plot, and the issue of equivocation played a key role at his trial, as it had in Southwell's. This time, however, it was linked with a plan so monstrous—to kill the king, his Protestant heirs, and most of the Protestant nobility of England—that it was forevermore tainted with treason, seen as trickery practiced only by the most dishonest, most depraved criminals.

Equivocation had unanticipated effects on the sacredness of the very oaths it was designed to protect. Eventually the doctrine became so entwined with Catholicism in the popular imagination that it was nearly impossible for a Catholic to swear and be believed. Even English Catholic authors began to decry the practice, complaining as the priest Christopher Bagshaw did in 1601 that, as a result, "they may charge us . . . with any treason whatsoever, and we have no way left unto us to acquit ourselves from it." Even a straightforward oath like "I swear I have not sheltered a priest" was assumed to include a mental reservation, an inward "so that it's any of your business," to deceive the authorities. No matter what accused Catholics said, the Protestant authorities thought they were guilty and practicing Jesuit trickery to save themselves. Equivocation, created to get Catholics out of one bind, inadvertently created another—the presumption of guilt. It also became a factor in the general decline of the power of oaths in this period.

If it is always possible to equivocate out of an oath, there is little point to swearing anymore; swearing itself is devalued as a means of guaranteeing the truth.

What the #%&* Is a Spiritual Body?

Another key factor that led to the weakening, the devaluing, of oaths was the rise of Protestantism itself. Protestantism made it impossible for people to touch God's physical body, in the Eucharist or by swearing, making oaths seem less effective.

The defining difference between Catholicism and Protestantism was the status of God's body in the Eucharist. For Catholics, as we saw in the previous chapter, God's body is really physically present in (or rather *as*) the Host. It looks like a wafer, but it has been transformed really and entirely into the body of God. For Protestants, the Host still becomes God's body after consecration, but in a spiritual sense, not a physical one. Though Protestant groups from Lutherans to Calvinists to the Church of England to the Anabaptists subscribed to a variety of contradictory opinions about many religious issues—the timing and role of baptism, what constitutes proper church adornment, even the precise nature of what the Host becomes after consecration—they all agree that a priest cannot transubstantiate a wafer into the physical body of God. At Communion God is not "bodily, naturally, and carnally . . . eaten," as the orthodox Catholics insist. The *Thirty-Nine Articles*, which codified Church of England doctrine, explain how the Eucharist is to be understood instead: "The body of Christ is given, taken, and eaten, in the Supper, only after an heavenly and spiritual manner." The wafer remains material bread, but God's body is also there "spiritually," "sacramentally," "figuratively," or "virtually," depending on which kind of Protestant is doing the describing. God's body was no longer capable of being touched, let alone broken and eaten by the faithful.

For Catholics, however, the concept of a spiritual Real Presence didn't make any sense. The early seventeenth-century Catholic controversialist Robert Parsons scoffed at the idea that God could be received "substantially, though yet spiritually only and sacramentally." For Parsons and his brethren, Real Presence meant physical presence—God is only (in) the wafer in some meaningful sense if he can be touched and eaten bodily, not spiritually or sacramentally.

Swearing, the other means through which people could touch God's body, underwent a parallel transformation, also moving from the physical to the spiritual realm. We have seen how certain kinds of medieval Catholic swearing could literally rip apart Christ's physical body, the same body that is on the paten during the Eucharist. Protestant swearing was thought to rip apart Christ's *spiritual* body, the same body that is there spiritually (and rather confusingly) on the paten during the Eucharist. Protestant William Vaughan described in 1611 how this was supposed to work: "When [people] forswear themselves . . . whether by God's body, by his blood, or by his wounds, they spiritually pierce his sides with their bloody weapons."

The Protestant Eucharist was supposed to be no less real and no less efficacious for being spiritual, and Protestant oaths were supposed to be no less capable of making God a witness and thus guaranteeing the truth of a person's statements. But an oath's power to affect God's spiritual body is nonetheless not as satisfactory as the power to compel him physically. Medieval Catholics knew that God's body was up in heaven, and sometimes on a paten during Mass, and they could reach out and touch it with their oaths, making sure he was paying attention. Where is God's spiritual body, though? *What* is his spiritual body? Just as the spiritual Real Presence of God during Communion caused epistemological problems for Catholics and for some Protestants—in what sense is God *really* there if not physically?—the Protestant mechanism of swearing cast doubt upon the extent of oaths' ability to secure the truth. Although Protestant writers stressed that swearing still worked to compel God to act as witness, oaths' new "spiritual" access to God called into question the certainty of their success.

All this weakened the power of oaths during the Reformation. The sheer number of oaths people were required to take during this period also contributed to the cultural sense that swearing by God was becoming meaningless verbiage instead of a sacred formula that guaranteed the truth of people's words. Henry VIII started the trend, arguably, with the 1534 Oath of Supremacy, which required various of his male subjects to swear that the king was the supreme governor of the Church of England. Elizabeth made her subjects swear a similar oath. In 1606, following the Gunpowder Plot, James I added the Oath of Allegiance, in which subjects had to swear loyalty to him and disavow the Pope. When the Civil War broke out, the oaths started to come thick and fast—the Protestation Oath (1641) of loyalty to king, Parliament, and Church of England; the Solemn League and Covenant (1643), declaring loyalty to the reformed (Protestant) religion; the Oath of Abjuration (1643 and 1656), disavowing, again, the poor Pope; the Engagement (1650), pledging loyalty now to the Commonwealth, since the king was dead; and in 1660, renewed Oaths of Allegiance to the new king, Charles II, and the Church of England. Historian Christopher Hill estimates that men might have had to take up to ten oaths of loyalty, all of them conflicting, between 1640 and 1660, with the effect that oaths lost much of their ability to do what the authorities kept imposing them in order to do. They stopped being a real guarantee that a person would be loyal or that he was telling the truth about something, and became a mere formula that could freely be recited for authority, irrespective of the swearer's real intentions and beliefs. What was like the rack "to a conscience that feareth God" in 1586 was a joke in a popular song by 1662:

> They force us to take
> Two oaths, but we'll make
> A third, that we ne'er meant to keep 'em.

From Feudal Lords to Boy Toys

One final cultural movement influenced the decline of oaths: the end of feudalism and the concomitant and related explosion of capitalism. In the feudal structure of medieval society, which had been eroding slowly for hundreds of years, oaths had delineated and guaranteed the relationships among lords, vassals, tenants, free peasants, and unfree peasants, linking them together in webs of mutual dependence and support. Central to the feudal system were the "great magnates"—nobles who held huge tracts of land, commanded private armies, and retained the personal loyalty of lesser nobles and gentlemen through networks of patronage. They were in effect minisovereigns, possessing the power to oppose or at least make life difficult for the supreme sovereign, the king or queen. By the time Elizabeth I acceded to the throne, the power of these magnates had already been severely reduced, and she implemented a program to shrink it even further. She might have served as inspiration for Louis XIV of France in the way she encouraged her nobles to bankrupt themselves in ever finer displays of clothing and spectacle. She insisted that they spend lots of time and money at court, making the dispensation of lucrative monopolies dependent upon their attendance and their (apparent) personal loyalty to her. They were thus unable to spend as much time on their own estates, cultivating their own networks of patronage. When Elizabeth took the throne, there was only one hereditary duke left in England, and she executed him (to be fair, he had tried to overthrow her). The next time there was a duke in England again, it was George Villiers, created 1st Duke of Buckingham in 1623 most probably because he had good-looking legs and was the lover of King James I. The great magnates and the feudal system they sustained were dead; long live a fine calf and nimble dancing.

What took over from feudalism as the structuring principle of society was capitalism. The market demanded honesty over and over, quicker and quicker—there was no time to swear by God before each transaction that the goods involved were of high quality, that the price was fair, and that they would be delivered on time. If they were, all was well, and the merchant or producer would thrive; if not, he'd go bust at a time in history when there was no unemployment insurance and people were regularly thrown into debtors' prison. As historian Christopher Hill puts it, "Supernatural sanctions became less necessary in a society in which honesty was manifestly the best policy, in which those who did not keep their covenants made were apt to have difficulties in business relationships." Hill describes the society taking form during the Restoration as a Hobbesian one in which the contract replaced the oath, where self-interest reigned and led to the discovery that "it paid a man to make his word his bond because of the rise in social importance of credit, reputation, respectability." For all these reasons—(1) the decline of feudalism, (2) the rise of capitalism, (3) the administration of too many oaths, (4) the overuse of equivocation to avoid them, and (5) the Protestant Reformation and the resulting idea that an oath based in God's spiritual body was less effective than one that exerted control over his physical one—people stopped swearing sacred oaths and started making promises and contracts.

This decline can be overstated. In the Renaissance people were still thinking and writing about oaths and were certainly swearing them, as of course we still do today, in court and in frustration. The scientist Robert Boyle, who discovered the eponymous law about the pressure and volume of gases, is less well known for his circa 1647 *Free Discourse Against Customary Swearing*. And Queen Elizabeth I even used profuse profane swearing as a way to strengthen her hold on the English crown. She liked to sprinkle her speech with "God's death!"—still one of the most shocking phrases a sixteenth-century Englishman could utter. *Man* is the operative word here—women's language was supposed to be both chaster and more devout than men's. As one poet who worked at Elizabeth's court put it, women should avoid indecent or irreligious words, because "the chief virtue of women is shamefastness . . . when they hear or see anything tending that way they commonly blush." Elizabeth, though, swore "God's death!" so often that even foreign ambassadors remarked on it.

When Elizabeth became queen, she found herself in a difficult situation—a young woman of twenty-five, she presided over a government of men who at best half thought and at worst were entirely convinced that women were not fit to rule. "It is more than a monster in nature that a woman shall reign and have empire above man" was the central thesis of *The First Blast of the Trumpet Against the Monstrous Regiment of Women*, a book popular at the time. In sprinkling her speeches with such a shocking oath, Elizabeth was asserting her right to rule. She was presenting herself as masculine, as having, as she liked to claim, "the heart and stomach of a *king*"—a fitting heir to the well-loved but extremely profane Henry VIII.

But despite tracts like Boyle's and expletives like the queen's, the great age of oath swearing was over, and the rise of obscenity was beginning.

All Things That Are to Be Eschewed

As we've seen, for hundreds of years people had worried that certain kinds of language—"foul words" or "words of ribaldry," for example—could lead their hearers or readers into sin. The very nature of "bad" language lay in its power to incite immoral behavior. During the Renaissance a different term began to come into use, for a different sort of bad language: *obscenity*. *Obscenus* had been in use in Latin during the Middle Ages—it is part of the definition for *foule* in the *Catholicon Anglicum*, for example. But in the closing decades of the sixteenth century, it began to appear in English. The first recorded English uses show a word finding its form—John Harington called it "obscenousnesse" when he defended his translation of the Italian epic poem *Orlando Furioso* (1591) against those who thought it an immoral project. "In all Ariosto," he claims, "there is not a word of ribaldry or

obscenousnes." (John Harington might serve as the presiding genius
of this book, for his dual interest in sex and scatology. Not only was
he one of the first people to use the word *obscene* in English, but he
also invented the flush toilet and wrote a treatise to publicize his invention, *The Metamorphosis of Ajax. Ajax* is a pun on "a jakes," slang
for privy at the time. He installed one of his new toilets at his manor
house at Kelston [now demolished], and his godmother, Queen
Elizabeth I, is supposed to have used it and liked it, but the idea
didn't catch on for another 250 years. It was cheaper and easier to
have your servants empty chamber pots and clean ordinary privies
than to install the plumbing necessary for Harington's system.)
Orlando Furioso (1532) is a wild story of knights questing after damsels in distress, Christians battling pagans, and magical creatures
giving aid to both sides. There is plenty of obscenous matter in Ariosto's poem, as Harington is the first to acknowledge: it appears in
the character of "the bawdy Frier, in *Alcina* and *Rogeros* copulation
. . . and in some few places beside" (including when the most beautiful of the distressed damsels is chained naked to a rock as an offering to a sea monster). But, Harington argues, vice is punished and
virtue rewarded in the poem—it is moralized so that the bawdy friar
comes to a bad end, adultery is punished, and so on. And, he adds,
the words that he and Ariosto use for these dirty deeds are as pure as
the driven snow.

This is a new distinction, between obscene words and the things
they represent. In the Middle Ages, broadly speaking, there was no
such difference. Any words that might lead to sin were bad, whether
they were *swive, cunt,* or "Thou art more beautiful than Aphrodite
herself." Now, Harington implies, it is worse to employ obscene
words in discussing wanton or immoral topics. Since Ariosto
describes his morally questionable plot points "with modest words
& no obscenous phrase," they cannot be deemed objectionable. This
appears to be very close to our contemporary notion of obscenity, in
which certain words are worse than others, even when they refer to
the same thing. For us today, certain words possess an offensive

power far in excess of their literal meaning, and we see the beginnings of this in Harington's "obscenousnesse."

A few years later, John Marston employed *obscene* in a similar way, making a distinction between *wantonness*, which is okay, and *obscenity*, which most definitely is not. He ends his 1598 erotic poem "The Metamorphosis of Pigmalion's Image" abruptly, just as the sculptor is really about to get into it with his living statue: "Peace, idle Poesie, / Be not obscene though wanton in thy rhymes."* For Marston, wantonness or sexual suggestiveness appears to be fine—before he breaks off he has described how Pigmalion and Galatea "dally" and "sport" with each other:

> Could he, oh could he, when that each to eyther
> Did yeeld kind kissing, and more kind embracing,
> Could he when that they felt, and clip't together
> And might enjoy the life of dallying,
> Could he abstaine mid'st such a wanton sporting
> From doing that, which is not fit reporting?
> What would he doe when that her softest skin
> Saluted his with a delightfull kisse?
> . . .
> Who knows not what ensues?

The details are left to the imagination. When it comes time to get graphic—to describe exactly how the key fits in the lock, as it were—Marston demurs. To say more, he argues, would be obscene.

A year later, the pamphleteer and satirist Thomas Nashe wrote a much less titillating mock encomium to the Herring in which he mentions in passing "the obscene appellation of *Sarding sandes*." (*Sard*, you remember, is the archaic word for "fuck" that appeared in the Lindisfarne Gospels.) This appears to be obscenity exactly as

---

*Pygmalion was a sculptor who carved a statue of a woman so beautiful that he fell in love with her. He prayed to Aphrodite to make the statue real, and she did.

we know it—*sard* is an obscene word, Nashe notes, making "sarding sands" worse somehow than "dallying dunes" or "bescumbered beaches" but perhaps still not as bad as the "fucking fells."* Thomas Thomas's definition of *obscœnus* in his 1587 Latin-English dictionary admirably sets out the new meanings accruing to the English word *obscene* by the end of the sixteenth century: "all things that are to be eschewed: filthie, foule, uncleane, wanton, bawdie, unchast, ribauldrie, abhominable, dishonest."

Along with the smallpox virus, obscenity was in the sixteenth-century air, especially among dictionary makers—a small subset of the population, perhaps, but one with inordinate influence. This was the Renaissance—it began in England two hundred years later than it did in Italy—and there was great cultural excitement over the rediscovery of ancient classical texts. Huge numbers of dictionaries were published in order to help readers whose command of Latin was less than solid glean the "pith and marrow" from these texts. Thomas Elyot's Latin-English *Dictionary* was revised and republished five times in twenty-one years; Thomas Thomas's *Dictionarium* was issued in fourteen editions over almost sixty years; *Riders Dictionarie*, bidirectional English to Latin and Latin to English, was revised eight times in fifty years. And these are only three of the most popular. Numerous other dictionaries were published at this time as well, giving readers of Cicero and Virgil a wide variety of choices.

But certain words presented a special problem for these new scholars of language, who were under the pressure of two competing imperatives. On one hand, dictionary makers subscribed to the classical principle of *copia*, defined by the great Renaissance rhetorician

---

* *Titillation* is only indirectly related to *tit*—it comes from the Latin *titillatio*, meaning "a tickling." *Bescumbered* means "covered in dung"; *to scumber* is "to evacuate the faeces," as the *Oxford English Dictionary* says, especially of a dog or fox. *Bescumber*, along with *bewray* and *beshit*, is one of those words that comes up a lot in the Renaissance but hardly ever anymore—all mean "to cover or spray with shit." Just as medieval people seem to have felt a need to spit that no longer impels us, people of the Renaissance appear to have been interested in the act of covering something with shit, which doesn't grab us today at all.

Erasmus (whom we met in the previous chapter as author of *On Civility in Boys*) in his 1512 *De duplici copia verborum ac rerum* (*On Copia* [abundance] *of Words and Ideas*). Erasmus argues that an author or speaker must be able to command a large vocabulary and be able to write in a wide variety of styles in order to teach and persuade effectively. Without this abundance "we shall also bore our wretched audience to death." Dictionaries must strive for a *copia* of words, both to allow their readers to understand as many of the Latin classics as possible and so that their readers may in turn use a wide variety of words in their own writing and speaking. Thomas Elyot listed as a selling point of his 1538 *Dictionary* that it contains "a thousand more Latin words, than were together in any one dictionary published in this realm." The more words, the better—the more definitions it supplies, the more useful his dictionary will be in helping readers understand vocabulary they might find in "any good author."

On the other hand, however, dictionary makers were faced with the problem that these "good authors" produced material that wasn't appropriate for all readers. "Good authors" included Catullus, despite the fact that his most famous poem begins "I will fuck you in the ass and make you suck my dick." And Martial is a "good author" despite the fact that his oeuvre consists solely of epigrams cynical, mocking, and often graphically obscene—"So I confess I thought you a Lucretia; but Bassa, for shame, you were a fucker. You dare to join two cunts and your monstrous organ feigns masculinity," for example. When Renaissance Englishmen read Martial, they were supposed to look for his "many commendable sentences and right wise counsels" and ignore the stuff about two cunts rubbing together. This was fine when it was grown men reading, who were learned and stable enough to have mastered Latin, the language of male initiates. What would happen, though, if young men or boys—or, God forbid, women—were to encounter some of Martial's vocabulary translated in a dictionary? In his famous treatise on education, *The Boke Named the Governour* (1531), Elyot explains what would result, warning that "there may hap by evil custom some pestiferous dew of vice to pierce the [brains and hearts] and infect the soft and tender buds, whereby the fruit may grown wild and some time contain in it fervent and mortal poison, to the utter destruction of a realm." Renaissance dictionaries, then, were supposed to include as many words as possible, but they also had a responsibility not to let any "pestiferous dew" poison young men by exposing them to words and ideas that they could not handle. *Copia* demanded, for example, that they include *cunnus*, because it is found in Marital, but didactic responsibility demanded that they leave it out. The way early modern lexicographers handled these conflicting imperatives gives us new insight into the development of modern obscenity.

Elyot broaches this conflict in a Latin epistle to his "truly learned readers" that prefaces his *Dictionary*. The topic of obscenity is itself so volatile that it can be discussed only in Latin. He declares: "If anyone wants obscene words, with which to arouse dormant desire while reading, let him consult other dictionaries and spurn mine, under this excuse, if he likes, that it lacks words of this very sort." Although *copia* is one of his guiding principles, and he boasts that his dictionary contains a thousand more words than the next man's, Elyot maintains that none of those words is obscene. "I knew how much human feelings are always ready for blazing up, once they are even moderately able to enjoy a little bit of half-hidden fire within a few lascivious little words," he writes. Therefore his dictionary will remove these little words and not "furnish raging Cupid with a torch."

This is very much the medieval view of foul words inciting other sins—a few lascivious little words ignite the blaze of desire, and pretty soon "Cupid" is running around with a "torch," sticking it who knows where. It differs from the medieval view, however, in that Elyot singles out "obscene words" (*obscæna uocabula*) as the ones that light the fires of sin. He seems to consider obscene words as more dangerous than other words, more capable of arousing that terrible and ultimately punishable desire.

Which words are obscene? Looking through Elyot's dictionary, we find that they correspond pretty closely to what we might expect, with some interesting exceptions. He includes the Latin *vulva* but explains quite chastely that it refers to "the womb or mother of any female kind, also a meat used of the Romans, made of the belly of a sow, either that hath farrowed [has had a litter], or is with farrow." He has deliberately censored the definitions found in earlier Latin-English dictionaries; Wynkyn de Worde's *Ortus Vocabulorum* of 1500, for example, defined *vulva* as "in English, a cunt." And he while he includes *cunnus*, he defines it not with its vulgar English equivalent but as "a womans wycket." In this case, Elyot judges all Latin words proper to print, accompanied by their circumlocutionary explanations in English, but decides that their straightforward English equivalents must be avoided. These plain English words evidently wield more power to arouse lascivious desires than their Latin equivalents or vulgar euphemisms.

That Elyot singles out obscene English words as the chief—almost the only—inflamers of concupiscence is even more apparent when we look at the words he includes for breasts. He starts off with the very factual *mamma*, "a dugge or pappe," and *mamilla*, "a little dugge or pappe," words that might apply either to people or to animals and which are described quite clinically, with no hint of the wanton uses to which these mammae could be put. Elyot goes on, however, to define *mammosus*, "having great dugges," and perhaps most strikingly *mammeata*, "a woman with greate dugges or pappes." The description Elyot provides for *mammeata* seems as likely as any word in his dictionary to stir up lust—after reading about "a woman with greate dugges or pappes" it seems hard not to picture one, and in deference to Elyot we won't speculate about where imaginations might go from there. But Elyot seems to have found nothing wrong, nothing dangerous to his readers' mental landscape, about including *mammeata* and words related to it in his *Dictionary*. We saw in the previous chapter how John Stanbridge, following the medieval model, censored anything tending toward licentiousness from his *Vulgaria*: remember *vulva* as "locus ubi puer concipitur." For Elyot, in contrast, only words such as *cunt* corrupt—words such as *pappe* or *dugge*, though they have sexual referents and might be thought to inflame the passions, are not obscene and are therefore less dangerous. There seems to be something magical about the way obscenities infiltrate the mind. They have an offensive (or erotic) power in excess of their literal meaning.

In other ways, though, Elyot's definition of obscenity is different from our own. Words for excrement are not on his forbidden list, because they have little chance of arousing any sinful desires. He defines the verb *caco*, for example, as "to shit." *Urina* is "urine or piss," while *vomo* is explained as "to vomit or parbrake." These words are not dangerous because they do not arouse lust and so lead to moral corruption, and instead the principle of *copia* reasserts itself. *Caco* is "to shit," but *cacaturio* is the more decorous "to desire to go to stool." *Urina* is either the blunt "piss" or the more polite "urine." With scatology, it appears important to master words of different registers—these might be useful to add to the rhetorician's rich store of vocabulary.

Other lexicographers abandoned didactic responsibility, or rather, refused to worry about their readers' moral education. John Florio, who published his Italian-English dictionary *A Worlde of Wordes* in 1598, and John Palsgrave, whose *Lesclarcissement de la Langue Francoyse* (The Clarification of the French Language) appeared in 1530, wanted instead to present their vernacular languages as they were really spoken, in all their morally dubious glory. In a preface, Palsgrave boasts that one could actually learn to speak French from his dictionary. Perusing these dictionaries, it quickly becomes apparent that obscene words must have played a vital part in early modern communication. Florio includes several terms that signify in some form or another "a mans privie member." There is the simple *cazzo*, the privie member itself. There is *cazzaria*, "a treatise or discourse of pricks,"* *cazzo ritto*, "a stiffe standing pricke," *cazzuto*, "a man that hath a pricke," and several more cognates. One of these words is intriguingly unlike its fellows— *cazzica*, "an interjection of admiration and affirming, what? gods me, god forbid, tush." Florio here chose to translate a word that derives from "penis" with a vain oath on God's name. Even in the Renaissance, it was still common to use oaths where we today— and the Italians of four hundred years ago—would use an obscenity. Florio and Palsgrave are writing at the birth of English obscenity, not yet its ascendancy.

The *Worlde of Words* includes *cunt* too, in *potta*, "a womans privie parts, a cunt, a quaint" and *pottaccia*, "a filthie great cunt."† Florio also freely uses *fuck* in his definitions of the Italian *fottere*. He assigns the verb itself the meanings "to iape, to sard, to fucke, to swive, to occupy," while *fottitrice* is "a woman fucker, swiver, sarder, or iaper" and *fottitore* the male equivalent. Palsgrave never prints the *f*-word in English, but translates *foutre* with *sard* and *swive*. He helpfully gives examples of how to use these words in conversation, such as "I will not swive her and she would pray me"—"I wouldn't fuck her if she begged me." Even worse, by the principle of didactic responsibility, might be his definition of *ie fringue*: "I frig with the arse as a queene doth when she is in japing," that is, "I rub with the ass as a prostitute does while she is fucking." I challenge you to read that without wading a little bit deeper into the ooze of sin.

Florio may have the most *fucks*, but his are not the earliest examples of the word. That honor goes to a piece of marginalia in a manuscript of Cicero, "O d fuckin Abbot," from 1528. An anonymous monk was reading through the monastery copy of *De Officiis*

---

* *La Cazzaria* is the title of a circa 1530 dialogue between two humanists who address questions ranging from "Why the asshole is behind the cunt" to "Why the common people don't understand the beauty of the Tuscan language."

† In Randle Cotgrave's 1611 *Dictionary of the French and English Tongues* there are no *cunt*s or *fuck*s, but there is a greyhound. A *levretée* is "an Hare-lipt, or blabber-lipt wench; also, a wench that hath beene buggered by a Greyhound."

when he felt compelled to express his anger at his abbot. (We can
be sure when this was because he helpfully recorded the date in
another comment.) It is difficult to know whether the annotator
intended *fucking* to mean "having sex," as in "that guy is doing too
much fucking for someone who is supposed to be celibate," or
whether he used it as an intensifier; if the latter, it anticipates the
first recorded use by more than three hundred years. Either is
possible, really—John Burton, the abbot in question, was a man
of questionable monastic morals. It is interesting as well that
while the annotator has no problem spelling out *fucking* (except
for the *g*), he refuses to write out a word that is most likely *damned*.
To this monk, *damnation* is the real obscenity, the one that can be
hinted at but not expressed in full.

There are at least two instances of *fuck* dated before that of our
monk, but scholars sometimes deny them the glory of first use
because one is Scottish and one appears in code, with a Latin verb
conjugation. The Scots poet William Dunbar (more of him later)
penned these lines sometime before his death, in 1513:

> He clappit fast, he kist and chukkit,
> As with the glaikis he wer ovirgane.
> Yit be his feirris he wald have fukkit . . .
> [He embraced fast [tight], he kissed and groped,
> As if he were overcome with desire.
> Yet [it seemed from] his behavior he would have fucked.]

The coded example is also from a poem, dated 1475–1500, this one
attacking the Carmelite friars of the town of Ely. It is macaronic, that
is, written partly in English and partly in Latin, with the dirty bits
"concealed" in the most basic of ciphers:

> Non sunt in cœli, quia gxddbov xxkxzt pg ifmk.
> . . .
> Fratres cum knyvys goth about and txxkxzv nfookt xxzxkt.

For each letter of code, you simply substitute the previous letter of the alphabet, and you get, making allowances for late medieval spelling, "fuccant wivys of heli"—"They [the monks] are not in heaven, because they fuck the wives of Ely." The third line unciphers to "swivyt mennis wyvis"—"Brothers with knives go about and swive men's wives." To this author, *swive* was apparently as bad a word as its synonym, also requiring at least the pretense of concealment. It is unclear whether the words are censored because *swive* and *fuck* are thought to be obscene, worse in themselves than the other words in the poem, or because the sexual sins of which the author accuses the monks are so horrible they cannot be stated outright. What is clear is that you didn't want to mess with any Carmelite friar looking for oppljf.

There are many theories on the etymology of *fuck*. It is popularly supposed to be an acronym. When England's population was decimated by the plague in olden times, the story goes, the king pondered how to get his subjects to reproduce. He issued proclamations demanding that they "fornicate under command of the king," or F.U.C.K. for short. This is not true, nor is pretty much any story that explains the origin of a swearword as an acronym. *Naff*, for example, is not an acronym of "not available for fucking." More familiar to Brits than to Americans, *naff* was a word in the gay slang language Polari in the 1960s, meaning "tacky." Princess Anne caused controversy when she told photographers to "naff off" in 1982. *Shit*, actually one of the oldest words in the English language, has produced perhaps the best of these stories: Before the American Revolution, people used to ship manure back and forth across the Atlantic for fertilizer. When the manure in the hold of the ship came into contact with seawater, it would start to ferment, producing methane gas. When an unfortunate sailor would go belowdecks with a lantern, the ship would explode. As a result, bundles of manure began to be labeled "Ship High in Transit," so that sailors would know to store them high enough that they wouldn't get wet and blow up.

If it's not an acronym, what is the etymology of *fuck*? The real answer is rather less interesting. It is a word of Germanic origin, related to Dutch, German, and Swedish words for "to strike" and "to move back and forth." It is also clearly not one of our good old Anglo-Saxon words, like *shit*, having come into use only in the late fifteenth century.

Florio and Palsgrave included words such as *fuck*, *arse*, and *swive* in their dictionaries because people used them in everyday life, despite the growing sixteenth-century sense that these words were obscene—worse, morally, than the other words around them. This increased use is reflected in court records of the period. Medieval insults that made it into suits of defamation and slander, as we saw in the previous chapter, overwhelmingly featured the words *false*, *harlot*, and *whore*, and various combinations thereof—"False whore-mongering harlot!" In the sixteenth century, the insults began to employ more of the words we would use today. In 1555, John Warneford and John a Bridges were at loggerheads over a piece of property, when John B. brought a defamation suit claiming that John W. had called him a "crooked nose[d] knave" and declared "shit upon his Crooked nose." When in 1597 Roger Jackson wanted to vilify William Hobson by suggesting he was an adulterer, he didn't use *adulterer* or *false*; he went straight to "he fuckes and sardes bothe Alen Sugdons wife of Stanley and her doghter." And in 1629 John Slocombe complained that George Bailey was going around telling people that he had shown him his "pricke" and told him "this pricke hath fuckt Ioan Pecke many times." Bailey was also spreading the rumor that Slocombe "did pisse or make water in the widdowe Tylles backside." This is less kinky than it sounds: Slocombe had apparently peed in her garden.

Some of this newfound obscenity probably reflects a change in the way speech was recorded in the various court rolls. In the Middle Ages, the records were often entirely in Latin and French, with the actual English words at issue included only occasionally. By the sixteenth century, the records were in English or in a mixture of English and Latin, so there was much more scope for insults to be written down at length. But these court records also reflect a move from oaths to obscenities as the language of emotive power. People didn't need to accuse each other of "fucking" in the Middle Ages, because the word *fuck* wasn't any worse than *lie with, have to do with*, or *adulteravit*. By the sixteenth century, *fucking* was becoming a more powerful word, so people began to employ it more and more frequently when they wanted to wound.

A genre of poetry called flyting exemplifies this new use of obscene words to injure and insult. Flyting was very much like the freestyle battles of today, in which rappers compete to insult each other in the most creative ways. While freestyle battling is a "street" art form, practiced mostly by disenfranchised youth, flyting was entertainment for the nobility. The most famous practitioner, William Dunbar, of the early *fukkit*, was a Franciscan friar, and even Scottish kings tried their hand. A typical example is this exchange between Friar Dunbar and Walter Kennedy, a court poet.

Kennedy to Dunbar:

> Skaldit skaitbird and commoun skamelar,
> Wanfukkit funling that Natour maid ane yrle . . .
> [Diseased vulture and common parasite,
> Weakly conceived foundling that Nature made a dwarf . . .]

Dunbar to Kennedy:

> Forworthin wirling, I warne thee, it is wittin
> How, skyttand skarth, thow hes the hurle behind.
> Wan wraiglane wasp, ma wormis hes thow beschittin
> Nor thair is gers on grund or leif on lind.
> [Deformed wretch, I warn you, it is known,
> How, you shitting hermaphrodite, you have diarrhea behind.
> Sad wriggling wasp, you have beshit more worms
> Than there is grass on ground or leaf on linden tree.]

The sixteenth century is a turning point in the history of swearing in English, as epitomized by Florio's *cazzica*, "an interjection of admiration and affirming, what? gods me, god forbid, tush." Where an Italian would employ an obscenity, an English person, Florio indicates, would still use a vain oath. But from this point on, the balance will tip heavily in favor of obscenity, until four hundred years later we get *motherfucker*, an interjection of admiration and affirming.

You Should Be Ashamed of Yourself

In the sixteenth century, obscene language was developing both as a moral phenomenon and as a social one. The moral aspect came from the Middle Ages and ultimately from the Bible, but the seductive force that used to be spread across an entire sinful sentence was becoming concentrated in a few lascivious little words for certain body parts and actions. The social aspect developed in the web of relationships at the new, nonfeudal court, where speech and writing were tools employed by courtiers as they jockeyed for the favor of the monarch on whom they were more and more dependent. This period saw a great "advance in the frontiers of shame," as Norbert Elias puts it. Sixteenth-century people were ashamed of more things than their medieval forebears, and ashamed in front of more people. It became more and more important to conceal these various shameful body parts and actions, in public life and in polite language.

Innovations in sixteenth-century architecture allowed for what scholars talk about as the "invention" of privacy, necessary for this increased delicacy of shame. Of course, solitude wasn't a Renaissance invention—people in the Middle Ages sometimes found themselves alone, though not as often as we do—but it was only after the proliferation of spaces in which people could reliably be alone that something like our notion of privacy developed, the feeling that there were certain things that belonged solely to an individual and that must not be shared with or shown before other people. Even confession, the most secret of all the sacraments, was not private, in our sense of the word, for much of the Middle Ages. You might have told your sins to the priest and God alone, but the priest very likely would have imposed on you a public penance—wearing sackcloth, missing Communion—to be performed in front of the entire community. The whole parish would thus have known about the "private" sins you confessed to the priest. Reading too was very often not private but a group activity: a poet reciting his poems to entertain the court, a lady reading from a book to entertain her friends, a monk reading from the Bible to his brethren in their monastery. Books were so rare, heavy, and expensive that no one ever curled up in an armchair to read to him- or herself. (Also, there were, as far as historians can tell, no comfortable chairs for most of the Middle Ages—you sat on either long benches or large, unpadded wooden chairs.) Even in the sixteenth century, people were suspicious of privacy—who knew what you could get up to all by your lonesome, with only the devil for company? In the Middle Ages, then, there was little that was private as we think of it, and even if people occasionally found themselves alone in the woods, this was not necessarily seen as a desirable thing.

In the Renaissance, people started building houses with more rooms. They needed more rooms, because suddenly they were accumulating more stuff. In a region of England called the Arden, to take just one small area, people amassed possessions at an astounding rate in the years between 1570 and 1674. Historian Victor Skipp calculates that possessions increased 289 percent among the wealthy, 310 percent among the "middling sort," and even 247 percent among the poorer classes during these years.* To see what this

---

*Historians don't like to use the terms *middle class* and *working class* to describe people of this period, as those words are too freighted with a Marxist sense of class opposition to delineate early modern social groups. "Middling sort" indicates people who were not wealthy and not poor, and who were for the most part merchants and low-level gentry. They were not "bourgeois," with all that term implies today. And the "lower sort" were not ill-educated factory workers who drank lots of beer on the weekends, the unfortunate connotations of *working class* today. (Also, there were no weekends—only Sunday, and you had better have spent that day in church.)

looked like in practice, Skipp compares the goods possessed by two farmers with approximately the same size landholding in 1560 and in 1587. Edward Kempsale, the first farmer, lived in a house with two rooms, and his household goods at his death consisted of six plates, three sheets, one coverlet, and two tablecloths. Thomas Gyll, in contrast, lived in a house with four rooms, and left more than twenty-eight pieces of pewter, five silver spoons, thirteen and a half pairs of sheets, six coverlets, and four tablecloths, as well as pillows, pillowcases, and table napkins. Master Gyll could build extra rooms to store and display his pewter and his thirteen and a half pairs of sheets thanks to a technological innovation—the fireplace. Around 1330, fireplaces were developed that would not collapse under the intense heat generated by a confined fire. The central open fire of the hall could be replaced with a fireplace and chimney; you could then add rooms above the hall, which previously had been impossible because the smoke needed to go out through a hole in the roof. These rooms could be given their own fireplaces, and could then be used even in the winter. Bill Bryson, shrewd observer of human nature, summarizes what happened next: "Rooms began to proliferate as wealthy householders discovered the satisfactions of having space to themselves. . . . The idea of personal space, which seems so natural to us now, was a revelation. People couldn't get enough of it." Houses began to have bedrooms, studies, dining rooms, and parlors—they began, slowly, to look more like houses as we know them today.

The notion of privacy evolved slowly, even with these extra rooms. People who used to sleep together in the straw of the great hall would now bed down in a bedroom, but they still likely would be sleeping with others. A (female) servant often slept on the floor of the room Samuel Pepys shared with his wife in the late seventeenth century; some of the servants found this arrangement perfectly normal, others, perhaps more attuned to the idea of privacy (or perhaps just more wary of Mr. Pepys), thought it odd. Privies were also spaces in which privacy could be achieved, as their name suggests. There were two kinds of places one might leave a sirreverence—the privies or garderobes, which were small rooms that hung out over the walls of a castle or house and allowed waste to drop into a moat or river or onto the ground below, and closestools, which were chamber pots enclosed and somewhat disguised by a piece of furniture. These were usually placed in a bedroom or dining room but could still be at least notionally private, surrounded by a curtain. (*Sirreverence* comes from "save-reverence," which people used to say before or after mentioning something likely to offend. The apology came to stand for the thing it excused, and so *sirreverence* came to mean "turd," as in these lines from Shakespeare's early rival Robert Greene: "His head, and his necke, were all besmeared with the soft sirreverence, so as he stunke worse than a Jakes Farmer," a person who cleans out privies for a living.) *Garderobe* looks as if it should refer to a place to put clothes—it is Norman French for "wardrobe"—but came to be applied to privies because they were often built off wardrobes. Privies were also called, in ascending order of politeness, *jakes* or *sinkes, latrines, places of easement,* and *houses of office. Jakes* especially was vulgar and impolite; in his *Metamorphosis of Ajax,* Harington relates the story of a flustered lady-in-waiting who introduces Jaques Wingfield as "M. Privy Wingfield." Privies were sometimes truly private one-seaters, where a person could read, think, sleep, or even, as King James I was rumored to have done, have sex. Often, however, they were still communal multi-seaters, though much less grand than those of ancient Roman times, maxing out at around seven or eight seats. While it is possible to imagine eight people staring resolutely into space while they used the facilities, these were more likely social spaces. In the late seventeenth century, the family at Chilthorne Domer, a manor in Somerset, would congregate daily in their six-seater.

In 1596, though, Harington had mocked this custom as "French," pretty much the worst insult an Englishman could throw at something in the Renaissance without resorting to sirreverence.

Harington suggests that multiseat privies are going out of fashion, that the most socially acceptable way to defecate is in privacy. A woodcut from his *Metamorphosis* illustrates this new custom of performing one's bodily functions in private, while pointing out the potential dangers of such solitude—the devil comes to annoy the defecator. Harington was a member of high society, a courtier and Queen Elizabeth's godson, and was ahead of the curve. He extolled the virtues of the private privy long before the country family, rusticated more than a hundred miles from London, thought to be ashamed of their bodily functions and started to discuss the day's events at the breakfast table, not in the shithouse.

For true privacy, a wealthy person could repair to his or her closet. In the Renaissance, this was not the room for storing clothes or books or your grandmother's sewing machine, but a small room like a study, used for reading or prayer. According to historian Mark Girouard, "it was perhaps the only room in which its occupant could be entirely on his own," since servants would likely be present even in a bedchamber. Closets, and the solitude they represented, were at first an elite phenomenon, seen only in the houses of the wealthy. But, as Thomas Gyll shows, the idea of privacy actually did trickle down. People of the middling and lower sorts also participated in the "Great Rebuilding," adding rooms to their houses where, eventually, they would seek to be alone.

These architectural changes are tied up with the development of privacy and the feelings of delicacy and shame we've linked to it. Some historians, such as Nicholas Cooper, suggest that "evolving civility showed itself in the desire for greater privacy and the need for more rooms"; others reverse the causation and see the increased number of rooms as creating spaces in which the modern notion of privacy could develop. Either way, privacy is inextricably linked to the advancing threshold of shame. Just as people started to wall themselves off physically from others in their new rooms, they began to wall themselves off psychically, as it were. Privacy created what we've seen Elias call "the invisible wall of affects," and with it the

A solitary defecator from *The Metamorphosis of Ajax*. The motto *Sprinto non spinto* is perhaps best translated as "I go quickly, I don't push or strain."

embarrassment and shame at the sight or mention of bodily functions that medieval people lacked.

The shame threshold trickled down too, like the idea of privacy, spreading from the upper classes to the middling and lower sorts. At first it was offensive to expose oneself or to use obscene language only if it was done before people of greater rank. In his influential treatise on manners, *Galateo* (1558), Giovanni Della Casa dictates that

> one should not sit with one's back or posterior turned towards another, nor raise a thigh so high that the members of the human body, which should properly be covered with clothing at all times, might be exposed to view. For this and similar things are not done, except among people before whom one is not ashamed. It is true that a great lord might do so before one of his servants or in the presence of a friend of lower rank; for in this he would not show him arrogance but rather a particular affection and friendship.

Della Casa is not talking about sexual relationships here. He means that it would be a sign of "condescension"—a mark of favor—to let a social inferior get a glimpse of, say, your balls. He introduces the (to us) quite foreign category of "people before whom one is not ashamed." At this point, in 1558, one could feel shame before equals or social superiors, but not before "inferiors" such as servants or even friends of lower rank.

The idea that people could be ashamed only before their social superiors led to some interesting fashion choices in the Renaissance. In portraits, Queen Elizabeth is buttoned up and surrounded by ruffs, poufy sleeves, and symbolic attributes of virginity, such as sieves and moons (symbols of Cynthia/Diana, virgin goddess of the hunt). In life, she liked to show her breasts to the French ambassador. André Hurault, envoy of King Henri IV, recorded his meetings with the queen in great detail, including one occasion when "she kept the front of her dress open, and one could see the whole of her bosom, and passing low, and often she would open the front of this robe with her hands as if she was too hot." Another time "she had a petticoat of white damask, girdled, and open in front, as was also her chemise, in such a manner that she often opened this dress and one could see all her belly, even to her navel." Hurault does not appear to record this with shock or even particular interest (he does note that "her bosom is somewhat wrinkled," but in the same tone in which he reports that she had pearls hanging down on her forehead, "but of no great worth"). Elizabeth's behavior was not a desperate attempt by a batty old woman to hang on to the threads of her sex appeal (she was sixty-four years old at this point) but was a gracious sign of condescension to her social inferior.

Under Elizabeth's successors James I and Charles I (until Puritans put a stop to the practice after the Revolution), women also routinely bared their breasts in court masques. These were plays put on by a combination of professional and amateur aristocratic performers; Queen Anne (James I's wife) and Queen Henrietta Maria (Charles I's) themselves took part. The architect Inigo Jones designed many of the costumes, and the drawings he made of his designs show clearly that many aristocratic bosoms were on display at these events.

Lavatorily, the same thing went on. Petitioners who sought to speak to James I could judge their perceived importance from the room in which the king received them. There was a hierarchy of chambers, starting with the public spaces for common visitors and ending with the king's closet. It was condescension, in the good, old-fashioned sense, if the king received someone before he got up from bed; it was only those petitioners who were kept to the more public throne room and audience chambers who might have reason to worry about their status and their requests. John Harington relates the story of another ambassador, this one a Venetian in France, who "hearing a Noble person was come to speak with him, made him stay til he had untied his points; and when he was new set on his stool, sent for the Noble man to come to him at that time; as

A dress for Queen Henrietta Maria, designed by Inigo Jones for the masque *Chloris* in 1631.

a very special favour." The ambassador untrusses his trousers and sits on his closestool—only then is he ready to receive his honored guest. Harington, though, disparages this as a "French courtesie," like the "French pox" (syphilis). The ambassador, like the family at Chilthorne Domer with their multiseat privy, is behind the times. According to Harington's elite courtly standards, receiving some-one while defecating is turning from gracious condescension to insult; defecation is turning into a private matter.

As the years progressed, society agreed more and more with Harington and less and less with the Venetian ambassador. As dis-tinctions of rank became more fungible, and as the middling sort acquired the material prosperity to emulate the aristocrats, the number of people in front of whom one had to be ashamed—to censor one's behavior and language—increased. By the eighteenth century, even kings and queens felt shame before their inferiors. Everyone began to be ashamed before everyone else.

The New Obscenity

As the shame threshold marched forward, obscenity became in-creasingly prevalent and important in the Renaissance. Dictionary makers such as Thomas Elyot had thought long and hard about it, in particular about which words should be avoided, while those such as Florio and Palsgrave almost reveled in the abundance of wanton words. In the wider literary world, some authors seem to have been more on Elyot's side, and some to have followed Florio. This lack of a consistent standard can be seen in the prefaces to the editions of two different poets, Chaucer and Homer, published at the turn of the seventeenth century. In the sixteenth century, Chaucer was be-ginning to be thought of as England's founding poet, its answer to the great Greek and Latin authors—Homer, Virgil, Horace, and others—of antiquity. Thomas Speght's 1598 edition of Chaucer was intended to burnish further the reputation of the medieval poet, who is "no less worthy than the best of them amongst all the

Poets of the world." Speght had a problem, however, in that some of Chaucer's language, as we saw so many times in the previous chapter, fell into the new category of obscenity. Speght had to defend his decision to reprint Chaucer's work at all, let alone make him out to be the founding father of English literature. Though Chaucer "is somewhat too broad in some of his speeches," Speght's preface admits, he is no more nor less obscene than the famous Roman "good authors" Ovid and Catullus, who were revered at the time. His obscenity—unremarkable in the Middle Ages—is by 1600 almost, but not quite, enough to disqualify him as England's premier poet.

In 1616, George Chapman published what he hoped would be the definitive edition of Homer, who had long been established as a canonical poet, perhaps *the* canonical poet. It is thus something of a surprise to read, in Chapman's preface, his attack on "a certain envious Windfucker." This person, Chapman complains, has spread rumors that he has translated Homer from Latin editions rather than from the original Greek. *Windfucker* is, arguably, just as bad a word as anything in Chaucer. (In Victorian editions of Chapman's Homer, it is replaced with *Windsucker*.) If on one hand Speght must explain away Chaucer's broad language while on the other Chapman can insult someone as a "Windfucker," it seems that there was no agreement about which words were acceptable and which were not in this period, even in such a narrow genre as literary prefaces to the works of canonical poets.

Playwrights were quick to take advantage of the new obscenity, but again the line as to which words were acceptable and which were not was blurry. Plays in this period, as any reader of Shakespeare knows, are full of double entendres (words or phrases that can be understood in two senses), puns, and other plays on obscene words. You can open Shakespeare's collected plays to just about any page and find dirty jokes and obscene innuendos; here is a tiny, tiny sampling. In *The Merry Wives of Windsor*, a Welshman examines a boy on the Latin "focative" (vocative) case, obviously a play on *fuck*. When, in the same play, a Frenchman announces, "If dere be one or two, I shall make-a de turd [third]," the Welshman replies, "In your teeth: for shame!" "Turd in your teeth," as we learned from the grammar school textbooks of the previous chapter, was a popular expression of defiance. In *Henry V*, there is an extended scene in which the French princess Katherine tries to learn some English and discovers that words innocuous in English are obscene in French. *Pied* is "le foot," as she pronounces it (sounding like the French for "fuck"), and *la robe* (the gown) is "le count" (*cunt*). Katherine is shocked by this and declares, "O Lord, those are bad words, wicked, coarse, and immodest, and not proper for well-bred ladies to use!" The title *Much Ado About Nothing* puns on "much ado about an o thing," *o* being Elizabethan slang for *le count*. Hamlet's line to Ophelia, "Do you think I meant country matters?" is so direct it almost doesn't qualify as innuendo. Her reply, "I think nothing, my lord" also plays on an o thing, or at least that's the way Hamlet takes it when he responds, "That's a fair thought to lie between maids' legs." Pretty much anything that might be bawdy in Shakespeare *is* bawdy, including the puzzling "to fill a bottle with a tun-dish" (sex; a tun-dish is a funnel), "to hide his bauble in a hole" (sex), and "to change the cod's head for the salmon's tail" (nobody is really sure what this one means, but it must have something to do with sex because *cod*, as in *codpiece*, means "scrotum," and *tail* means "genitalia," either male or female).

As bawdy as he is, Shakespeare never employs a primary obscenity. Other Renaissance dramatists had fewer qualms about using them, however, like Shakespeare's contemporary Ben Jonson. In his plays you get, to name just a few, "Windfucker," as well as "turd i' your teeth . . . And turd i' your little wife's teeth too," "Marry, shit o' your hood," and "Kiss the whore o' the arse." As with literary prefaces, it seems, there was no accepted standard of what sort of language was appropriate for drama.

Renaissance drama is an especially interesting place to examine the period's attitudes to obscenity, because we have fairly extensive records of its censorship. Plays were licensed for performance and sometimes for print by the master of the revels, a functionary appointed by the king or queen. Theater companies had to submit every script to the master, who looked it over and decided whether it was fit to be performed. Sir Henry Herbert left the most complete records, covering the years 1623 to 1642, and from his comments we can infer that what rendered plays unfit was, first of all, too pointed political commentary or scenes that might offend powerful people; second, oath swearing; and only then obscenity. The master had in fact a legal duty to censor oaths in plays. In 1606 Parliament had passed the Act to Restrain Abuses of Players, which made it illegal to "jestingly or profanely" use God's name onstage. Any expletives involving God's name—*by God, God's blood,* and even the minced forms *'sblood* and *zounds* (God's wounds)—were forbidden in drama. (In 1623, "profane oaths" were banned in real life as well, on penalty of a fine, or of the stocks if a swearer could not pay.) You can see this 1606 law reflected everywhere in printed playbooks. Since printed editions of plays were often based on the scripts used by actors, plays published before 1606 tend to contain a great deal of swearing; those published after, very little. In *The Famous Victories of Henry V* (1598), Prince Hal and his friends can't get through two lines of dialogue without an oath. Here is a speech by the prince, early in the play:

> Gogs [God's] wounds how like you this Jockey?
> Blood [God's blood] you villains my father robbed of his money abroad
> . . .
> Gogs wounds you lamed them fairly.*

Shakespeare's own Henry plays, which were based partly on *The Famous Victories,* also contain a fair number of oaths, including

---

* If you want to see Shakespeare's genius in action, compare *The Famous Victories* with the Henriad.

zounds and *'sblood*. By the time his later tragedies are published, however, *zounds* and *'sblood* have disappeared, and in plays such as *Othello*, most references to God have been replaced by references to heaven.

Sir Henry Herbert is so concerned about oath swearing in the drama he is charged with regulating that he is willing to risk a formal disagreement with King Charles I. As was his usual practice, Herbert had cut the oaths from a play, *The Wits*, written by the courtier William Davenant. Davenant and his friends complained to the king, who called Herbert into his rooms and told him that "*faith* and *slight* [were] asseverations only, and no oaths." Herbert has no choice but to allow these words into the play, since the king has commanded it, but he records his disgruntlement in his book: "The king is pleased to take *faith, death, slight* for asseverations . . . [but I] conceive them to be oaths, and enter them here, to declare my opinion and submission." There is no question of *God's blood* or *God's wounds* being allowed in a play by this time, in 1633. Herbert feels strongly that even the most mild of minced oaths should be censored, but he cannot cross the king. And so playgoers received the pleasure of hearing *faith, death*, and *slight* used by various characters more than a hundred times when they saw *The Wits*.

Herbert once burns a play he receives "for the ribaldry and offense that was in it," but scholars argue that he censored the play more for its "offense"—political satire—than for its bawdy language. Scholars argue that obscenity alone was not reason enough to ban a play in this period. The first acknowledged case of censorship on grounds of obscenity occurred a century later, with the prosecution of Edmund Curll in 1727. (He was accused of "obscene libel" and "disturbing the King's peace" by publishing the pornographic novel *Venus in the Cloister*.) More often, Herbert links "ribaldry" with oath swearing, as in "oaths, profaneness, or obsceneness," or "oaths, profaneness, and ribaldry." These two kinds of bad language often appear together, and both must be avoided. In this respect, Herbert's attitude is closer to the Victorian than to the medieval. In the Middle

Ages, we have seen, the sins of the tongue were numerous and varied, from scolding your neighbors to singing hymns of praise with
too much expression. By the nineteenth century these "sins" have
been narrowed down to two, which are almost constantly associated, as they are in Herbert's record book—oaths and obscene
language.

What best sums up the period's mixture of oaths and obscenity,
its shifting combination of Holy and Shit, is a religious group from
the 1650s called the Ranters. Ranters are like witches—the popular
imagination had a firm image of them, and many tracts were written
that revealed their evil dealings, but it is unclear whether anyone
actually self-identified as one. Ranters, it was thought, believed that
God manifested himself in each individual believer; therefore, any
impulse a person had was holy. It thus became impossible to sin,
and the Ranters became the seventeenth-century id let loose. They
had orgies, they masturbated in public, they kissed each other's
naked buttocks, they entered polygamous "marriages." One of their
songs prefigures the 1960s sentiment of "Love the One You're
With":

> The fellow Creature which sits next
> Is more delight to me
> Than any that I else can find;
> For that she's always free.

Equally shockingly, however, the Ranters also performed the Eucharist themselves, interrupted church services to preach their gospel,
and swore. They were famous for their profane oath swearing, which
they supposedly saw as the fullest realization of God in man. They
swore so virulently that people who heard them were supposed to
become prostrate with shock, as did one innkeeper who tried to
throw a Ranter out of her house: "it put the woman into such a fright,
to hear his curses and blasphemies, that she trembled and quaked
some hours after."

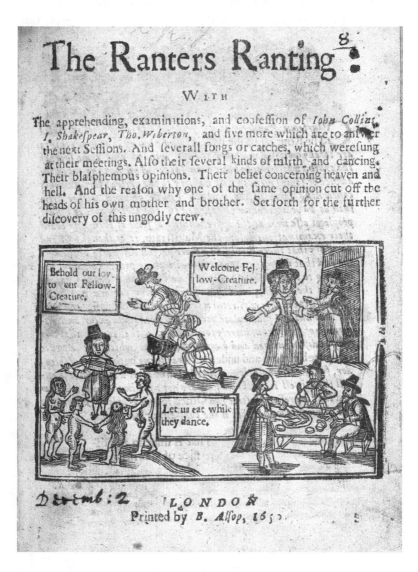

The Ranters Ranting, 1650. This pamphlet details some of the Ranters' horrible practices and helpfully illustrates them with a woodcut.

As the example of the Ranters indicates, the sixteenth and seventeenth centuries presented a mix of the Holy and Shit. The Holy was declining in power, the Shit gaining it. Oaths had lost their ability to access God directly, and had begun to lose their power to shock and offend, but had not yet been eclipsed as the most powerful kind of language. Obscenity was beginning its rise to the position it has today, but it was still in the process of being defined, with obscene words sometimes avoided and sometimes ignored or even celebrated in the same contexts. It would take the extreme repression of the Victorians finally to secure obscene words their place as the "worst" in the English language.

Chapter 5

The Age of Euphemism

The Eighteenth and Nineteenth Centuries

In 1673, John Wilmot, Earl of Rochester, composed a poem attacking his mistress for the criteria she used in choosing other lovers. While his subject matter perhaps fails to strike a chord, Rochester's vituperative language is instantly recognizable. "Much wine had past with grave discourse / Of who Fucks who and who does worse," he begins this poem, his most famous, "A Ramble in St James's Park." Drunk, and looking for some lechery himself, he wanders into the park, which is "Consecrate to Prick and Cunt" because it is so full of people meeting up for assignations. Even the trees are sexualized—their "lewd tops Fuckt the very Skies." In this promiscuous landscape the poet sees his lover, Corinna, go off in a carriage with three fops, and complains:

> Gods! that a thing admir'd by me
> Shou'd fall to so much Infamy.
> Had she pickt out to rub her Arse on
> Some stiff prickt Clown or well hung Parson,
> Each job of whose spermatique sluice
> Had filled her Cunt with wholesome Juice,
> I the proceeding should have praisd . . .
> But to turn damn'd abandon'd Jade
> When neither Head nor Tail persuade
> To be a Whore in understanding
> A passive pot for Fools to spend in. . . .

He is angry that Corinna has taken up with fools, though neither "head nor tail" inspired her choice—she was motivated by social snobbery, not intellectual interest or sexual desire. A good old country boy the poet could accept, or a parson with a large "spermatic sluice," because the decision would be driven by pure desire. But when Corinna seduces the ridiculous men-about-town based partly on a calculation of social advantage, she becomes a whore, in the poet's system of values.

Rochester concludes with one of the best curses ever:

> May stinking vapours Choke your womb
> Such as the Men you doat upon;
> May your depraved Appetite
> That cou'd in Whiffling Fools delight
> Beget such Frenzies in your Mind
> You may goe mad for the North wind,
> And fixing all your hopes upon't
> To have him bluster in your Cunt,
> Turn up your longing Arse to the Air
> And perish in a wild despair.

May you go crazy, fall in love with the wind, stick your ass in the air, and die. It's practically Yiddish, and a literal description of the Renaissance insult *windfucker*. This is followed by one of the best threats ever written down:

> But Cowards shall forget to rant,
> School-Boys to Frig, old whores to paint,
> The *Jesuits* Fraternity
> Shall leave the use of Buggery,
> Crab-louse inspir'd with Grace divine
> From Earthly Cod to Heaven shall climb,
> *Physicians* shall believe in *Jesus*
> And Disobedience cease to please us

E're I desist with all my Power
To plague this woman and undo her.

Cowards will stop boasting, schoolboys will stop boxing the Jesuit, whores will stop putting on makeup, Jesuits will stop boxing the schoolboys, and genital lice will crawl from the scrotum up to heaven before the poet will stop tormenting Corinna for her lapses in amorous taste.*

This is modern obscenity. Though some of the sentiments and language are foreign to readers today, *cunt, fuck, frig, prick, arse,* and other words are employed in order to provoke, to offend, to add insult to injury.† Rochester does not write "when your lewd Cunt came spewing home" because *cunt* is the most direct word for what he's talking about and he values clarity of thought and expression. He uses it because it has become a derogatory, offensive, obscene word, and he wants to shock and offend.

Rochester's poems heralded a brave new era of obscenity. Words such as *cunt* had been employed for hundreds of years, as we have seen, and in the Renaissance had begun to accrue the power being lost by oaths. In the sixteenth and seventeenth centuries, the Holy and the Shit were mixed, neither one nor the other predominating. In the eighteenth and nineteenth centuries, however, the balance swings entirely toward the Shit. Obscenities experienced a tremendous growth in strength, even as they disappeared almost entirely from public discourse. Obscene words for body parts and actions (sex and excrement) took oaths' place as the words that shocked and

---

* "Boxing the Jesuit" was eighteenth-century slang for masturbation. As Francis Grose explains in his 1785 dictionary of slang: "to box the Jesuit, and get cock roaches" is a "sea term [used by sailors] for masturbation. A crime it is said much practiced by the reverend fathers of that society."

† *Frig* as an obscene word is perhaps more familiar in Britain, where it refers to masturbation. If you come across it in America, it may occasionally be a misspelling of *fridge*, meaning "refrigerator." I walked into my daughter's school one morning and saw a sign posted: "Note: small frig needed Tuesday."

offended; that insulted; that expressed extremes of emotion, positive or negative. To a degree, obscene words even adopted oaths' ability to signify the truth of a statement, a capability that harks back to the "plain Latin" of ancient Rome. Toward the end of the nineteenth century, obscene words began to be used nonliterally, for their emotional charge alone; at this point they completed their transformation into swearwords.

Rochester and his libertine companions were reacting to the Puritanism of the Commonwealth (1649–1660), when chastity, modest dress, and sober behavior reigned, except, of course, among the Ranters. When Charles II was restored to the throne in 1660, the merry monarch and his friends threw themselves into an opposite world—they wore beautiful clothes, took countless mistresses (one hopes it was on the basis of desire and/or intellectual interest), and practiced jolly pranks such as kidnapping heiresses and trying to marry them by force. (When he was eighteen, Rochester abducted the fourteen-year-old Elizabeth Malet from her grandfather's coach. He was caught and sent to the Tower of London, and the girl was returned to her family. Elizabeth was apparently impressed—she married him of her own volition two years later.) After the riotous Restoration, however, a form of Puritanism came back, though its motivations were not religious this time, but social. The bourgeoisie developed in the eighteenth century—a middle class of merchants who seized on the "civilizing process" that had started in the Renaissance and made it their own. Good manners and refinement of language became an indication of social and moral worth, a sign of distinction that differentiated the middle classes from the great unwashed outside and below. Delicacy of speech and propriety of dress became increasingly important, to such a degree that chickens lost their *legs* and developed *limbs* (and later *white* and *dark meat*), lest the bird be so rude as to remind someone that people have legs too. These two trends account for obscenity's great power in the eighteenth and nineteenth centuries. Obscene words violated class norms—they were seen as the language of the lower classes, the uneducated—and accessed the deepest taboo of Augustan and Victorian society, the human body and its embarrassing desires, which had to be absolutely hidden away in swaths of fabric and disguised in euphemisms.

Eighteenth- and nineteenth-century English also needed to be purified to reflect the greatness of the growing British Empire. Latin had served Rome well; English had likewise to be made to conform to rules and shorn of slang (often code for obscenities) so that it could help to promote British imperialism and monumentalize the empire's achievements forever. The growing empire paradoxically created the last category of obscenity—racial slurs. Many of these arose as cultures intermixed on a scale never seen before, as the empire stretched its arms across the ocean to America and then around the world, and the United States expanded westward.

From Oath to Affirmation

Vain and blasphemous oaths didn't disappear all at once in the eighteenth century—theirs was a slow but steady decline, which is still going on today. In surveys of the American and British publics, oaths are now ranked among the mildest but most common swearwords. In a 2006 study of speakers of American English, *hell, damn, goddamn, Jesus Christ,* and *oh my God* were five of the ten most frequently used swearwords, with the top ten making up 80 percent of the swearing recorded. *Oh my God* alone accounted for 24 percent of women's swearing.* In the early eighteenth century, vain and blasphemous oaths were even more numerous than they are today, as the obscenities were just starting to take their place in the lexicon of swearing. A character in Alexander Pope's *The Rape of the Lock*

---

* The results for British swearing are similar—*God* and *hell* are two of the most frequently used swearwords, among all social classes.

(1712) provides an extreme but not unrealistic example of the way oaths were employed at this time:

> My Lord, why, what the devil?
> Z——ds! Damn the lock! 'fore Gad, you must be civil!
> Plague on 't! 'tis past a jest—nay prithee, pox!
> Give her the hair.

Sir Plume, just the kind of fop that Rochester's Corinna would have opened her legs for, is defending his beloved Belinda from the evil baron who has just cut off a lock of her hair—the "rape." The swearing in this poem presents a striking contrast to the way oaths were treated in the seventeenth century, when they were banned onstage and struck from most published texts of plays, including Shakespeare's. By the end of the eighteenth century, *zounds* was still in use but had become a completely meaningless expletive. It even had to be defined in dictionaries of slang for those who might hear it said but fail to understand it. Francis Grose's 1785 *Classical Dictionary of the Vulgar Tongue* explained it as "an exclamation, an abbreviation of God's wounds" (Grose also defined such obscure terms as "crinkums, the foul or venereal disease" and "feague, . . . to put ginger up a horse's fundament, to make him lively and carry his tail well.") Eighty years later, John Hotten even got the definition slightly wrong in the 1865 edition of his *Slang Dictionary*: "an abbreviation of God's wounds,—a very ancient Catholic oath." Like all swearing by God's body parts, it was not particularly Catholic, but had been nondenominational.

One final example must serve to indicate the frequency with which vain oaths were sworn in the eighteenth century, and the decline in their potency. When Captain Basil Hall visited the Comoro Islands off the coast of Africa in the 1820s, he was welcomed by an islander with the memorable words: "How do you do, sir? Very glad to see you. Damn your eyes! Johanna man [a man from Anjouan, one of the islands] like English very much. God damn!"

The man had learned English from sailors who had visited the islands previously, and had retained what seemed to him to be the essential phrases of polite conversation: "Damn me," "Damn you," and "God damn."

The decline in the potency and eventually in the frequency with which people used vain oaths goes hand in hand with falling church attendance throughout the eighteenth and nineteenth centuries. The Church was still very rich and politically powerful, but religion occupied a less central role in the average person's life. "The terrors of supernatural vengeance had steadily receded" since the seventeenth century, as historian Keith Thomas puts it, and with these terrors went much of the Church's control over people's inner and outer lives. (Of course this is a broad generalization; the nineteenth century also saw the rise of numerous evangelical movements that put God and religious obligations firmly at the center of life.) The number and prominence of people over whom the Church had no hold at all also began to increase—"freethought," code for atheism, was a contentious but growing movement in the second half of the nineteenth century, and people who didn't believe in God had little incentive to use his name, even in vain.

The same conditions that initiated the slow decline of vain oaths paradoxically inspired huge battles over sincere swearing in the nineteenth century. In the Victorian era, as today, oaths had to be sworn when giving evidence in court and upon certain important occasions, such as assuming public office or becoming a doctor or lawyer. Historically these oaths had been taken before God, on a Bible, and as a Christian, "profess[ing] faith in Jesus Christ." By the late seventeenth century, laws had begun to chip away at the Christian-fits-all nature of these oaths—the 1689 Toleration Act gave the Quakers the right to affirm their intentions before God, not to swear (if you remember, they believed that Christ was speaking literally when he said "Swear not at all" in Matthew). But in 1847, Lionel de Rothschild, a Jew, was elected to Parliament. To take his seat and begin his term, he was supposed to swear the parliamentary oath on a Bible including the New Testament and "upon the true faith of a Christian." No Quakerly affirmation before God and by Jesus would help here. Rothschild didn't believe in the New Testament and had no Christian faith. A bill was introduced to soften the oath into a form Rothschild might be able to swear, but it was rejected by the House of Lords. This set up a pattern repeated for ten years—Rothschild was elected repeatedly and overwhelmingly by his constituents, but he would not swear the oath as it stood. Bills to change the oath were proposed, only to be repeatedly and overwhelmingly rejected by the House of Lords. Meanwhile, another Jew was elected to Parliament. David Salomons saw that Rothschild's approach wasn't working, and so he swore the oath when he took his seat, simply omitting the words "on the true faith of a Christian." He was able to participate in three votes in the House of Commons before being thrown out by the sergeant-at-arms and fined five hundred pounds for voting illegally.

In 1880, the people of Northampton chose someone even more scandalous as their MP—an avowed atheist, Charles Bradlaugh. Like Rothschild, Bradlaugh refused to swear the parliamentary oath. He wanted to give an affirmation—and not before God, like the Quakers—upon taking his seat. When it was decided that he could not affirm, he offered to swear the oath even though it was meaningless to him, "as a matter of form." The House decided that since he was not a believing Christian, he couldn't swear the oath, and so he was arrested and imprisoned when he attempted to take his seat without having sworn. Like Rothschild and Salomons, he was elected by his constituents over and over, and each time he was prevented from doing his job by the oath he first would not, then would but couldn't, swear.

These oaths were a point of controversy because they so clearly enshrined England's status as a believing Protestant nation, a status under threat in the nineteenth century. Victorian England had no shortage of people making arguments, familiar to us from the Middle Ages and Renaissance, that "the sacredness of oaths is essential to the existence of society," or "that from the earliest times of a Christian Legislature no man has ever been permitted to take part in it, except under the sanction of a Christian oath." Cardinal Henry Manning warned against the dangers of allowing atheists to affirm: "Deny the existence of God, and nine thousand affirmations are no more than nineteen or ninety thousand words. Without God there is no law-giver above the human will, and therefore no law; for no will by human authority can bind another. All authority of parents, husbands, masters, rulers, is of God."

Manning, and others like him, were worried about two things. First of all, they believed that an affirmation was not as secure as an oath. Without supernatural sanction, without God to strike down liars and allow honest men to flourish, an affirmation is nothing but empty words. But more important, affirmation would allow atheists to participate in public life, defend themselves at trial, make wills that could be supported in court, and so forth. It would be a public acknowledgment that Britain was not a God-fearing Christian nation but a plural society, Christian, Jewish, and nonbelieving.*

These arguments were roundly rejected by the thousands of people who elected the Jews and the atheist to Parliament, again and again. Cardinal Manning could protest all he wanted, but British society was changing and oaths, which had publicly cemented Britain's status as a Christian nation, had to change with it. Rothschild finally took his seat in Parliament in 1858 after the passage of the Jewish Relief Act, which allowed him to swear "so help me Jehovah" on the Old Testament. Bradlaugh was finally allowed to swear the oath and take his seat in 1886, despite his nonbelief, and in 1888 he secured the passage of the Oaths Act, which allowed anyone who either had no religious belief or believed that swearing was religiously forbidden

---

*As literary critic and historian Joss Marsh writes, "Not to be competent to give evidence in a legal system that had come to rely upon evidence . . . was tantamount to nonexistence." An atheist whose nine-year-old son was killed before his eyes by a reckless cabby was unable to give evidence at the inquest, as he couldn't take the oath; atheists charged with blasphemy couldn't speak at their own trials, as they could not be sworn.

to "solemnly, sincerely, and truly declare and affirm" in almost all cases where an oath had previously been required.

In the nascent United States, oath swearing was a much less contentious issue. The framers of the Constitution allowed affirmation from the get-go, without hinging its use on exceptions for religious or nonreligious belief. The president's promise is the only one actually spelled out in the Constitution, and it is a marvel of ecumenical brevity compared to the numerous oaths specified in such discriminatory detail in British law:

> Before he [the President] enter on the execution of his Office, he shall take the following Oath or Affirmation: "I do solemnly swear (or affirm) that I will faithfully execute the Office of President of the United States, and will to the best of my Ability, preserve, protect, and defend the Constitution of the United States." (Art. 2, Sect. 1)

The oath or affirmation to be taken by other public officials is not set out specifically in the Constitution, but Article 6 declares that they "shall be bound by Oath or Affirmation to support this Constitution; but no religious Test shall ever be required as a Qualification to any Office or public Trust under the United States." Rather than pass successive amendments granting exceptions for Quakers, then for Unitarians, then for Catholics, then for Jews, then for atheists, the Constitution got it all over with at once. If you wanted to affirm, whether from an abundance of religious belief or from none at all, you could.* George Washington undercut the really quite astonishing secularity of the presidential oath when he took it in 1789, adding "So help me God" and kissing the Bible upon which he swore. "So help me God" has since become an official part of

---

* British laws that granted rights to religious minorities, including the right to swear or affirm according to their beliefs, include the Toleration Act (1689) for Quakers and other dissenters who believed in the Trinity, the Doctrine of the Trinity Act (1813) for Unitarians, the Roman Catholic Relief Act (1829), and the Jewish Relief Act (1858).

other public oaths and affirmations in the United States, such as those sworn by judges and witnesses giving evidence (the exact form of courtroom oaths varies from state to state, and even from judge to judge).

To Call a Washtub a Washtub

As vain oaths were on the decline and sincere oaths were consumed by controversy, obscene words began to take on some of their functions. Most obviously, obscenities took the place of vain oaths to become our swearwords—words that shock, that offend, and that express strong emotion, positive or negative. But, in a limited way, obscene words also assumed oaths' privileged relation to facts— they became the words that a man (especially a man) used when he wanted to tell the truth. As God's body receded from contact, the human body supplied its lack as a generator of taboos and as a guarantor of the truth.

This is signaled in two popular metaphors in seventeenth- and eighteenth-century England—"the naked truth" and "to call a spade a spade." When the truth is naked, it is obvious, without disguise, fully revealed to the eyes and understandings of hearers, viewers, or readers. Many authors of this period thought such openness was a fundamental characteristic of obscene language. More directly than do euphemisms or other polite expressions, obscene words were thought to *reveal* the body parts and actions that morality or modesty dictates must be concealed, and are thus able to convey the reality, the truth, of those things more immediately. Using obscene words characterized a speaker as direct, honest, the kind of person who would not mince words to spare someone's feelings or sense of decency.

The association between obscenity and honesty goes back to ancient Rome. We saw in the first chapter how Martial praised the emperor Augustus's liberal use of *futuo* in an epigram—the emperor knew "Romana simplicitate loqui," how to speak with Roman plain-ness. In the late seventeenth century, the biographer John Aubrey declared that he wrote "the naked and plaine truth, which is here exposed so bare that the very pudenda are not covered, and affords many passages that would raise a Blush in a young Virgin's cheek." He made good on his word by describing a lawyer as having "got more by his Prick than he had done by his practise" and recounting a tale of Sir William Fleetwood, who was surprised by violent diar-rhea ("loosenesse") while out walking: "He turned up his breech against the Standard [a pub] and bade his man hide his face; For they shall never see my Arse again, sayd he."* Throughout the eigh-teenth and nineteenth centuries, obscenities continued to be seen as the best words to use when displaying "the naked truth." Such thrusters-forth of the scantily clad truth were, normally, imagined to be masculine—for around two hundred years (1600–1800) a common word for "expurgate" was *castrate*. "Remov[ing] obscene or objectionable passages," as the *Oxford English Dictionary* terms it, was seen as cutting off the manly bits.

The other metaphor that associated truth-telling with the use of bad words was "to call a spade a spade." This proverb seems to have been invented by Erasmus, whom we also have to thank for the idea of *copia* and for his tract on civility in young boys. In his *Adages*, a huge collection of Greek and Roman proverbs, he lists "ficus ficus, ligonem ligonem vocat": "he calls a fig a fig, and a spade a spade." He glosses that this "is an iambic line from the comedies of Aristophanes adapted for use as an adage. It suits a man who speaks the truth in a

---

* This was a popular motif. It also appears in a 1613 epigram by Henry Parrot:

> *Cacus* constrain on suddaine to untrusse,
> Turn'd up his podex in the open street
> But hid his face and to them answerd thus
> That passed by, and told him t'was unmeet,
> Ther's none (quoth *Cacus*) by mine arse that knows me,
> How beastly els soever they suppose me.
> —*Laquei ridiculosi*

simple and countrified style, who tells of things as they are, and does not wrap them up in ornamental verbiage. . . . Men of more homely mother-wit speak more crudely and more plainly, and call things by their true names." In this form, the proverb addresses both obscene words and vulgar ones. *Ficus* literally means "fig" but is metaphorically used for "anal sore" and in late Latin came to refer to the vagina. A person of scrupulous politeness might thus avoid using even the proper term for the fruit to prevent any possible innuendo; a more straightforward, more manly person would not hesitate to use the word *fig* despite its sexual undertones. *Ligonem* is a vulgar word, one that, as Erasmus explains, "will strike the hearer as rather too common for the dignity of the context" and which is adopted from the vocabularies of "low trades and occupations, like bath-attendant, cook, tanner, and eating-house keeper." Someone who calls a spade a spade is not afraid to use the proper but lower-class word for a lower-class thing. The Roman historian Tacitus exemplifies the opposite of this plainspoken style, with his literal refusal to call a spade a spade: "Telling of a Roman army hard pressed in Germany and forced to dig emergency fortifications by night, he says that in their hasty retreat they had 'to a great extent lost the implements by means of which earth is dug and turf is cut.'" Tacitus's refusal to mar the otherwise elevated style of his history with such a vulgar word perhaps prompted Erasmus to (mis)translate the proverb from the Greek as he did. The Greek actually means "he calls a fig a fig and a wash-tub or kneading-trough a wash-tub or kneading-trough."

These two metaphors reveal how, in a small way, obscene words came to be seen as telling the truth like oaths. (In a 2005 study, intrepid researchers showed that swearwords actually do "increase the believability of statements." Testimony that contained words such as *God damn it*, *shitty*, *fucking*, and *asshole* was perceived by test subjects to be more credible than the same testimony minus the swearwords.) By the eighteenth century, obscene words had assumed both functions of oath swearing. They possessed the offensive and emotive charge for which people of the past had turned to oaths by God. And they had, in a limited form, acquired oath's ability to "guarantee" the truth. It would take until the late nineteenth century, however, before obscene words were actually referred to as "swearing."

Gwendolen: I am glad to say that I have never seen a spade. (*The Importance of Being Earnest*, Oscar Wilde, 1895)

By the Victorian era, it is possible to find people who were so distant from the bluff, obscene truth-tellers of earlier centuries that they had never seen a spade, let alone discussed one. Gwendolen's line from *The Importance of Being Earnest* is a joke, but, according to historian and literary critic Joss Marsh, it is true that by the mid-1800s, "hardly anyone called a spade a spade." According to William Dean Howells, an American author whose most famous novel, *The Rise of Silas Lapham*, was published in 1885, "Generally, people now call a spade an agricultural implement." And Henry Alford, theologian, critic, and poet, advised fellow authors to avoid euphemism in his 1863 *A Plea for the Queen's English*: "Call a spade a spade, not *a well-known oblong instrument of manual industry*." Such delicate souls were not dedicated simply to avoiding vulgar words such as *spade*; obscene ones, and those body parts that inspired them, were under even stricter taboos.

History is silent as to whether John Ruskin, the eminent Victorian art critic, had ever met with a spade, but he had apparently never seen the naked body of a woman before his wedding night. He had by all accounts fallen in love with Effie Gray and fought hard to marry her over the objections of his family—hers was bankrupt. They married in 1848 and embarked on their honeymoon in Blair Atholl, Scotland. But when it was time to consummate the marriage, Ruskin balked. (He continued to balk for another six years, until Effie left him. She went on to marry the painter John Everett Millais and have eight children.) Effie explains why in a letter to her parents, asking them to help her get her marriage annulled:

> He alleged various reasons, Hatred to children, religious motives, a desire to preserve my beauty, and finally this last year told me the true reason (and to me this is as villainous as all the rest), that he had imagined women were quite different to what he saw I was, and that the reason he did not make me his Wife was because he was disgusted with my person the first evening April 10th [their wedding night].

Ruskin offers the same reason in a statement he gave to his lawyers at the time of the annulment: "It may be thought strange that I *could* abstain from a woman who to most people was so attractive. But though her face was beautiful, her person was not formed to excite passion. On the contrary, there were certain circumstances in her person which completely checked it." In order for the annulment to succeed, Effie had to undergo a virginity test; she was examined by doctors who found that "she is naturally and properly formed." We can infer, too, that the father of her eight children wasn't disgusted by her person. What did Ruskin find so abhorrent about her, and why? The prevailing theory blames her pubic hair. Ruskin was familiar with the idealized forms found in Greek and Roman statues of women, but they to a headless torso were hairless, or strategically veiled. According to Ruskin's biographer Mary Lutyens, Effie was very likely the first naked woman he ever saw, and the fact that she had hair down there was a shock from which the aesthete couldn't recover.*

---

* Another speculation was that she was menstruating and that nothing had prepared Ruskin for this either. Other scholars have argued that it would be impossible even for Ruskin to be this ignorant, citing a letter he wrote to his parents that some aristocratic young men possessed pictures of "naked bawds." It seems unlikely that Ruskin, who very much wanted to burn the erotic paintings of his idol J. M. W. Turner, would have wanted to examine the naked bawds, even if offered. He described Turner's erotic works as "painting after painting of Turner's of the most shameful sort—the pudenda of women—utterly inexcusable and to me inexplicable." He could only explain their production as "having been assuredly drawn under a certain condition of insanity."

The Venus de Milo, not Ruskin's wife.

Ruskin's reaction to his wife's body offers a striking illustration of the degree to which sexual matters were repressed, at least in "proper" Victorian society. The faintest allusions to sexuality were so deeply forbidden and bodies were so swathed in fabric that it was possible for a man to reach the age of thirty and have no idea that his wife, like all women, had pubic hair.

Ruskin is not an isolated case; other Victorians were strikingly ignorant of things improper. The eminent poet Robert Browning seems not to have recognized a common obscenity. In his 1841 poem *Pippa Passes*, he writes:

Then owls and bats
Cowls and *twats*
Monks and nuns, in cloister's moods,
Adjourn to the oak-stump pantry.

Browning had encountered this word only once before, in a seventeenth-century satirical ballad. Reading these lines—"They talk't of his having a Cardinalls Hat, / They'd send him as soon an Old Nuns Twat"—he assumed that *twat* referred to some item of nunly apparel, like a wimple, rather than a part of nunly anatomy. Other Victorians also failed to recognize *twat* as one of the oldest obscene words for "vagina." None of the twenty-three or so Victorian editions of Browning's dramatic poem omit it, even while editors of the era were busy expurgating naughty words like *harlot* and *damn'd* from the poems of Alexander Pope (1859), and *womb* and *prostitute* from those of Walt Whitman (1855).

The first use of *twat* recorded in the *Oxford English Dictionary* is from a 1656 translation of Martial, the epigram that begins "Catching me with a boy, wife, you upbraid me harshly and point out that you too have an arse" and ends "Don't give masculine names to your things, wife. Think you have two cunts." Robert Fletcher translates the last lines as "Give not male names then to such things as thine, / But think thou hast two Twats o wife of mine." The word was in common use during the late seventeenth and early eighteenth centuries, but the *OED* has no record of it from 1727 to 1919. It could be, then, that the *twat* came back, after a period of abeyance, in the twentieth century. Browning would then appear less of a sheltered innocent, unfamiliar with an everyday obscenity. There is tantalizing evidence that *twat* did remain in use during the later eighteenth and nineteenth centuries, however, though it more or less disappears from written records. It appears in Thomas Wright's 1857 *Dictionary of Obsolete and Provincial English* (defined as "pudendum f."). And in 1888, a concerned reader wrote to the journal *The Academy* about a "distressing blunder" he had noticed in Browning's poem. His note is a masterpiece of indirection—nowhere in it does he mention what the blunder actually is. He simply wants to point out that "the word in question is probably still in provincial use, and may be found in its place in Wright's Dictionary." The editor of *The Academy* has seen fit to add that, "Like many other provincialisms, it is also in use in London." From this correspondence, at any rate, it seems that *twat* was still in use as an obscenity in the Victorian period, that Browning didn't know what it meant when he employed it, and that everyone concerned decided that the situation was really much too delicate to discuss—better to leave things alone and not call attention to it.

Browning failed to recognize a well-known obscenity, as Ruskin failed to realize that his wife would have hair where the Venus de Milo doesn't. How is it possible that two such intelligent, well-traveled, well-read men had two such areas of ignorance? The nineteenth century saw the apogee of the rise of civility that began in the Renaissance. Throughout the eighteenth century, it had become more and more taboo to reveal certain body parts and actions in polite society or to mention them in polite conversation. Even to hint that they existed became a terrible faux pas. All this linguistic and vestmental concealment had its desired effect in Ruskin and Browning—it covered up *twat* and the rest of the female body so thoroughly that they disappeared altogether for our two eminent Victorians. This is not to say that Victorian men never swore, or never saw naked women before they married—this is in fact very much *not* the case, as we will see a bit later. Ruskin especially was perhaps unusually naive, having asked his parents to move in with him at college. But it is true that the Victorian cultural climate was one in which sex and excrement were very rarely mentioned in polite society, where, in fact, people hesitated even to point vaguely in their direction. It was the great age of euphemism.

Euphemisms

To the Victorians they were *inexpressibles* (1793), *indescribables* (1794), *etceteras* (1794), *unmentionables* (1823), *ineffables* (1823), *indispensables* (1828), *innominables* (1834–43), *inexplicables* (1836), and *continuations* (mid-nineteenth century). What were they? Perhaps this citation from the *OED* will help: "Shoes off, ineffables tucked up" (1867). No? What about this one: "Liston, in a pair of unmentionables coming half-way down his legs" (1823). Yes, they are trousers, "an article of dress not to be mentioned in polite circles," as *The Century Cyclopedia* of 1889 cautions. (Ironically, *etcetera* had in centuries past been a euphemism for words much more unmentionable than *trousers*. In Randall Cotgrave's 1611 French-English dictionary, *con* (cunt) is defined as "a womans *etc.*" And in *Romeo and Juliet*, it substitutes for the word *arse* in one of Mercutio's double entendres—"O that she were / An open *et caetera*, thou a pop'rin peare!")*

What was so wrong with saying *trousers*? First of all, when you took them off, you were naked. And their shape revealed a man's legs, and a man's having legs implied that he very likely had other body parts up there, and . . . *please*, remember yourself. The women! The children! *Leg* was another word that was not supposed to be

---

* *Open-arse*, we have seen, was a synonym for *medlar*, which was itself sometimes substituted for *vagina*. A *poperin pear* is a kind of pear that came originally from Poperinghe, in Flanders. In Shakespeare, though, of course, a pear is never just a pear.

used in polite society. *Limb* was the preferred term, which was further euphemized to *lower extremity*. Captain Frederick Marryat, an English sea captain turned writer, had much to say about *limbs* versus *legs* in his 1839 *Diary in America*. (He had traveled to the United States to "examine what were the effects of a democratic form of government and climate upon a people which, with all its foreign admixture, may still be considered as English," and to get away from his wife. As his contemporaries noted, in practice he found it difficult to make observations about the democratic form of the climate.)

> When at Niagara Falls, I was escorting a young lady with whom I was on friendly terms. She had been standing on a piece of rock, the better to view the scene, when she slipped down, and was evidently hurt by the fall; she had in fact grazed her shin. As she limped a little in walking home, I said, "Did you hurt your leg much." She turned from me, evidently much shocked, or much offended; and not being aware that I had committed any very heinous offence, I begged to know what was the reason of her displeasure. After some hesitation, she said that as she knew me well, she would tell me that the word *leg* was never mentioned before ladies. I apologized for my want of refinement, which was attributable to my having been accustomed only to *English* society, and added, that as such articles must occasionally be referred to, even in the most polite circles of America, perhaps she would inform me by what name I might mention them without shocking the company. Her reply was, that the word *limb* was used; "nay," continued she, "I am not so particular as some people are, for I know those who always say limb of a table, or limb of a piano-forte."

From Marryat's account too comes evidence that at least some Victorians covered up the limbs of their furniture. He continues his narration:

> A few months afterwards I was obliged to acknowledge that the young lady was correct when she asserted that some people were

more particular even than she was. I was requested by a lady to escort her to a seminary for young ladies, and on being ushered into the reception room, conceive my astonishment at beholding a square piano-forte with four *limbs*. However, that the ladies who visited their daughters, might feel in its full force the extreme delicacy of the mistress of the establishment, and her care to preserve in their utmost purity the ideas of the young ladies under her charge, she had dressed all these four limbs in modest little trousers, with frills at the bottom of them!

Several widespread Victorian assumptions about language are crystallized in this account. Marryat associates euphemisms with women, and with women of a particular social class—the middle. Such women, like the mistress of the seminary, see delicate language as a way to advertise their delicate sensibilities, which are themselves supposed to be an indication of social and moral worth. Marryat is also poking fun at these women who cannot bring themselves to say *leg*, and this is a perennial theme—Victorian euphemisms went hand in hand with a discourse that ridiculed them. There is scholarly debate about the number of people who really sewed inexpressibles for the limbs of their pianos, or whether Marryat's seminarian was an exception or even his invention. But it is hard to deny that such coverings are the logical consequence of the thought process that led society to deem trousers and legs as beyond the pale. Marryat's story reveals something about Victorian society, even if most people chose to show off, rather than cover up, the ornately carved legs of their mahogany furniture.

Marryat's account also makes clear that he sees *limb* as an American euphemism. He, "having been accustomed only to *English* society," would use the more straightforward word *leg*. In fact, many nineteenth-century Brits thought that euphemism was a particularly American affectation. They pointed out that while Americans talked about their *roosters* and *faucets*, Brits still had *cocks* in their barnyards and bathrooms. While Americans picked at the *bosom* of a chicken,

Why Americans say *faucet*.

Brits tucked heartily into the *breast*. The Englishman Thomas Bowdler censored Shakespeare in 1807, but the American Noah Webster castrated the Bible itself in 1833, inserting "euphemisms, words and phrases which are not very offensive to delicacy, in the place of such as cannot, with propriety, be uttered before a promiscuous audience." (*Promiscuous* may seem like an unfortunate adjective to choose when one's project is to get rid of "language which cannot be uttered in company without a violation of decorum, or the rules of good breeding," but in 1833 the word meant "wide and diverse," not "sexually indiscriminate." It attained its current meaning only in the late nineteenth century.) Even John Farmer and William Henley, authors of the magisterial 1890–1904 slang dictionary that contains thousands of euphemisms, accused Americans of being overly euphemistic. Henry Wadsworth Longfellow's use of the word *benders* for *legs* prompts a series of recriminations from them: *bender* is "a euphemism employed by the squeamishly inclined for the leg. A similar piece of prudishness is displayed in an analogous use of 'limb.' With a notorious mock-modesty, American women decline to call a leg a leg; they call it a limb instead. . . . Sensible people everywhere, however, have little part in such prudery."

But there were plenty of people willing to bemoan the British affection for euphemism too, and plenty of examples to give them cause. In the 1874 edition of his *Slang Dictionary*, John Hotten took issue with British euphemism, condemning words such as *inexpressibles*— which were as British as meat pies and orderly queues—as "affected terms, having their origins in a most unpleasant squeamishness." Henry Alford, dean of Canterbury, noted biblical scholar, and editor of John Donne, had much to say about the evils of euphemism in his *Plea for the Queen's English*. "In the papers," he complains—newspapers are in his view responsible for much of the euphemistic inundation—"a man does not now *lose his mother*: he *sustains* (this I saw in a country paper) *bereavement of his maternal relative*." No one *goes* anywhere anymore—a man going home is set down as "an individual proceeding to his residence." Nor does anyone *eat* when it is possible to *partake*, or *live in rooms* when the option is to *occupy eligible apartments*.

Some of Alford's complaints are not about euphemisms per se but about an overly inflated style, diction that has come to be known, probably to Alford's shame, as "Victorian." It is not particularly Victorian, either—Alexander Pope had already been calling fish "finny prey" and the "scaly tribe" in the early eighteenth century. When Alford complains about *partake*, he is objecting not to a euphemism for *eat*, but to an ameliorative term, a word with more or less the same meaning that is employed because it is more formal, more elevated—fancier. (Actually, as Alford points out, *partake* is not a synonym for *eat*. It means "to share in something," whether food, a military expedition, or a joint visit to the privy.) *Proceed* was likewise an ameliorative term for *go*—it makes the ordinary act sound better. The line between euphemisms and ameliorative terms is thin and hard to keep to, however—both serve the same purpose of substituting for a word or disguising a topic that is too vulgar, or sometimes just too ordinary, for the context.

Even the pornography of the period embraced this elevated style. In 1749, John Cleland wrote his way out of debtor's prison with a pornographic novel that contained not a single obscene word. *Memoirs of a Woman of Pleasure* (*Fanny Hill*) is basically a series of sexual encounters between Fanny and various men, other women and various men, Fanny and various women, other women and various women, and, once, two men. A typical scene has Fanny taking revenge on her own unfaithful lover by seducing a young man with a huge "machine," who is so "full of genial juices" that he can orgasm twice in a row:

> Not once unsheathed, he proceeded afresh to cleave and open himself an entire entry into me, which was not a little made easy to him by the balsamic injection with which he had just plentifully moistened the whole internals of the passage. Redoubling, then, the active energy of his thrusts, favoured by the fervid appetency of my motions, the soft oiled wards can no longer stand so effectual a picklock, but yield and open him an entrance.

This passage is actually about Christ's love for his Church. No, not really. It does use the biblical metaphor of sex as opening a locked door, though.

A surprisingly large number of other authors went for "botanical porn," which involved learned comparisons of the genitalia to plants. Erasmus Darwin, Charles Darwin's grandfather, was one such author, who produced the only very mildly titillating *The Loves of the Plants* in 1789. Other botanists were more explicit than Darwin, but always in the most refined of language. The author of a mid-eighteenth-century poem called *Arbor Vitae* ("The Tree of Life") describes the tree this way:

> The tree of Life, then, is a succulent plant, consisting of one only stem, on the top of which is a *pistillum* or *apex*, sometime of a glandiform appearance, and not unlike a May-cherry, though at other seasons more resembling the Avellana or filbeard tree. Its fruits, contrary to most others, grow near the root; they are usually two in number, in size somewhat exceeding that of an ordinary nutmeg, and are both contained in one Siliqua, or purse, which together with the whole root of the plant, is commonly beset with innumerable fibrilla, or capillary tendrils.

If you don't recognize this as a description of the penis, you haven't been paying attention. *Fanny Hill* and works of botanical erotica contain obscene subject matter—almost nothing *but* obscene subject matter, in fact—without offensive or low language. They are porn with pretensions, the product of an age with a craze for euphemisms, an era that prized delicate and learned diction whatever the occasion.

Euphemism is the opposite of swearing. Swearwords work because they carry an emotional charge derived from their direct reference to taboo objects, orifices, and actions. Euphemisms exist to cover up those same taboos, to disguise or erase the things that prompt such strong feelings. These anti-obscenities, if you will, are formed by several processes, including indirection, Latinization, and employing French. A word such as *inexpressibles* works as a euphemism because it completely disguises the thing to which it refers—it hides its referent, as do *confinement, situation,* and *condition* ("interesting" or otherwise), which were popular Victorian euphemisms for *pregnancy.* Latin, with its irreproachable reputation as the dead language of the well educated, also gave rise to many euphemisms. In the Renaissance, a man could freely piss in public; now he had to *micturate* (c. 1842) behind closed doors. Other bodily functions got Latinized as well, and so we have *defecate* (to shit), *osculate* (to kiss), *expectorate* (to spit), and *perspire* (to sweat). Of perspiration, the *Gentleman's Magazine* of 1791 records: "It is well known that for some time past, neither man, woman nor child . . . has been subject to that gross kind of exudation which was formerly known by the name of *sweat*; . . . now every mortal, except carters, coal-heavers and Irish Cahir-men . . . merely *perspires.*" Linguists Keith Allan and Kate Burridge call Latinate terms such as these *orthophemisms* rather than *euphemisms.* Orthophemisms are "more formal and more direct (or literal)" than euphemisms. *Defecate,* because it literally means "to shit," is an orthophemism; *poo* is a euphemism, and *shit* is a dysphemism, the taboo word the others were created to avoid. According to Allan and Burridge, both euphemism and orthophemism arise from the same urge: "they are used to avoid the speaker being embarrassed and/or ill thought of and, at the same time, to avoid embarrassing and/or offending the hearer or some third party. This coincides with the speaker being polite."

French also contributed a number of popular euphemisms, including *accouchement* for having a baby, *lingerie* for underwear, and *chemise* for *shift,* a word that itself had replaced the even more indecent *smock* (which is a long dress or shirt that served as an undergarment). The poet Leigh Hunt recorded his difficulties in finding a title for his version of a medieval story about a knight who fights in a lady's chemise to prove his valor. He attempted to call it "The Three Knights and the Smock" or "The Battle of the Shift," but public outcry forced him to expunge any mention of the offending clothing. He marveled that he could not even employ the word *chemise*—"not even this word, it seems, is to be mentioned, nor the garment itself alluded to, by any decent writer!" Hunt eventually called the 1831 poem "The Gentle Armour." As late as 1907, *shift* was a powerfully taboo word. When an actress spoke it onstage during the premiere of John Millington Synge's *The Playboy of the Western World*, the audience began to riot. The play is about life in an isolated village in Ireland, and premiered in Dublin at the National Theater; in these circumstances, the use of *shift* was seen as an insult to Irish Catholic womanhood. A decent woman would not be mentioning her unmentionables at all, let alone using the vulgar word *shift*.

Let's focus now on one taboo area to show the great range of eighteenth- and nineteenth-century euphemisms, and how our three drivers—misdirection, Latin, and French—team up in creating them. Consider the toilet. In the eighteenth and nineteenth centuries, *house of office* was still in common use, thanks perhaps to its entirely mystifying literal sense. *House* was also involved in a number of related euphemisms, such as *necessary house, house of commons*, or just *commons*—a haven of democracy to which everyone had to resort, rich or poor, male or female, old or young.* There was also the less frequently employed *mine uncle's* (house). Chamber pots were still employed for relieving oneself in the middle of the night, or when suffering a disinclination to proceed to the privy, and continued to be called *chamber pots*, or just *chambers*. This shortening occasions a joke in the Victorian collection of erotica *The Stag*

---

*An anonymous author waxed poetic on this theme in 1697 in "On Melting Down the Plate: Or, the Piss-pot's Farewell":

Presumptuous Piss-pot! How didst thou offend?
Compelling Females on the hams to bend?
To Kings and Queens, we humbly bow the Knee;
But Queens themselves are forc'd to stoop to thee.

Party (ca. 1888, edited by the American author of children's verse Eugene Field, most famous for *Wynken, Blynken, and Nod*):

> The newly wedded country gent was registering at the Grand Pacific. The urbane clerk suggested the bridal chamber. Groom did not seem to take. The clerk again repeats his question, "Don't you want a bridal chamber?" Countryman—Wall, you might send one up for her, I guess, but I can piss out the window.

The clerk, of course is suggesting the bridal room; the groom assumes he means the bridal chamber pot. Such a pot was also called a *jerry*, probably short for *jeroboam*, a large bowl, goblet, or wine bottle. *Commode* was also a popular euphemism, being French. A *commode* was originally any kind of elaborate and delicate piece of furniture with drawers and compartments. (It was also eighteenth-century slang for

A mid-nineteenth-century chamber pot, complete with poetry and brown frog.

a woman's headdress, which at the time would have been a huge tower of real and false hair, feathers, ribbons, and powder—certainly also elaborate and delicate.) Its meaning narrowed to indicate a piece of furniture that could enclose chamber pots, hiding them from view, until finally it came to designate the pot itself. And *po* was in use by 1880—*pot* sounds so much decenter in French.

In the late eighteenth century, improvements in plumbing technology led to the wider adoption of flush toilets and a concomitant change in nomenclature. (John Harington, if you remember, had invented a flushing toilet in 1597 and wrote a mock heroic poem about it.) Flushing toilets, and the rooms they were in, began to be called *water closets*. Running water and ideas of cleanliness and hygiene later gave rise to *washroom* and *bathroom*, a masterpiece of misdirection, for, as British people love to point out to Americans, there is very often no bath involved. *Loo*, a common British word for *bathroom*, might also derive from the water component of the water closet. In Scotland, it had been polite to cry "Gardy-loo" when emptying your chamber pot out the window, a corruption of *gardez l'eau*—"watch out for the water." *Loo* might also be a corruption of the French for "place," *lieu*, as in *place of easement*. One final candidate etymology has *loo* coming from *bourdalou*, a portable chamber pot for ladies. The seventeenth-century French preacher Louis Bourdaloue was so popular that people would assemble hours in advance of his sermons. Ladies brought their *bourdalous*, which they could use under their skirts, so that they didn't have to lose their seats by getting up to find the privy. (Bourdaloue often preached at Versailles, so the ladies very likely would have had trouble finding a privy anyway. The palace was plagued by people defecating in the corners of rooms and urinating into potted plants, fireplaces, staircases, etc., perhaps out of carelessness, perhaps from a lack of privy-cy.)

Latin makes its contribution to toilet words with *lavatory*, *latrine*, and *urinal*. *Lavatory* is like *washroom*—in the Middle Ages it had referred to a vessel for washing the hands, and came to indicate the room in which you wash your hands, because you've just used the toilet. *Latrine*, like *lavatory* from the Latin for "wash," has always referred to a privy or set of privies in a camp, barracks, or hospital. *Urinal* was a glass used by medieval physicians to collect urine for examination, and also by the fifteenth century a plain chamber pot. By the mid-nineteenth century it had attained the meaning it has today—a fixture attached to a wall, used by men for urinating (or a room containing such fixtures).

Finally we go back to French for the most common toilet word, *toilet* itself. It originated in the French word *toilette*, meaning "little cloth." The *toilette* covered the dressing table while makeup was applied and hair was coiffed; eventually it came to stand for the articles on the dressing table used in grooming, then the process of getting dressed. From there, it came to refer to the room in which the getting dressed happened, which was often furnished with a bath. Hence, as can be seen in the *OED*, *toilet* came to indicate a bathroom, a lavatory, and then the ceramic pedestal itself.

In American English, the euphemism treadmill has turned for *toilet*, and it has now become a vulgar word instead of a decorous one used to disguise an unpleasant fact of life. Polite Americans would be hard-pressed to ask "Where's the toilet?" as is commonly heard in Britain. In Britain, though, *toilet* is vulgar in the original sense of the term—it has class connotations, employed by people of the middle class on down. *Loo* is the word used by upper-class Brits. In a reflection on social class that he composed for the *Times* of London, the Earl of Onslow admitted that "I find it almost impossible to force the word toilet between my lips." (He found it impossible to spell as well, going for the French *toilette*.) And when Prince William and Kate Middleton broke up briefly in 2007, the British press blamed it on Kate's mother's use of the word *toilet*, creating a scandal called, not surprisingly, "Toiletgate." The prince could never marry a girl whose mother said "toilet" (and did other irredeemably middle-class things such as chew gum and say "Pardon?" instead of "What?" or "Sorry?"). Toiletgate fizzled out, of course—the prince married his commoner, and Mrs. Middleton probably now makes sure she uses the facilities before she goes out.

These are, believe it or not, just a few of the more popular euphemisms for *toilet* that were in use in the eighteenth and nineteenth centuries, showing how misdirection, Latin, and French allowed English-speakers to create new, polite words that allowed them to discuss things they were not supposed to mention. To be fair, there were also dysphemistic names for toilets, words intended to make a thing sound worse than it is. *Shit-house* first appeared in 1795, according to the *OED*, while *bog-house* was popular in the eighteenth century, ceding ground to the shortened form *bog* in the nineteenth. (There was also a brief flowering of *boggard* in the seventeenth century.) The *bog-* words evidently derive not from *bog* in the sense of "wet, swampy ground" but from a verb meaning "to exonerate the bowels; also *trans.* to defile with excrement" (another one of those "to spray someone or something with shit" verbs, which we no longer seem to need today). In its definition, the *OED* makes clear that *bog* in this sense is not a polite word—it is "a low word, scarcely found in literature, however common in coarse colloquial language." *John* started to compete with *jakes* as the masculine name of choice for the facilities in the eighteenth century—a 1735 list of rules for students at Harvard College includes the biblical dictum that "No freshman shall mingo [piss] against the College wall or go into the fellows' cuzjohn." "Cuzjohn" is "cousin John"; the word is still in use as just plain *john* and remains mostly an Americanism.

Crapper, another dysphemistic use, is almost unique in the realm of bad words in that it is the subject of an etymological legend that turns out to be (mostly) true. The story is that a man named Thomas Crapper invented the flush toilet, and that it is called "the crapper" in his honor. There was indeed a Thomas Crapper (1836–1910), and while he did not invent the flush toilet, he did manufacture them and patent many improvements to the design, always printing his name boldly in his bowls and on his cisterns. *Crap* itself is an old word, first appearing in the fifteenth century and indicating "the husk of grain,

Pedestal Wash-down Closets.

The "CEDRIC."

Combination No. 4

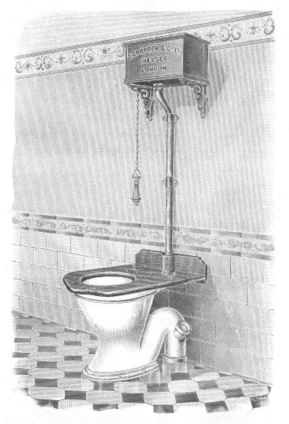

No. 4 Combination, comprising White "Cedric" W.C., with No. 211 Polished Mahogany Seat with Back Board, 2 gallon Porcelain Enamelled Iron (No. 220) Syphon Water Waste Preventer with 1¼ in. Fittings, and China Pull and Porcelain Enamelled Iron Brackets, as shown

Crapper model #4, "The Cedric."

chaff." By the Victorian era, it had developed its contemporary meaning of bowel exoneration, the process or product, but was used mostly in America. Simon Kirby, managing director of Thomas Crapper & Co. Ltd.—which is still in business today—explains how the vulgar American word and the venerable English plumber collided to give us "the crapper": "During World War I, American servicemen stationed in London were so amused that the ancient and vulgar word for faeces was printed on so many water closets, that they began to call the W.C. a 'crapper.' Though crude, the soubriquet made sense and it stuck. . . . In etymological circles, this process is called 'back formation,' which sounds rather like a sewer problem!"

Alternatively, one could take the Roman view and see it as nominative determinism ("Nomen est omen")—Thomas Crapper was destined to work with toilets, just as much as A. J. Splatt and D. Weedon ("wee'd on") were fated to publish an article on urinary incontinence ("The Urethral Syndrome: Experience with the Richardson Urethroplasty"), or Usain Bolt to become the fastest man alive.

Class and Swearing

Euphemisms enjoyed such prominence because the eighteenth and especially the nineteenth centuries were the age of decorum. The civilizing process that began slowly in the Middle Ages reached its height during these years; the shame threshold was at its widest extent. Bodily functions that formerly were performed unashamedly in public were now done only behind closed doors; the same functions had been discussed openly but were now subject to a parallel cloaking in language. As one historian writes, "Excretion was an accepted and semipublic event that Chaucer rarely used for comedy. In the last [i.e., nineteenth] century, these body functions have become rites performed in the shamefast privacy of a closed room, the excreta being immediately laved away by sparkling rivulets, to be seen and smelled no more." Likewise, the words used to discuss these topics were washed out of public discourse—*shit* became *defecate*, and Victorian readers were embarrassed by the use of *piss* in the King James Bible. All things sexual were hidden away to an even greater degree, including things such as trousers that were not themselves taboo but lay adjacent to taboo areas.

The newly emerged middle class was responsible for a great deal of this increased delicacy. The biggest social change of the eighteenth century was the development of the bourgeoisie—historical linguist Suzanne Romaine observes that "the transition from a society of estates or orders to a class-based society is one of the (if not THE) great themes of modern British social history." In the Middle Ages, society had been rigidly hierarchical and divided by social function— those who fought (the landed gentry and knights), those who studied and prayed (the clergy), and those who worked (the peasants). You could go from the gentry to the clergy—many second and third sons did exactly this in England, because primogeniture left them little to inherit—but otherwise social mobility was almost impossible. In the Renaissance, merchants and craftspeople began to be seen as "the middling sort"—they were not noble, but neither were they poor peasants. By the eighteenth century, the industrial revolution, colonization, and global trade had made many of the middling sort extremely rich, forcing a reevaluation of their place in society. Economic criteria replaced social function as the determiner of social status, giving us what was coming to be called "class," the upper, lower, and middle. Since class membership was determined to a great extent by money, class boundaries were much more fluid than those between the old estates. As one's power, wealth, and influence increased, one moved up; if one went bankrupt, one moved down. The upper classes were more or less secure, with their ancestral lands and titles, but the middle classes felt themselves to be in a constantly precarious position. They needed to shore it up by broadcasting their differences from the lower classes—they moved to the suburbs, behaved with what they saw as greater moral probity, and, most relevant to us, spoke differently. "The middle class . . . sought an identity for themselves predicated in asserting their social and moral superiority over the working classes," as linguist Tony McEnery puts it. They strove to "establish a personal ascendancy above the herd as right minded, responsible and successful citizens, and at the same time to impress their worth upon their social betters, including God."

The civilizing process was thus co-opted by the middle class as a way of differentiating themselves from the lower classes. They asserted their "civility" through language—the euphemisms they chose drew attention to an extreme delicacy that shrank from anything even pointing vaguely in the direction of taboo, marking them off from the lower classes, who, it was thought, still called a spade a spade, a water closet a shithouse.

The opposite of euphemism—swearing and other sorts of "bad language"—was identified as morally wrong, partly because it spoke freely of taboo subjects, and partly because it was thought to be lower class. Obscene words such as *fuck* and *cunt* and also merely vulgar words such as *thing* and *half pay* came to be seen as the language of the uneducated, who were also ipso facto the morally sketchy—people who would violate linguistic decency, it was thought, would not hesitate to commit any sort of outrage against moral decency.

But let us allow a few Victorian grammarians to speak for themselves. Richard Chenevix Trench lamented in 1859: "How shamefully rich is the language of the vulgar everywhere in words which are not allowed to find their way into books, yet which live as a sinful oral tradition on the lips of men, to set forth that which is unholy and impure." George Perkins Marsh declared confidently around 1859 that "purity of speech, like personal cleanliness, is allied with purity of thought and rectitude of action." And Alfred Ayres had nothing good to say in his 1896 *The Verbalist* about people who use the word *gentlemen* where a simple *men* would do:

> Few things are in worse taste. . . . The men who use these terms
> most . . . belong to that class of men who cock their hats on one side
> of their heads, and often wear them when and where gentlemen

would remove them; who pride themselves on their familiarity with the latest slang; who proclaim their independence by showing the least possible consideration for others; who laugh long and loud at their own wit; who wear a profusion of cheap finery, such as outlandish watch-chains hooked in the lowest button-hole of their vests, Brazilian diamonds in their shirt-bosoms, and big seal-rings on their little fingers; who use bad grammar and interlard their conversation with big oaths.

It is difficult to pick apart the tangle of class and linguistic prejudices in Ayres's stylistic advice. To say "gentlemen" when you mean "men" is low-class but aspirational, not the choice of someone who is content with his station. Such a man is trying to look middle- or upper-class, without a firm grasp on the lingo. He is very likely nouveau riche, with lots of money to buy Brazilian diamonds and large rings, but no taste. He is also morally suspect (here is the link between class and virtue), the kind of person who shows "the least possible consideration for others." Finally, such a person is uneducated, with little knowledge of grammar and a propensity to swear.

Perhaps no one in the twenty-first century would put it quite like Mr. Ayres, but the attitudes he reveals still exist, particularly about swearing. Swearing is frequently connected with ignorance—swearers are depicted as uneducated people who lack the verbal resources or imagination to think of any other words to use. And, with some empirical justification, swearing is thought to be a low-class habit. Tony McEnery analyzed 8,284 recorded examples of swearing, then broke them down by class. He found that members of the working class swore the most and used the strongest words. Members of the upper middle and middle middle classes swore the least but used stronger words (e.g., more *fuck*s than *God*s) than members of the lower middle class. McEnery speculates that this might be "evidence of hypercorrection . . . in attempting to copy the linguistic habits of the AB [upper middle and middle] social class, the lower-middle-class speakers exaggerate what they view to be a feature of AB speech." This modern empiricism gives some support to the proverbs about swearing and social station mentioned in the introduction: "he swears like a lord" and "he swears like a tinker." Excessive swearing was proverbially associated both with the aristocracy, who were more or less secure in their social position and could say and do what they wanted, and with what we'd now call the lower classes, who supposedly didn't know any better. When in *Henry IV, Part One*, Lady Percy swears what her husband, Hotspur, considers a mealy-mouthed oath—"in good sooth"—he tells her to swear "as a lady . . . a good mouth-filling oath," not as a merchant "comfit-maker's wife." Even in Shakespeare's day, the middling sort were marking themselves off with their more delicate language.

The links between social class and swearing are complicated. It is true that on average, the lower classes swear more than the upper and middle classes. It is probably true in some cases that people who swear frequently are uneducated, with impoverished vocabularies and imaginations. And it may very well be true that some sorts of swearing are morally wrong. But it is also important to remember that these attitudes were brought to us by the same people who declared that it was a sin to boldly split an English infinitive (Latin infinitives, like *futuere*, can't be split) and informed students that they can't use no double negatives (according to the principles of logic, they cancel each other out, despite centuries of usage during which they were perfectly well understood). Like many of our most prescriptive points of grammar, modern attitudes toward swearing and social class are the legacy of Victorian social climbers who were afraid to look working-class.

Shit, That Bloody Bugger Turned Out to Be a Fucking Nackle-Ass Cocksucker!

The eighteenth and nineteenth centuries' embrace of linguistic delicacy and extreme avoidance of taboo bestowed great power on those words that broached taboo topics directly, freely revealing what middle-class society was trying so desperately to conceal. Under these conditions of repression, obscene words finally came fully into their own. They began to be used in nonliteral ways, and so became not just words that shocked and offended but words with which people could *swear*.

The definitive expletive of the eighteenth century was *bloody*, which is still in frequent use in Britain today, and is so common Down Under that it is known as "the great Australian adjective." *Bloody* was not quite an obscenity and not quite an oath, but it was definitely a bad word that shocked and offended the ears of polite society.* It is often supposed to be a corruption of the old oaths *by our lady* or *God's blood* (minced form: *'sblood*), but this is another urban legend that turns out to be false. Either it derives instead from the adjective *bloody* as in "covered in blood" or, as the *OED* proposes, it referred to the habits of aristocratic rabble-rousers at the end of the seventeenth century, who styled themselves "bloods." "Bloody drunk," then, would mean "as drunk as a blood."

The career of *bloody* is interesting, because one can clearly see either its perjoration (becoming a worse and worse word) or the rise of civility in action—or perhaps both. In the late seventeenth century, dramatists had no problem including the word in plays seen by genteel audiences, and printers had no problem spelling it out in their editions of those plays: "She took it bloody ill of him," is just one example, occurring in the 1693 *Maids Last Prayer*. Henry Fielding, author of *Tom Jones*, uses it in one of his plays in 1743: "This is a bloody positive old fellow." And Maria Edgeworth has her hero exclaim of another man, "Sir Philip writes a *bloody* bad hand," in 1801's *Belinda*. If Miss Edgeworth—who wrote novels about young women finding love and good marriages for a largely female readership, as well as morally improving children's literature (six volumes of *Moral Tales for Young People*)—had her young hero say "bloody,"

---

* The *Gentleman's Magazine* of 1891 contains an article titled "Some English Expletives," in which it discusses "that most characteristic of English epithets." *Bloody*, it argues, "is often classed as profane or obscene . . . but does not properly fall within either of such categories."

it can't have been that bad a word. Miss Edgeworth gets her "bloody" in at almost the last moment it is possible, however. At around this time, the word starts to get more offensive: it begins to be printed as *b——y* or *b——* and falls out of polite use, where it continues through the Victorian era. When George Bernard Shaw wanted to create a scandal, but not too big a scandal, in his 1914 *Pygmalion*, he had Eliza Doolittle exclaim in her newly perfect posh accent, "Walk! Not bloody likely! I am going in a taxi." The first night's audience greeted the word with "a few seconds of stunned disbelieving silence and then hysterical laughter for at least a minute and a quarter," and there were some protests from various decency leagues, but on the whole a scandal never materialized. *Bloody* became "the catchword of the season" and *pygmalion* became a popular oath itself, as in "not pygmalion likely." Had he scripted Eliza to say "Not fucking likely!" (which he very well could have in 1914) there in all likelihood would have been a real scandal, akin to that generated by *shift* in *Playboy of the Western World.*

This was *bloody* at the turn of the century—a bad word, but not so bad that it was not in common use, according to Shaw, "by four-fifths of the English nation." Perhaps because of this somewhat equivocal status, *bloody* comes in for more than its fair share of opprobrium from Victorian language mavens. In their definitions for *fuck* and related terms, for example, Farmer and Henley do not editorialize, merely defining the terms ("to copulate," etc.) and providing examples of use. But they go off on poor *bloody*. It is

> an epithet difficult to define, and used in a multitude of vague and varying senses. Most frequently, however, as it falls with wearisome reiteration every two or three seconds from the mouths of London roughs of the lowest type, no special meaning, much less a sanguinary one, can be attached to its use. In such a case it forms a convenient intensive, sufficiently important as regards sound to satisfy those whose lack of language causes them to fall back upon a frequent use of words of this type.

Note the typical association of bad language with low social status and lack of education—the London roughs say "bloody" a lot because their vocabulary isn't rich enough to furnish them other options. The original *OED* (1888) takes a similar line—*bloody* is "now constantly in the mouths of the lowest classes, but by respectable people considered 'a horrid word,' on a par with obscene or profane language, and usually printed in the newspapers (in police reports, etc.) as 'b——y.'" Perhaps the *OED* would have had similar things to say about *fuck*, but the Victorian editors decided not to include it, along with *cunt*. And Julian Sharman, whose 1884 *Cursory History of Swearing* does not include any obscene words, attacks *bloody* for several pages. A sampling:

> We cannot disguise to ourselves that there is much in its unfortunate associations to render its occurrence still exceedingly painful. Originating in a senseless freak of language, it has by dint of circumstances become so noisome and offensive . . . Dirty drunkards hiccup it as they wallow on ale-house floors. Morose porters bandy it about on quays and landing-stages. From the low-lying quarters of the towns the word buzzes in your ear with the confusion of a Babel. In the cramped narrow streets you are deafened by its whirr and din, as it rises from the throats of the chaffering multitude, from besotted men defiant and vain-glorious in their drink, from shrewish women hissing out rancour and menace in their harsh querulous talk.

(*To chaffer* is "to bargain, haggle, bandy words.") Again, *bloody* is portrayed as a word beloved by the ignorant, morally degenerate lower classes. *Bloody*, unlike a word such as *fuck*, was perfectly placed to attract the anger from society's growing intolerance of obscenity—it was "a swear-word," as the *Pygmalion* press described it, yet it was not quite profane and not quite obscene. This made it offensive, but not so bad that one couldn't with any decency draw attention to it.

Bugger was the other early obscenity used nonliterally, with the true flexibility of a fully developed swearword. It was, in the past as now, a blunt, direct word for anal intercourse (or for the person who does the penetrating during said anal intercourse, the *pedicator*, if you will remember your Latin). Randall Cotgrave used it this way when defining *levretée*, the girl "buggered" by a greyhound. Even more frequently, however, the use of *bugger* was divorced from its literal meaning, in examples such as these: "God damn him, blood and wounds, he would bugger his Soul to Hell, and these words he used frequently to Man, Woman, and Child, *bugger, bugger, bugger*" (1647, reported); "Go, get thee gone ... thou frantic ass, to the devil, and be buggered" (1693); "B——st [blast] and b-gg-r your eyes, I have got none of your money" (1794); "Damn 'em bugger you an' your ballast" (1854); "Take the bugger off, he is knifing me" (1860); "Previous to this the soil had, in the expressive phrase of the country, been 'buggered over' with the old cast-iron plows" (1868). One final example shows that the biblical epidemic of crotch grabbing had not entirely died out in the Victorian era. A witness for an 1840 divorce petition described how Susan Shumard "came out and met him [Francis Shields, her brother], and as she came up to him, she grabbed him by his private parts; there was considerable of a scuffle; she held tight, and he hollowed to her, you bugger you, let go." (This was evidence that Susan had slept with her brother; her husband wanted a divorce because she had supposedly married him without informing him that she was four months pregnant with her brother's child. The General Assembly of Ohio refused to grant the divorce— they felt that the testimony on both sides was so fantastical and unreliable that they could make no determination about the truth of the matter.) It is interesting that in the nineteenth century, *bugger* was apparently a term that could be applied equally to men and women, while today it is used almost exclusively toward men. Along with Francis Shields and the gentleman who called "*bugger bugger bugger*" to "Man Woman and Child," we have evidence from the masterpiece of Victorian pornography, *My Secret Life* (1888), in which the protagonist reports that a low-class prostitute with whom he is consorting calls her landlady "bugger."

This movement contradicts two trends in swearword evolution. With the development of feminism, many swearwords have become more equal-opportunity, not less. *Bitch* can now be applied to men and women, as can *cunt*. In the nineteenth century *shit* as a noun was reserved exclusively for men—the *West Somerset Word-book* defines it as "a term of contempt, applied to men only," as in "He's a regular shit." Now, women too can work, vote, own their own property, and be called a shit.

When swearwords don't become more equal-opportunity, they often begin to be used solely for women—Geoffrey Hughes calls this the "feminization of ambisexual terms." Words such as *scold, shrew, termagent, witch, harlot, bawd,* and *tramp* were all at one point in their histories terms for men; furthermore, the terms were usually neutral and sometimes even adulatory. *Scold,* for example, comes from the Old Norse word for "poet." When these terms were feminized, they perjorated, going from neutral or positive to insulting. *Bugger* bucks this trend, too, going from a word used of men and women equally to an insulting term reserved almost exclusively for men.

In these examples, *bugger* shows great grammatical flexibility. Geoffrey Hughes categorizes swearing into eight classes, while Tony McEnery finds sixteen; either way, the above *bugger*s can occupy many of the slots. The word can be personal: "you bugger you!"; personal by reference: "take the bugger off"; a curse: "bugger you!"; destinational: "bugger his Soul to Hell"; and a figurative extension of literal meaning: "the soil was 'buggered over.'" Hughes notes that "as terms become more highly charged, so they acquire greater grammatical flexibility."* As words become charged—obscene—they are

---

* These schemas work better with verbs than with nouns. Few would argue that *cunt* is one of the most highly charged words in the English language, yet it can fill at most two of Hughes's slots, *personal* and *personal by reference.*

able to be used in more and more ways. Once the worst word in the language, *fuck* can be used in all eight of Hughes's categories and in fourteen of McEnery's sixteen.

As we can see with *bugger*, most categories of swearing require the word *not* to be used in its literal sense. When Francis yells "you bugger you" at his sister, he is not suggesting that she goes around having anal intercourse—he means "I have a strong negative emotion toward you, let go of my balls!" When soil is described as "buggered over," no one is suggesting that teams of sodomites traversed the field, doing their thing—it means, figuratively, "really messed up." Along with grammatical flexibility, this figurativeness is the hallmark of a fully obscene word, a word used not as a literal descriptor but to shock, offend, or otherwise carry emotion—a swearword.

Bloody and *bugger* were the two most prevalent swearwords in the eighteenth and nineteenth centuries. There is ample evidence of their use, from multiple sources, because they were employed frequently (remember Shaw's contention that *bloody* is "in common use as an expletive by four-fifths of the English nation") and because they were considered less offensive than many other obscene words. It was possible to print the two, even if they had to be disguised as *b——y* and *b-gg-r*, where *f——k* would have been impermissible. But there is tantalizing, if sparse, evidence that our other modern swearwords were making the same transition at the same time, becoming not just obscene words but swearwords, used where one once would have used an oath. By the 1860s, swearing probably sounded much as it does today, with obscene words doing much of the work of swearing, and with religious words—*damn it, Jesus, oh God*—employed frequently but to less effect.

The evidence for the most part comes from records of court proceedings, where people's spoken language was recorded verbatim; from pornographic books, where obscene language went hand in hand with obscene doings; or from dictionaries whose editors were brave enough to include bad words. Let's take *fuck*, for example. Around 1790, a Virginia judge named George Tucker wrote a poem in which a father argues with his son the scholar, "'G—d— your books!' the testy father said, / 'I'd not give ——— for all you've read.'" According to Jesse Sheidlower and Geoffrey Hughes, the third ——— is replacing "a fuck," producing the first recorded example of the modern teenage mantra, "I don't give a fuck." This poem didn't see the light of day until a scholarly edition of Tucker's work in 1977. Tucker's great-granddaughter published some of his poems in 1895, but she somehow didn't see her way to including this one. By 1879, the evidence is less equivocal. A character in the mock Christmas pantomime *Harlequin Prince Cherrytop and the Good Fairy Fairfuck* (1879) declares, "For all your threats I don't care a fuck. / I'll never leave my princely darling duck." (The panto relates the story of Prince Cherrytop, who has become enslaved by the Demon of Masturbation. The Good Fairy Fairfuck helps him conquer his addiction to self-abuse, so he can embrace the joys of holy matrimony with his betrothed, the Princess Shovituppa. It was written by an eminent journalist for the *Daily Telegraph*, whose work had also been published by Dickens and Thackeray.)

In 1866, a man swore in an affidavit that one Mr. Baker had told him he "would be fucked out of his money by Mr. Brown." The notary who recorded the testimony editorializes, "Before putting down the word as used by the witness, I requested him to reflect upon the language he attributed to Mr. Baker, and not to impute to him an outrage upon all that was decent." Luckily for us, the witness insisted he copy it down, outrage or no, and so we have the first recorded use of *fuck* meaning "cheat, victimize, betray." In 1836 Mary Hamilton was charged with using "obscene language" in the street—she followed a group of other women, called them "bloody whores," and "[told] them to go and f . . . k themselves." An 1857 abolitionist work relates the story of a slaveholding doctor who whipped one of his slaves on Sunday. The woman "writhed under each stroke, and cried, 'O Lord O Lord!'" The doctor "gazed on the Woman with astonishment" and said "Hush you ****** b h, will you take the name of the Lord in vain on the Sabbath day?" ("****** b h" = "fucking bitch"). Again we have circumstance to thank for the preservation of this insult. The authors of the antislavery tract were invested in making slaveholders appear as foul and morally bankrupt as they could, and one easy way to signal that was with obscene language. And though they provide no examples in their slang dictionary, Farmer and Henley describe both the adjective and adverb forms of *fucking* as "common." The adjective, they note, is "a qualification of extreme contumely" ("fucking bitch" is a pretty good example of that), while the adverb ("I am fucking furious!") is "intensive and expletive; a more violent form of BLOODY." If *fucking* was "common" in 1893, when the volume containing *F* was published, it was probably in pretty wide use for some years before that, as the 1857 example implies.

So by the mid- to late nineteenth century, we have many forms of *fuck* being used just as they are today—"he fucked me over," "go fuck yourself," "you fucking bitch," "I don't give a fuck," et cetera. What about our other swearwords? *Shit* was apparently used in modern ways back then too. In an investigation of voting fraud from 1882, one man was recorded as telling another, "Shit, that't nothen [that ain't nothing]; get your father to swear that you are twenty-one." This is *shit* as an interjection, just as we use it today: "Shit, I got a parking ticket." And we've already seen the *West Somerset Word-Book* of 1886 record *shit* as a "term of contempt," which, it notes, is "very com. [common]."

The same dictionary includes a definition for *nackle-ass*, an adjective meaning "poor, mean, inferior, paltry: applied as a term of contempt to both persons and things indifferently," as in "Why do you not buy yourself a knife worth something; (and) not keep about such a [nackle-ass] thing as that?" or "A *plat-vooted* [flat-footed], nackle-ass old son of a bitch!" While *nackle-ass* in particular doesn't seem to have made much of an impression beyond West Somerset, it is strikingly reminiscent of our own modern and widespread *-ass* constructions—*big-ass, bad-ass, dumb-ass,* and so on. It is different, too, from the Renaissance construction *burnt-arsed*, as in "burnt-arsed whore." This was a literal use—it meant "infected with venereal disease."

One final example will have to suffice: in 1894, a New York man murdered an acquaintance partly because the acquaintance wouldn't stop calling him "cock-sucker." It's not clear who started the bad blood originally, but the deceased escalated things by ordering drinks for a group of men but excluding his murderer with the words "Treat them five and leave that cock-sucker out." He then smacked the defendant on the nose and called him "cock-sucker" several more times. When at one point the defendant didn't have enough money to pay for another drink, the deceased also butted in with "Let him stick it up his ass." Eventually the defendant left the bar, came back with the gun, and shot the man who had repeatedly called him "cock-sucker."

These examples sound practically contemporary. The words in question, *fuck*, *shit*, *ass*, and *cocksucker*, were chosen for their emotive charge, not to denote as directly as possible some part of the body or action. They were employed to shock and offend, or to express the speaker's emotional state. Most of these are also figurative uses, not literal—*nackle-ass* has nothing to do with the buttocks, to be "fucked out of your money" has nothing to do with sex. It is possible that *cocksucker* was meant literally; the defendant repeatedly asserted that he was *not* a cocksucker. It was still an extremely offensive word, however, with a shock value out of proportion to its literal meaning—it led, after all, to murder. Examples of words like these are much scarcer than ones involving *bloody* and *bugger*. They are considered to be worse today, and were probably more offensive in the past as well ("an outrage upon all that was decent," as the notary put it in 1866). Whether or not they were used less frequently in life—and they probably were not, given that *fucking* and *shit* were both described as "common" by their dictionary editors—they made it into print far less often. An essayist for the *Gentleman's Magazine* of 1891 echoes the lexicographers' insistence that these words were common, opining that "the 'bad language' of the present day must be characterized as obscene rather than profane." The flexibility of *bugger* reveals that the contemporary grammar of obscenity existed in the early nineteenth century; the ubiquity of *bloody* shows that nineteenth-century people used bad words with abandon. Coupled with the tantalizing but few Victorian examples of obscenities that have come down to us, it seems safe to say that by the 1860s, and perhaps even earlier, people in America and Britain were swearing much as they do today.

Another, related question is when obscene words started to be identified as "swearing," along with oaths. Many works of the period that address swearing refer to "profane swearing and obscene language," as if these are still considered to be separate but related kinds of speech. The entry on *swearing* in *Chambers's Encyclopædia* of 1892, however, notes that "by oaths are loosely understood many terms and phrases of a gross and obscene character, as well as those words the use of which implies profanity proper." And the Boston magazine *Liberty* identified both obscenity and profanity as types of swearing in 1887: "We say that it is no worse to swear by the realities of nature as exemplified in the human body than to swear by a holy ghost. One is obscenity; the other profanity." Certainly by the early twentieth century, we achieve our confused state in which "profanity"—originally a religious concept indicating the opposite of sacred—refers almost exclusively to obscene words, and "swearing" includes both oaths and obscenities.

Gamahuche, Godemiche, and the Huffle

Though Victorian people were swearing in much the same way that we do today, not all the bad words of the time are as familiar as *fucking bitch*. Many of these words rich and strange are not swearwords per se but terms for topics so esoterically taboo that they would never have come up in polite conversation. In his 1785 *Classical Dictionary of the Vulgar Tongue*, Francis Grose includes *to huffle*, which is "a piece of bestiality too filthy for explanation." (The 1788 and 1823 editions decide that discretion is the better part of valor and fail to mention the bestial practice at all.) Grose also lists "to bagpipe, a lascivious practice too indecent for explanation." Even Farmer and Henley, brave champions of obscenity who boldly explained *fucking*, refuse to define *to bagpipe* in their dictionary—they simply repeat Grose's definition manqué. One hopes for something really spectacular from these words, but they are simply the Victorian version of *blow job*, slang for fellatio, a practice evidently much more shocking one or two centuries ago. Another popular Victorian word for this lascivity was *gamahuche*. It derives from French, so it probably was a euphemism used in order to lift the tone of *huffle* and *bagpipe* out of the gutter. It more properly means "mouth on genitals," as it can be used for both fellatio and cunnilingus.

Larking is another "lascivious practice that will not bear explanation," according to Grose in 1785. (It also disappears from later editions of his dictionary.) It is a bit harder to figure out to what *larking* refers. Farmer and Henley go with fellatio again, but Gordon Williams argues persuasively that *larking* is having sex with the man's penis between the woman's breasts. In an 1800 engraving called "The Larking Cull," the man is shown in just this position.

A practice considered less horrifying, in that it gets a real definition, is *to tip the velvet*. In the eighteenth century, this apparently meant "French-kiss"—Grose describes it as "tongueing a woman," or "to put one's tongue into a woman's mouth." A hundred years later, Farmer and Henley are defining it as cunnilingus. It is possible that the meaning changed in the intervening years, or that it was already ambiguous in the eighteenth century—"tongueing a woman" could refer equally to either action. Such kissing does seem to have been considered deviant; *Harris's List of Covent-Garden Ladies*, a guide to London prostitutes published annually between 1757 and 1795, mentions how "a velvet salute of this kind" from Miss H—lsb—ry "had nearly disgusted Lord L——." For two guineas they worked it out, however: "he found that her tongue was attuned to more airs than one." (Covent Garden was a well-known center of prostitution. According to Grose, *covent garden ague* was venereal disease, a *covent garden abbess* was a bawd, and a *covent garden nun* was a prostitute.)

Other wonderful words that may be unfamiliar to you include *godemiche*, another French import, meaning "dildo." A dildo, Grose helpfully explains, is "an implement resembling the virile member, for which it is said to be substituted, by nuns, boarding school misses, and others obliged to celibacy, or fearful of pregnancy. Dildoes are made of wax, horn, leather, and diverse other substances, and if fame does not lie more than usually, are to be had at many of our great toy shops and nick nackatories." Grose is wonderfully able to describe what a dildo is while denying any firsthand knowledge of them. *Lobcock* is "a large relaxed penis, also a dull inanimate fellow." A *rantallion* is "one whose scrotum is so relaxed as to be longer than his penis, i.e. whose shot pouch is longer than the barrel of his piece." *Fartleberries* are "excrement hanging to the hairs about the anus, &c, of a man or woman." (Here *&c*, "et cetera," is back to being slang for the private parts.) And then there is *burning shame*, "a lighted candle stuck into the parts of a woman, certainly not intended by nature for a candlestick." Why this lascivious practice bears mention when larking and huffling don't is not completely clear. Grose defines *cunt* as "a nasty name for a nasty thing"; perhaps he was simply unable to deny himself the pleasure of the pun: *burning shame* is "terrible shame/shame (cunt) on fire."

There were many vulgar slang words for the penis and the vagina themselves as well. *Pego* was popular, as were words that depicted the penis as splitting the woman's anatomy or plugging a hole: *arse-opener*, *arse-wedge*, *beard-splitter*, *chinkstopper*, *plugtail*. It was also *Thomas* or *man Thomas*, *machine*, and *tool*, which are still in use today. The vagina was the *monosyllable* (Grose's default word), *quim*, or *pussy*, a woman's *commodity*—what a woman has to offer in the free market—or her *madge* (Madonna's nickname is more appropriate than we thought). Slang for sexual intercourse included *roger* (also eighteenth- and nineteenth-century slang for the penis;

popular in Britain today), *screw*, and *have your greens*, the last putting a different spin on a phrase I have shouted at my children for years.

Breasts and *bubbies* were the standard terms for breasts in the eighteenth and nineteenth centuries. *Bubbies* was pronounced "bubbies," as in Jewish grandmothers, not "boobies," as in our own juvenile word for breasts. *Harris's List* finds many occasions to describe bubbies and breasts—Mrs. B-ooks, who lodges next to the pawnbroker on Newman Street, for example, "is tolerable well made, with well formed projecting bubbies, that defy the result of any manual pressure, panting and glowing with unfeigned desire, and soon inviting the gratification of the senses." Betsy Miles, at a cabinetmaker's in Old Street, Clerkenwell, is "known in this quarter for her immense sized breasts, which she alternately makes use of with the rest of her parts, to indulge those who are particularly fond of a certain amusement"—larking, it sounds like. (She does it all, actually, "backwards and forwards." "Entrance at the front door" is "tolerably reasonable," but she gets "nothing less than two pound for the back way.")* *Diddeys* was another word for the breasts themselves, while *bushelbubby* was slang for a woman like Betsy Miles, who had large breasts. When the *List* describes the "two young beautiful tits" of Mrs. Mac-tney, Great Titchfield Street, however, it is referring to her teenage protégées, not her breasts. *Tit* came into its modern meaning only in the early twentieth century; from the seventeenth to nineteenth centuries, it indicated a young girl. (*Tit* as a variant of *teat* was used in the early Middle Ages—a tenth-century vocabulary defines *mamilla* [breast] as "tit" and *papilla* [nipple] as "titt-strycel.")

---

*It is worth noting that Betsy, Miss H—lsb—ry and Mrs. B-ooks are extraordinarily well paid. Betsy gets two pounds for the backdoor, Miss H receives two guineas (slightly more than two pounds) a pop, and Mrs. B-ooks gets a banknote, the lowest denomination of which was £5. In the mid-eighteenth century, a housemaid could expect to earn £6 a year; Mrs. B-ooks can earn that practically every night she chooses to work. Even well-off, thoroughly middle-class (male) lawyers only earned around £165 a year—two to three months' work for our ladies. Of course, not all the women did so well from their commodities. Many on Harris's list sold themselves for a few shillings. Even these "cheaper" women outearned housemaids by a wide margin, however.

Racial and Ethnic Slurs

The eighteenth and nineteenth centuries were the age of decorum, but also the age of nationalism, with the expansion of the British Empire and the growth of America as an industrial powerhouse. Nationalistic pride was reflected in the desire of grammarians and lexicographers to "fix" the English language, making it a fit vehicle for imperial ambitions, as Latin had been for Rome. "Fixing" English meant two things—preserving it from change, so that Englishmen of the future would be able to understand the language of their forebears, and correcting its faults, getting rid of transitory slang and low terms that sullied the purity of the national language. Samuel Johnson sums up the aims of many lexicographers, as well as his own: he wants to create "a dictionary by which the pronunciation of our language may be fixed, and its attainment facilitated; by which its purity may be preserved, its use ascertained, and its duration lengthened." Noah Webster had similar aims for his dictionaries of American English—they should promote America's distinct national character and, as he saw it, cultural superiority. He wrote in 1789:

> As an independent nation our honor requires us to have a system of our own, in language as well as government. Great Britain, whose children we are, and whose language we speak, should no longer be our standard. For the taste of her writers is already corrupted, and her language is on the decline. But if it were not so, she is at too great a distance to be our model and to instruct us in the principles of our language.

It was Webster who was in large part responsible for getting rid of the *u* in *honor*, giving Americans something of a spelling system of our own.

This nationalistic desire to "fix" the English language worked hand in hand with rising civility to banish slang, vulgar words, and taboo topics from polite public discourse. Paradoxically, it also led to the creation of a whole new category of swearing—racial and ethnic slurs. Before the era of empire, people had of course been in contact with other cultures, felt pride in their own culture, and experienced xenophobia. For centuries, the English had shared their small island with the Welsh and the Scots (and they had colonized Ireland since the mid-1500s). Renaissance drama had made some use of ethnic stereotypes—Shakespeare's rather obscure "leek" references mock the supposed Welsh penchant for this vegetable, for example, and the Welsh love of cheese is also ridiculed during this period. The Scots and the Irish came in for their share of such insults as well, and we've already seen Shakespeare mock the French with "I shall make-a de turd." There were, however, "comparatively few terms of abuse" among these groups, as Geoffrey Hughes notes.

It was only with the development of nationalism, and the great mixing of people brought about by trade and colonialism, that racial and ethnic insults really took off. By 1682 the Irish were no longer gently ridiculed for mispronouncing *is* as "ish" but were being denigrated as *bogtrotters* and *boglanders*. Abusive terms for other ethnicities arose around the same time, in quick succession: *frog* (a Dutch or a French person, 1652), *hottentot* (originally a term for the African "Bushmen," then for any "uncivilized" person, 1677), *dago* (Spanish or Italian person, originally a U.S. term, 1723), *macaroni* (a foppish and effete foreigner, especially Italian, 1764), *yankee* (a derogatory term from the southern United States for New Englanders, or, used by the British, for Americans generally, 1765), *nigger* (a black person, 1775), and *kaffir* (originally a Muslim term for "heretic," which came to refer to black Africans; predominantly a South African term, 1792).

A bit later we get *sheeny* (a Jewish person, 1816), *coon* (a black person, 1837), *wi-wi* (the French, in Australia and New Zealand, 1841), *mick* (an Irishman, 1850), *yid* (Jewish again, 1874), *jap* (Japanese, 1880), and *limey* (an Englishman, used by people from the British colonies, 1888). By 1940, our lexicon of slurs is pretty much complete, with *ofay* (a derogatory term for whites, used by

U.S. blacks, 1898), *wop* (a U.S. term for an Italian or other southern European, 1912), *spic* (a Spanish-speaker from South America or the Caribbean, 1913), *wetback* (an illegal immigrant from Mexico, 1929), *wog* (a foreigner, especially of Arab descent, 1929), and *gook* (a foreigner, especially East or Southeast Asian, 1935). *Honky* (a white person) first appears a bit later, in 1946, and the last important entrant is *paki* (1964), British slang for a person of South Asian descent. *Paki* is not commonly heard in America, but in Britain it is one of the top-ten swearwords, ranked in 2000 as number ten in order of offensiveness—below *cunt* and *motherfucker* but well above *arse* and *bugger*.

Some of these words were originally neutral terms, including, surprisingly, *nigger*, which had been used since 1574 to designate dark-skinned people from Africa. In early examples such as "the Nigers of Aethiop [Ethiopia] bearing witness" (1574), the word is used without intent to wound; its derogatory sense dates from around 1775. Most, however, were originally intended to be insulting—they were slurs. They were immediately offensive to their targets. It took much longer, however, for them to become offensive to others, for society to decide that they too were "bad words" or swearwords. Farmer and Henley, the pioneering authors of the late nineteenth-century *Slang and Its Analogues*, include entries such as *nigger in the fence*, "an underhand design"; *nigger-driving*, "exhausting with work"; and *nigger-luck*, "very good fortune," as well as *sheeny* and *yid*. Farmer and Henley define these racial and ethnic slurs without comment, even though they editorialized about the coarseness, lowness, and vulgarity of *bloody* and *bugger*.

Even the first edition of the *OED* failed to note the potential offensiveness of racial epithets, though it had refused to include *fuck* and *cunt* at all, and editorialized about many it did include. *Arse*, for example, was "obs. [obsolete] in polite use" in 1888; *bugger* was "in decent use only as a legal term." Even *boghouse*, which, as we have seen, was a euphemism for a privy, was qualified as "dial. [dialect] and vulgar." *Bogtrotter*, *frog*, *kaffir*, and other racial epithets, in contrast, were defined without comment, though it did note in 1908 that *nigger* was a colloquial use and "usually contemptuous."

By the end of the nineteenth century, English-speakers were firmly stuck in the Shit. Obscenities had become the most offensive words in the English language, the ones with which people preferred to swear. A new category of swearing arose during this era as well, though it would take a further fifty years or so until society as a whole began to condemn the use of racial epithets, making them too into obscene words.

Chapter 6

"Fuck 'Em All"

Swearing in the Twentieth Century and Beyond

A young soldier comes home to his family after World War II. His grandmother asks him how his time in the army was. The truth is that he has seen many men, friends and enemies, die horrible deaths, and he returns with a heavy heart. He doesn't want to burden his family, though, so he says, "The boys sure were funny, Grandma—they had so many great jokes." "Tell us one, tell us one," his family begs. He says, "Oh, I can't do that. You see, the boys also used an awful lot of bad language." His family really wants to hear a joke, though, so someone suggests that he just say "blank" whenever he comes to a bad word. He agrees, and tells a joke: "Blank blank blank blankity blank. Blank blank blank blank, blankity blanking blank blank. Blanking blankity blanking blank, blank blank blank blank fuck."

I will confess that this is my favorite joke. I love the idea that there are so many words more unsayable than *fuck*. What could these be? But the joke also suggests that language changed as a result of the war, that some words started to be considered less obscene than they had been in the Victorian era, and that—like *bloody* and *bugger*—they started to reenter the world of public discourse. Some scholars have argued that during and after World War I and World War II, people began to swear *more* than they had in the past. The particular horrors of these wars—the constant threat of death by poison gas and machine guns, trench warfare, incendiary bombing—led to feelings of rage and helplessness that needed an outlet in frequent swearing. Soldiers brought what they heard in the barracks and in the field home with them and into print (and later radio and TV) to a degree that hadn't been seen before.

Swearing in the armed forces was so ubiquitous that *fuck* really wasn't such a bad word. John Brophy and Eric Partridge, who in 1930 published a collection of British songs and slang from World War I, claimed that soldiers used *fucking* so often that it began to mean nothing more than "a warning that a noun is coming." "It became so common," they explain, "that an effective way for the soldier to express emotion was to omit this word. Thus if a sergeant said, 'Get your —— ing rifles!' it was understood as a matter of routine. But if he said, 'Get your rifles!' there was an immediate implication of urgency and danger."*

The soldiers brought this language home to Grandma. Simultaneously, a new, more realistic style of reporting was taking hold that recorded the speech men actually used on the battlefield, obscenities and all. In 1929, the Australian Frederic Manning published a fictionalized account of his experiences as an infantryman in World War I, neither expurgating nor euphemizing the constant swearing. Just one example: "'Oo's the bloody shit 'oo invented this way o' doin' up a fuckin' overcoat?" Manning's book was published anonymously, in a small edition—evidently either he or his publisher was worried that the public was not ready to hear the unvarnished truth about how its soldiers spoke.

Others who wrote about their experiences during the wars were more circumspect and their books best sellers. Robert Graves's 1929 memoir *Goodbye to All That*, for example, records soldierly swearing

---

*Despite preserving these songs for posterity, Brophy and Partridge (who a few years later published one of the best slang dictionaries and even a book devoted exclusively to bawdiness in Shakespeare) felt the need to go Victorian on the obscenity they contained. These words, they declared, "are ugly, in form and in sound. They are sexual but utterly unvoluptuous. Their use will coarsen and degrade, but it will not soften or seduce. . . . They are unshriven and, seemingly, past redemption. In *Lady Chatterley's Lover* D. H. Lawrence experimented with two of them [*fuck* and *cunt*]. . . . The experiment was a failure: the two words instead of interweaving with the texture of his prose, rear their unlovely heads out of the page, gibbering abominably." The inspiration for *Alien*?

mostly with euphemisms and elisions: "Sir, he called me a double effing c——." In his 1948 war novel *The Naked and the Dead*, Norman Mailer famously substituted *fug* and *fugging*, leading Tallulah Bankhead to quip upon meeting him, "So you're the young man who can't spell *fuck*." *Fug* was back to *fuck* a few years later when James Jones published *From Here to Eternity* in 1951, though he had to cut his *fuck*s down from 258 in the manuscript to only 50 in the final book. But whether they spelled obscenities out nakedly, hid them with dashes and dots, or cloaked them as *fug* or *effing*, these best-selling writers and reporters brought obscenities out into the public sphere where they hadn't appeared for centuries.

Songs and Slang of the British Soldier contains in its various songs "I shall tell the Sergeant-Major / To stick his passes [up his arse]," eunuchs who want "balls" for Christmas, and a soldier who would prefer to stay in England and "[roger/fuck] my bloody life away" (the words in brackets are not printed out in the text, but represented by a dash). In 1928 Allen Walker Read—like Eric Partridge an early researcher of words that most academics wouldn't deal with for another sixty years—traveled around the western half of the United States, collecting graffiti he found in public bathrooms. The writings he recorded look quite contemporary, yet at the same time seem to come straight off the walls of Pompeii. A man was moved to write on the wall of a bathroom in the Municipal Auto Camp in Red Bluff, California, that "me and my wife had a fuck," reminiscent of "Hic ego cum veni futui / deinde redei domi"—"I came here and fucked, then went home." Other graffiti writers give advice about evacuation, like the Seven Sages of Ostia: "When you want to shit in ease / Place your elbows on your knees / Put your hands against your chin / Let a fart and then begin." Still others comment on the graffiti they read: "I'm proud to say this crapper has less vulgar poet[ry] in it than the past dozen I've been in. It shows only people with brains use this crapper."

Fuck, to take just one obscene word, was by World War II used with much of its modern variety: *dumbfuck*, (I don't give a) *flying fuck, motherfucker,* and *motherfucking.* A popular song from World War II was "Fuck 'Em All," the chorus of which goes:

> Fuck 'em all!
> Fuck 'em all!
> The long and the short and the tall;
> Fuck all the Sergeants and W.O.1's,
> Fuck all the corporals and their bastard sons;
> For we're saying goodbye to them all,
> As up the C.O.'s arse they crawl;
> You'll get no promotion this side of the ocean,
> So cheer up my lads, fuck 'em all!*

As we saw in the previous chapter, we have tantalizing hints that by the mid- to late nineteenth century, people were swearing in much the same ways as we do today. By 1945, the evidence for this is ample and incontrovertible—people were *absofuckinglutely* (1921) using the same obscenities, in similar ways, with similar frequency.

What the brave members of the Greatest Generation started, the counterculture of the 1960s finished off. We saw in the previous chapter how in the Victorian era, anything potentially provocative or offensive—parts of the body in particular—had to be covered up and banished from speech. "In the 1960s," as Geoffrey Hughes puts it, "the floodgates opened"—those Victorian walls of shame were breached. The Vietnam War also helped to increase public swearing, since protesters made it a point to use obscene language—the phrase "Fuck the draft" was the subject of an important court case in 1971, as we'll see later—to express their rage at the government.

When talking about postwar America and Britain, it becomes more and more difficult to pick out the really important causes of societal change. We could discuss film production codes, radio and TV broadcast licensing, the baby boom and increasing numbers of people

---

* *W.O.1* stands for "warrant officer first class," *C.O.* for "commanding officer."

becoming middle class and thus more permissive (or "a change of emphasis from a production-based economy to a consumption-based one," which "has been assumed to have affected a change in attitudes, with continence being rejected in favour of indulgence," as one scholar puts it), dozens of court cases that eroded laws against obscenity, Mary Whitehouse and the Viewers' and Listeners' Association (which campaigned in Britain for strict TV broadcasting standards), declining church attendance, and the growing importance of black culture, with its game of "the dozens," rap music, and hip-hop.

Whatever the particular causes, by the beginning of the twenty-first century, people had gotten used to seeing and talking about naked bodies and sex acts again, in movies, on TV, and in pornographic (and "ordinary") magazines sold openly on newsstands. We are not back where we were in the Middle Ages—no doctor is going to write about the "cunt" in an article for the *New England Journal of Medicine*, no new translation of the Bible is going to include "bollocks" or "the parts of the body by which turds are shat out" (not even the *Jesus Loves Porn Stars Bible*). But we have reached a point where we are comfortable enough with sexual swearing that we no longer consider the old obscenities to be the worst words in the English language. When graffiti collector Allen Walker Read published his groundbreaking article on *fuck* ("An Obscenity Symbol") in 1934, he declared that it was "the word that has the deepest stigma of any in the language." By the 1990s, however, many people in America were making the same argument for *nigger* or, in Britain, *paki*. Christopher Darden, a prosecutor in the O. J. Simpson trial, called *nigger* the "filthiest, dirtiest, nastiest word in the English language." And Dictionary.com declares that "*nigger* is now probably the most offensive word in English." Given the depth of feeling about the *n*-word, it is perhaps surprising to see how recently it achieved its taboo status. It is only within the last sixty years or so that it has become a word that offends (or is supposed to offend) everyone, not just the people who are its targets, and that should not be used in polite speech.

A story about the 1939 film *Gone with the Wind* illustrates the recentness of this change in attitudes. There is a familiar anecdote about swearing in the film—that producer David Selznick was fined $5,000 because Rhett Butler walks out on Scarlett O'Hara at the end of the movie with the words "Frankly, my dear, I don't give a damn." Actually, the film production code had changed shortly before the movie's release, so Selznick was never fined. As with Eliza Doolittle's "Not bloody likely!," "I don't give a damn" was more of a scandal manqué than a real cause of concern.

The real, less well-known scandal involved the word *nigger*. The producers of the film wanted to preserve the "true southern flavor" of the book and so decided to include dialogue in which various characters use the word—Mammy speaking disapprovingly of "shiftless niggers," for example. The 1930 Motion Picture Production Code forbade the use of profanity in films, including "God, Lord, Jesus, Christ—unless used reverently—Hell, S.O.B., damn, Gawd" (except when a quotation from a literary work, hence the exception for Rhett's "damn"). It outlawed "obscenity in word, gesture, reference, song, joke, or by suggestion (even when likely to be understood only by part of the audience)." It stipulated that "the use of the Flag shall be consistently respectful." It even mandated that "the treatment of bedrooms must be governed by good taste and delicacy." But it did not forbid or discourage the use of racial epithets such as *nigger*. Only when the film's African American actors refused to say the word and hundreds of letters poured in objecting to its use did producer Selznick agree to take it out of the script.

The fact that hundreds of people objected to the filmmakers' decision to use the *n*-word shows that by the 1940s there was a growing sense that it was out of bounds, an offensive word that no one should say. But while the *n*-word was becoming more and more taboo across a broader swath of society, there were still pockets of resistance. As late as 1992 (and presumably today as well), a genteel elderly white woman could tell her neighbor in North Carolina that she was looking for a "yard nigger." (This particular lady happened to be speaking to a philosopher interested in derogatory speech, and so her words were recorded for posterity.) While such a person would most likely shrink from using sexual obscenities and profane oaths, she had no problem casually dropping America's worst racial slur. For her, having grown up white in the American South, that was simply what one called black people; the term "carried no explicit contempt" (though plenty of condescension) and was not meant to shock or be impolite. She simply wanted someone to do her yard work; the term for such a person in her racially stratified world was "yard nigger."

Despite such holdouts, *nigger* is an obscene word for most Americans and Brits today. One might say it is our most dangerous word. People have lost their jobs for saying other words that are completely unrelated but sound like it. David Howard, for example, told his staff that they would have to be "niggardly" with the budget of their municipal agency, as money was tight. *Niggardly* means "parsimonious" or "miserly," and *niggard* first appears two hundred years before *nigger*, deriving from an old Scandinavian word, *nig*, for a miserly person. Nevertheless, several employees took great offense and Howard was forced to resign. A British acquaintance of mine was castigated for using the word *niggling*, meaning small or petty, in a work email. (*Niggling* is also unrelated to *nigger*, though *to niggle* was slang for sexual intercourse in the nineteenth and eighteenth centuries.)

But *nigger* isn't always a negative word. Especially when used by African Americans among themselves—and pronounced and spelled *nigga* to differentiate it from the slur—it can be a sign of belonging, an expression of respect and affection, a claim to an identity that is, as Randall Kennedy puts it, "real, authentic, uncut, unassimilated, and unassimilable."

Them's Fightin' Words

As we have seen in previous chapters, swearing has had a patchy history of official regulation. Oaths were regulated by the Church and occasionally by the state, as in the 1606 Act to Prevent the Abuses of Players and a 1623 law against general profane swearing and cursing.

Obscene words, since they began to be thought of as shocking only in the Renaissance, suffered less control. The first prosecution for obscenity, as we've seen, was Edmund Curll's in 1727, and he was singled out because he had published an anti-Catholic pornographic novel—*Venus in the Cloister* actually contains little if any obscene language. In the twentieth century, the legal regulation of obscenities became more complicated and more thorough, with the doctrine of "fighting words," and with legal cases that focused not just on obscenity in its more general sense as "things offensive to decency" but on particular obscene words themselves.

In the United States in the 1940s, some swearwords were legally recognized as having a power in excess of their literal meaning, much as oaths possessed six hundred years ago. These "fighting words" are so offensive that they "by their very utterance inflict injury or tend to incite an immediate breach of the peace," and as such are not protected by the First Amendment.

The fighting-words doctrine was articulated in a 1942 U.S. Supreme Court case, *Chaplinsky v. State of New Hampshire*. Walter Chaplinsky was a Jehovah's Witness proselytizing in Rochester, New Hampshire. He stood on a public sidewalk, attacking organized religion as a "racket," and attracting a large, generally hostile crowd. When the town marshal warned him that the crowd was getting restless, Chaplinsky shouted, "You are a God damned racketeer" and "a damned Fascist and the whole government of Rochester are Fascists or agents of Fascists." He was promptly arrested.

Chaplinsky sued because he felt that the arrest violated his right to freedom of speech, his constitutional right to criticize organized religion and call people fascists. The Court disagreed, exiling his words to the ghetto of unprotected speech along with "the lewd and obscene, the profane, and the libelous"—the kinds of language that can be regulated by Congress. "Resort to epithets or personal abuse," the high-minded judges unanimously declared, "is not in any proper sense communication of information or opinion safeguarded by the Constitution."

This decision led to great confusion in the lower courts about exactly what counts as a fighting word and thus could be illegal, and what is merely offensive speech and thus protected. Chaplinsky himself questioned whether "damned Fascist" was "bad" enough to be a fighting word; the Court countered that the determining factor is "what men of common intelligence would understand would be words likely to cause an average addressee to fight." If someone called me a fascist today in über-liberal Cambridge, Massachusetts, I would be more bemused than insulted, but in the middle of World War II in small-town New Hampshire, the word was probably much more directly relevant and offensive. Still, it seems that Chaplinsky had a point. One need only look at some lower-court cases to see that men (and women) of common intelligence are nowhere near to agreement.

In 2006, Connie Watkins screamed at city employees who were pruning trees in front of her house, "Fuckin' treetrimmers you're butchering my trees." Four years later the Arkansas appeals court determined that these words were fighting words, upholding her arrest for disorderly conduct. *Fuck* is not automatically a fighting word, though. When a police officer asked John Kaylor to move his truck, which was blocking an alley, Kaylor called him a "fucking asshole" and refused to move the vehicle. A court in Ohio decided that these were *not* fighting words—police officers are legally supposed to exercise more restraint than private citizens and so should not react to the provocation of insults. If you're going to call someone a "motherfucking bastard," choose a police officer, not a gardener. On second thought, don't. The officer and his partner took Kaylor out with pepper spray and arrested him, even though Kaylor's swearing was constitutionally protected.

In Michigan, Thomas Leonard was arrested for referring to "a God damn lawsuit" at a town meeting. (Coincidentally, the lawsuit was his, and he was suing the police department.) An appeals court determined that these were not fighting words. *Whore, harlot,* and *jezebel* are, though, at least according to a Wisconsin appeals court.

Ralph Ovadal was part of a group that had been protesting nude bathing at a Wisconsin beach for several years. When one of his friends tried to give Nancy Erickson a Gospel tract, she swore at him. Then Ovadal and his friends surrounded Erickson and called her "whore," et cetera, for six minutes, in accordance with a little-known part of the gospel of Matthew: "I say unto you, Love your enemies, bless them that curse you, do good to them that hate you, and call anybody who looks like they might go swimming naked 'harlot' at least thirty times."

Nigger is the fighting word par excellence. Jerry Spivey, an elected district attorney in North Carolina, was overheard at a bar saying, "Look at that nigger hitting on my wife," and he was removed from office. The North Carolina Supreme Court ruled that Spivey's "repeated references to Mr. Jacobs [the man who supposedly hit on his wife] as a 'nigger' presents a classic case of the use of 'fighting words' tending to incite an immediate breach of the peace which are not protected." The court goes on: "No fact is more generally known than that a white man who calls a black man a 'nigger' within his hearing will hurt and anger the black man and often provoke him to confront the white man and retaliate." The North Dakota supreme court found that a white high school student's use of "stupid nigger" to a black classmate constituted fighting words; a similar decision was handed down by an appeals court in Arizona, in a case in which a white teenager shouted at a black woman at a bus stop, "Fuck you, you god damn nigger." The Arizona court ruled that "few words convey such an inflammatory message of racial hatred and bigotry as the term 'nigger.'"

The *n*-word does not always fit the definition of a fighting word, however. When a telemarketer twice insulted people who had refused his offer of home improvement services as "dumb nigger," a New York court ruled that these were *not* fighting words. "Venting anger and frustration by hurling insults may be unpleasant and crude," the opinion states, but unless there is a strong presumption that such words will result in violence, even racial slurs are protected speech.

The other key case in which the United States Supreme Court has addressed fighting words is *Cohen v. California* (1971). In 1968, Paul Robert Cohen wore a jacket with "Fuck the Draft" written on it into a California municipal court. He was arrested and sentenced to thirty days in jail for disturbing the peace through offensive conduct. The Supreme Court ruled that his conviction had been unjustified. His jacket was not obscene, because under American law obscenity must clearly be erotic, and "it cannot plausibly be maintained that this vulgar allusion to the Selective Service System would conjure up such psychic stimulation in anyone likely to be confronted with Cohen's crudely defaced jacket." The Court is not disputing that *fuck* is "an obscenity" or an "obscene word," as we've been discussing for two-hundred-odd pages, but rather is saying that the jacket doesn't fall into the legal category of "obscenity," which, as we will see, is related to but distinct from obscene language.

"Fuck the Draft" was also not a case of fighting words, because the slogan was unlikely to provoke an immediate breach of the peace. The Court's opinion stresses that this is the real concern about fighting words—they are likely to cause immediate violence, like falsely shouting "fire" in a crowded theater. To provoke such a strong reaction, they must usually be directed at an individual, to be "personally abusive epithets." No one could have taken "Fuck the Draft" as a personal insult, so the words are not fighting words. No matter how much legislators in California hated swearing (or hated hippie protesters), they could not simply ban the use of *fuck*. The Court's opinion also recognizes that some words carry an emotive content that may be more important than their cognitive content, and that is also constitutionally protected. When Cohen wore his jacket, he was not offering a reasoned account of why the draft should be abolished. He was communicating the strength of his opposition, which the First Amendment allows him to do.

American law has long recognized that society has an interest in regulating words that might incite people to commit violence. The difficult question with fighting words is figuring out which words count. Not all people subscribe to the same standards of decorum; not all people are shocked and offended by the same things. "One man's vulgarity," as Justice Harlan put it in the *Cohen* decision, "is another man's lyric," and courts must be careful not to censor speech simply because they don't like the music. America is a "rough-edged society," as other opinions point out, and sometimes people must tolerate views they find distasteful or insulting, even when those views are expressed through racial epithets.

The situation is different in Britain, where laws specifically forbid "hate speech"—verbal attacks based on race, ethnicity, religion, and/or sexual orientation. Freedom of speech is protected in Britain under the Human Rights Act of 1998 and under common law, but hate speech exemptions have what courts in the United States would likely call a "chilling effect" on freedom of expression. In 2012, for example, Welsh university student Liam Stacey was found guilty of racially aggravated harassment and sentenced to fifty-six days in jail for his Twitter posts about a black soccer player, Fabrice Muamba. Muamba had suffered a cardiac arrest during a game, moving Stacey to tweet "LOL [laugh out loud], Fuck Muamba. He's dead!!!" When various other Twitter users reproached him for his comment, sometimes with their own obscene and possibly racist language—for example, "You must be fucking barmy [crazy] if you think a greasy little welsh sheep shagger could take on a fucking cockney you silly fat wanker"—Stacey responded with lines such as "I ain't your friend, you wog cunt. Go and pick some cotton."* While his tweets are extremely offensive (as are the ones tweeted to him in response), it is difficult to see how, as the trial judge put it, they "aggravated [the] situation"—Muamba was recovering in the hospital—or incited anyone to violence or racial hatred. Few people have been

---

* *Wanker* is quite taboo in Britain, though almost unused in the United States. The etymology is unknown; it was first employed around 1950, and means "masturbator," or figuratively "loser" or "jerk." *Jerk* (*jerk off*) is one of our few contributions to the "masturbation as insult" category, while Brits also have *tosser* and *frig*, which, as we have seen, are obscene terms for the act.

charged with employing racist language in Britain under the several laws banning its use, but the possibility is always there anytime someone uses a racial slur. It would perhaps be best to follow the advice of the judge who presided over the trial of Matthew Stiddard, who, like Stacey, was charged with racially aggravated harassment. Stiddard had called a respected police surgeon "a fucking Paki" and was advised by the judge, "Next time call him a fat bastard and don't say anything about his colour."

Fighting for the Phallic Reality

The law has also attempted to regulate obscene words through obscenity prosecutions. As we've already discussed briefly, "obscenity" as a legal concept is not the same as "obscenities" or "obscene words." In fact, the legal category of "obscenity" often does not even involve any obscene words. Pictures or videos can be legally obscene without any words at all, and text can be obscene without any obscene words, as we saw with *Fanny Hill* and nineteenth-century botanical pornography. But two of the most famous twentieth-century obscenity cases did center on obscene words and sped the entrée of these words into public discourse and into wider and more frequent general use. These were the trials of *Ulysses* and *Lady Chatterley's Lover*.

James Joyce's *Ulysses* is now seen as a classic, perhaps *the* classic, of modern literature. It was ranked number one on Modern Library's list of the "100 Best English-Language Novels of the 20th Century" and appears in nearly every such list, whether or not the ranking is English-language only, and whether the books are limited to the twentieth century or from all of literary history. But when it was first published in 1922, it was number one on a different sort of list— called "the most infamously obscene book in ancient or modern literature." British poet Edmund Gosse announced that Joyce was "a sort of Marquis de Sade, but does not write so well." Even Virginia Woolf tut-tutted that "the directness of the language and the choice of incidents, if indeed there *is* any choice, have raised a blush even upon such a cheek as mine."

So what was the problem with the greatest novel of modern literature? The book contains a fair number of obscene words, most of which are put into the mouths of two soldier characters. These two privates give voice to Joyce's version of the language of the common soldier, as recorded in Frederic Manning's fictionalized memoir and in Robert Graves's *Goodbye to All That*. Like Manning and unlike Graves, Joyce spells it all out: one private threatens, "I'll do him in, so help me fucking Christ! I'll wring the bastard fucker's bleeding blasted fucking windpipe!" and exclaims, "God fuck old Bennet. He's a whitearsed bugger. I don't give a shit for him." The other private tells his companion, "Bugger off, Harry. Here's the cops!" The critical reaction to this language—denouncements of the book as "infamously obscene"—is what Manning was afraid of when he published his memoir anonymously in a small edition, and what Graves managed to avoid with his euphemisms.

But "I'll wring the bastard fucker's bleeding blasted fucking windpipe" wasn't even the main problem. The section that actually resulted in the book being made illegal in the United States was this:

> And she saw a long Roman candle going up over the trees, up, up, and, in the tense hush, they were all breathless with excitement as it went higher and higher and she had to lean back more and more to look up after it, high, high, almost out of sight, and her face was suffused with a divine, an entrancing blush from straining back and he could see her other things too, nainsook knickers, the fabric that caresses the skin, better than those other pettiwidth, the green, four and eleven, on account of being white . . . And then a rocket sprang and bang shot blind blank and O! then the Roman candle burst and it was like a sigh of O! and everyone cried O! O! in raptures and it gushed out of it a stream of rain gold hair threads and they shed and ah! They were all greeny dewy stars falling with golden, O so lovely! O so soft, sweet, soft!

If you were paying attention, you probably noticed the similarities to the Song of Songs: Roman candle = penis, burst = ejaculate, stream of rain = et cetera, et cetera. This is an elaborate allegory of masturbation, the main character Leopold Bloom pleasuring himself while watching a girl on the beach, who is herself watching fireworks. If you weren't paying attention, though, it is easy to miss (and, after 350 pages already, your attention might well be wandering). Certainly twelve-year-old boys aren't going to pass this around if they can get their hands on a copy of *Romeo and Juliet*.

The book was being published serially in the United States without any problems until this section came up.* In 1920 alert reader John Sumner, head of the New York Society for the Suppression of Vice, did notice the masturbation and sued to have publication stopped on grounds of obscenity. In Britain the book was banned by order of the Home Office after critic Shane Leslie pointed out the ways in which it was blasphemous and detrimental to the morals of society. *Ulysses* was banned in the United States from 1920 to 1933 and in Britain from 1922 to 1936. (It was still freely published in France, though.)

Random House possessed the rights to publish *Ulysses* in the United States and figured that such a scandalous book would sell. First, though, it needed to create a trial, one that would declare the book not obscene and thus legal to be published. The publisher tried to get the book impounded by customs, but this proved difficult, even for such an "infamously obscene" work. According to the story, Random House arranged for someone to bring an illegally published copy from France into the United States. When the "mule" went through customs, however, it was too hot for the inspector to bother opening anyone's luggage. The man insisted that there was contraband in his luggage until the inspector was forced to search his

---

* Ezra Pound had censored the first few sections, taking out Joyce's phrase "the grey sunken cunt of the world" and removing Leopold Bloom's trip to the outhouse—perhaps the first noncomical depiction of defecation in literary history. It is possible that these would have brought down the censors earlier.

bag. When the inspector discovered the copy of *Ulysses* instead of a bottle of rum or a packet of opium, he refused to seize it, telling the Random House man, "Oh, for God's sake, everybody brings that in. We don't pay any attention to it." (An estimated thirty thousand illegal French editions had already been "smuggled" in.) The customs chief had to be called in, and he eventually did his duty and impounded the book, paving the way for Random House's long-sought trial.

The trial happened in 1933 (with a favorable appeals court ruling in 1934) and was a success for Random House, for James Joyce, and for literary obscenity in general. The two courts' judgments overturned the Hicklin Rule, which had governed obscenity trials in America and Britain since 1868. (In a wonderful piece of nominative determinism, this rule had been set out by Lord Chief Justice Cockburn—"cock burn" being the result of indulging one's libidinous leanings with a poxy whore.) This rule stated that if one part of a work was obscene, it *all* was—a book that contained a single obscene word was thus always in danger of being banned as obscenity. Instead, the American courts insisted that a book be judged in its entirety: "The question . . . is whether a publication as a whole has a libidinous effect." If a work contains a few obscene words or suggestive passages, this is no longer enough to push it into the category of obscenity. As the appeals court pointed out, most of Western literature could be indicted for obscenity under the Hicklin Rule, from the *Odyssey* to *Hamlet* (not forgetting the Bible). The Hicklin Rule also reflected the Victorian obsession with preserving the innocence of the lower classes and children—it stated that courts must consider "whether the tendency of the matter charged as obscenity is to deprave and corrupt those whose minds are open to such immoral influences and into whose hands a publication of this sort may fall." If a work excited lust in those least able to resist such base urges, it was obscene. The U.S. courts insisted instead that the law deal only with a book's effect on a "normal person," equivalent to the "reasonable person" posited in tort law, not with its effects on the parts of the population most liable to libidinous excitation, whether those be the poor, the uneducated, or the boys. Given these considerations, the courts found that *Ulysses* was too sincere a portrait of lower-class life in Dublin, too artful a re-creation of people's sometimes frustrating and often boring inner monologues, and just too dang long—it is of "such portentous length," one judge noted—to be obscene.*

D. H. Lawrence's *Lady Chatterley's Lover* was the subject of another key obscenity trial, this one in Britain, in 1960. It tested the new British Obscenity Act of 1959, which, influenced by the American *Ulysses* cases, stipulated that works had to be considered as a whole, not in part, and that the literary merit of a work, evaluated by a panel of experts, should also be taken into account in determining whether it is obscene. Where four-letter words were only part of the problem with *Ulysses*, they were the heart of the problem with *Lady Chatterley's Lover*. One of Lawrence's projects in writing the book in the late 1920s was to free obscene words from their social stigma, paving the way for a healthier acceptance of sexuality, and healing what he saw as a cultural separation of intellect and body. Or as he put it: "If I use the taboo words, there is a reason. We shall never free the phallic reality from the 'uplift' taint till we give it its own phallic language, and use the obscene words." In any case, the phallic reality remained chained until 1960, when Penguin Books decided to publish an unexpurgated edition of *Lady Chatterley's Lover*, complete with swearwords and all.

The book had been published in several editions since 1928, but all had been censored except the first edition, published in Italy. These editions removed passages such as the one in which the gamekeeper Mellors, representing the fully sexualized phallic reality, discusses anatomy with his lover Lady Chatterley, who carries the heavy weight of representing both the eternal feminine and the transition from the bodiless and barren world of intellectuals and the

---

* The British ban was lifted in 1936, largely as a result of the American court cases.

aristocracy to the profound, embodied sensuality of a person who has thrown off the conventions of society:

> "Th'art good cunt, though, aren't ter? Best bit o' cunt left on earth.
> When ter likes! When tha'rt willin'!"
>   "What is cunt?" she said.

Mellors goes on to explain to the good lady the difference between *fuck*, which is what animals do, and *cunt*, which is "the beauty o' thee, lass!"

The crown was hampered in its case by a prosecutor who seemed more in sympathy with Cockburn's original 1868 views than with the revised obscenity law. He famously asked the jurors, "Is it a book that you would even wish your wife or servants to read?" A panel of esteemed literary scholars gave their views that *Lady Chatterley's Lover* was an important novel and that the obscene words were a necessary part of Lawrence's project, not an add-on intended to promote lust among wives and servants. The book was declared not obscene and Penguin's unexpurgated edition sold 2 million copies in its first year and 1.3 million in its second.

The trial of *Lady Chatterley's Lover* is often seen as heralding an era of new openness in public discourse. People had been speaking together in private like Mellors and Lady Chatterley for a hundred years, but the publication of their Penguin edition signaled a new acceptance of this language in the public sphere. The trial offers a handy symbol for the cultural liberalization taking place, in which obscene words became more socially acceptable, because the parts of the body they represented were themselves becoming less shocking.

By 1973, the words thought to be so shocking in *Lady Chatterley's Lover* were being said openly on public radio at two o'clock in the afternoon, prompting another key legal case. In 1972, George Carlin had identified "the seven words you can never say on television" and made these the basis of a monologue he performed on a comedy tour. The monologue basically consists of him swearing, with occasional disquisitions into the strange ways we use these seven words—*shit, piss, fuck, cunt, cocksucker, motherfucker,* and *tits*. He has this and more to say about *shit*, for example:

> The word shit, uh, is an interesting kind of word in that the middle class has never really accepted it and approved it. They use it like crazy but it's not really okay. It's still a rude, dirty, old kind of gushy word. [*Laughter*] They don't like that, but they say it, like, they say it, like, a lady now in a middle-class home, you'll hear most of the time she says it as an expletive, you know, it's out of her mouth before she knows. She says, Oh shit oh shit [*laughter*], oh shit. If she drops something, Oh, the shit hurt the broccoli. Shit. Thank you.

A man heard part of this monologue, broadcast by a California radio station, while he was driving with his young son. He complained to the Federal Communications Commission (FCC), which is responsible for regulating what is broadcast on the radio and on television in the United States. In the United States, obscene material, which (1) appeals to the prurient interest, (2) depicts sexual conduct in a patently offensive way, and (3) lacks serious value, cannot be broadcast at any time.

What was at issue with Carlin's monologue, however, was not obscenity but whether the FCC had the power to regulate indecency. Legally, indecency is "language or material that, in context, depicts or describes, in terms patently offensive as measured by contemporary community standards for the broadcast medium, sexual or excretory organs or activities." This is pretty much code for obscene words. The FCC threatened the local radio station with disciplinary action if more complaints were received. The Pacifica station sued, complaining that the FCC was chilling Americans' right to free speech. The case went all the way to the Supreme Court, where the FCC won—in 1978 the Court declared that the FCC did have the power to regulate indecency on television and the radio. Material broadcast into people's homes or cars is subject to less First

Amendment protection than are books, stand-up comedy tours, or personal conversations, because it is harder to avoid offensive material in such a situation. The FCC can ensure that indecent language is broadcast only between 10:00 p.m. and 6:00 a.m., when the most vulnerable listeners—children—are supposed to be asleep.

We have only to look at TV today to see that the Supreme Court and the FCC were less like Moses commanding the Red Sea to part and more like King Canute ordering the tide not to come in and watching helplessly as his shoes got wet. The tide of swearing has come in—of Carlin's original seven words you can't say on TV, you can now say all but three, depending on when you are talking and how you use the words. And this is only on network TV. On cable, there has been a show, *Deadwood*, whose entire raison d'être appeared to have been swearing, as extreme and as frequent as possible. A group of fans has calculated the "fucks per minute" from the show at 1.73 for the final season and 1.76 for the previous one. And these figures are just for *fuck*, not for *cocksucker*, *chink*, and the other swearwords in common use on the show. The HBO crime drama *The Wire* featured a scene where two policeman converse about a crime scene using only variations on the word *fuck* in different tones of voice, managing to express frustration, surprise, pain, compassion, and insight with dialogue that is basically "fuck . . . motherfucker . . . the fuck? Fuckity fuck fuck fuck fuck. . . . fuckin' A." Once you hit the Internet, all bets are off. On YouTube you can find any number of paeans to profanity, including "the Fucking Short Version" of dozens of movies such as *The Departed, The Big Lebowski,* and *Die Hard II.* The title is pretty descriptive—these are the movies pared down to a single word. There is the little boy who can't say *truck*—it's a "fire fuck." There is the Teletubbies doll that says "Faggot faggot faggot bite my butt!" (Actually, unfortunately, it says "faster faster faster" in Cantonese—a language mix-up.) And there are many, many swearing parrots.

On Urban Dictionary.com, the most popular website about contemporary language usage, obscenities receive far and away the most attention. People vie to come up with the best definitions and identify or invent new slang based on them. *Fuck*, as of this writing, has collected more than 200 different definitions and more than 150,000 "thumbs-up" and "thumbs-down" votes on their quality. (*Mother*, in contrast, has 33 definitions and 4,500 votes.) It has also inspired approximately 6,000 entries based on it, from *fucabomb* to *fuczoid*. *Cunt*, impressively, has acquired 414 definitions and somewhere around 200,000 votes while inspiring 2,500 entries, from *cuntabilia* to *cuntzor*. There are also Web pages that list all the bad words in the Bible that explain, sometimes correctly, the etymologies of swearwords; and that describe the most popular obscenities among rappers, the prison population, and gay men.

In March 2011, three of the top-ten hit songs on the *Billboard* pop music chart had obscenities in their titles (bleeped, courtesy of the FCC, when played on the radio). Cee Lo Green told various people off with "Fuck You!," Enrique Iglesias begged pardon for his rudeness in announcing "Tonight (I'm Fuckin' You)," and Pink told listeners that they needn't be "Fuckin' Perfect." The *New York Times* called this "*some* kind of milestone," as top-ten pop music had in the past at least theoretically shied away from such blatant swearing. (*New York Times* best-selling books have been ahead of the curve in this respect. The list included Randall Kennedy's *Nigger* way back in 2003, followed by Harry Frankfurt's *On Bullshit* [2005], Justin Halpern's *Shit My Dad Says* [2009], and Adam Mansbach's *Go the Fuck to Sleep* [2011].)

Rap music, in contrast to pop, is marked by an exuberant and near-constant use of swearwords. Much of rap music deals with boasting and bragging (or, as rappers and critics call it, "braggadocio," derived from a character in Edmund Spenser's 1590 epic poem, *The Faerie Queene*); battling or "beefing," like the flyting of fifteenth- and sixteenth-century Scotland; and "hustling," making money, usually through illicit means. "Lighters," by Eminem and Royce da 5'9", is a 2011 example of braggadocio—"Had a dream I was king, I woke up, still king," Eminem boasts. The song is so full of obscenities that bits of it are almost unintelligible when heard on the radio, particularly when Eminem points out, among other things, that "You stayed the same, 'cause cock backwards is still cock, you pricks." Rap battling evolved most directly from "the dozens," a game originally played by young African American men. In the dozens, contestants show off their verbal dexterity and wit by trading insults, particularly of the "yo momma" variety—"Yo momma so ugly, they filmed *Gorillas in the Mist* in her shower." As Scottish flyting shows, though, this kind of organized obscenity has evolved over and over in society—it must represent a fairly universal human urge. Hustling, as rapper Jay-Z puts it, is "the ultimate metaphor for the basic human struggles: the struggle to survive and resist, the struggle to win and to make sense of it all." Rap music depicts these basic human struggles in the coarse language of the street. Obscenities are particularly useful in these contexts because they are the words with the most emotive force. They are the go-to words for expressing aggression, for putting someone else down, for resisting "the system" and the dominant culture that expects certain kinds of "good" language and behavior.

The Science of Swearing

As swearwords have become more prevalent and less taboo in society, this more relaxed cultural climate has opened up swearing as a (mostly) socially acceptable field of study. Brain scientists, psychologists, linguists, and sociologists now all do research into different aspects of swearing. The discovery of Tourette's syndrome in the late nineteenth century really sparked scientific inquiry into our topic, although at that point in time doctors had to conduct their research through euphemisms and elisions and had to fight against the idea that understanding swearing was unworthy of real intellectual effort.

On July 10, 1890, a mother brought her thirteen-year-old daughter to the Johns Hopkins Hospital in Baltimore because the girl could not stop her body from jerking and she was making loud barking sounds.

Doctors tried hypnosis to calm her down, but it was unsuccessful. A few months later, her case took a turn for the worse. Her mother wrote the doctors: "Mary makes use of words lately that make me ashamed to bring her to you or to take her out of the house; it is dreadful, such words as ———, ———, ———, etc. She was always a modest child, and it almost kills me for to hear her use such words." It is fairly obvious that the worrisome words are obscene—the mother implies that they are the opposite of modest—though the doctor can't mention what they are in a late-nineteenth-century medical journal. (The thirteenth-century English translator of Lanfranc's *Science of Chirurgie*, say, would not have had such scruples.) Mary was suffering from Tourette's syndrome, described by two French doctors in 1885.

Tourette's syndrome is characterized by physical and vocal tics such as eye blinking, coughing, shrugging the shoulders, twitching of the limbs, and clearing the throat. The most famous symptom, though, is what got Mary's mother so upset—coprolalia, the uncontrollable utterance of obscene words. (Touretters also occasionally suffer from copropraxia, which involves obscene gestures such as giving the finger or crotch grabbing, and coprographia, the urge to make obscene drawings.) Only 10 to 30 percent of people with Tourette's experience coprolalia, but it causes great embarrassment to them and can lead to even greater misunderstandings with the general public. Sometimes the tic is relatively harmless—someone mentions ducks, and the Touretter feels compelled to repeat "fuck a duck." Other times the outbursts are more meaningful, directed at a person's race, weight, or sex, in what might seem to be the most hurtful way possible.

In the 1890s, no one had any idea what caused Tourette's syndrome, or why anyone might be compelled to vocalize the words locked down by society's strongest taboos. The problem was thought to lie, probably, with the mothers—they were too rigid and didn't let their children indulge in enough free play, so the children never learned to control their bodies and language. Or they were too indulgent of temper tantrums, with the same result. If it wasn't the mother's fault, you could always blame penis envy, as in the case of Alice, a child with uncontrollable movements and strange vocalizations who had the bad luck to draw a picture of a tower in her psychiatrist's office in the 1940s.

Now, however, we have an idea of how Tourette's syndrome really works, thanks to advances in the fields of psychology and neuroscience. This in turn gives us insight into what goes on in "normal" brains when people swear. Scientists have found that swearing most likely originates in the right hemisphere of the brain, and within that half, in the "primitive" part of the brain, the limbic system. The right half of the brain is responsible for nonpropositional or automatic speech, which includes greetings, conventional expressions such as "not at all," counting, song lyrics, and swearwords. Propositional speech—words strung together in syntactically correct forms to create an original meaning—occurs in the left hemisphere. The limbic system, particularly the amygdala, records the emotional content of words—their connotations, as opposed to denotations. The amygdala "lights up" during brain scans when subjects read taboo words, and this increased activity can also be measured through the skin with electrodes. Like my grandmother, aphasiacs who have lost their ability to create propositional speech because of Alzheimer's or problems in their left brain often retain their ability to swear. Medical literature abounds with cases such as that of a man whose entire left hemisphere was surgically removed due to cancer, leaving him with the ability to say "um," "one . . . three," and "goddammit." (In contrast, one patient whose right brain had atrophied could carry on a conversation more or less normally but had lost the ability to sing "Happy Birthday" or say the Pledge of Allegiance.)

Swearing, though, is a combination of left and right brain, executive and lower functions. When you swear, you do not say just any old bad word—you choose the one calculated to do the most insult, to relieve the most stress, or perhaps to relieve the most stress without offending your Mormon neighbor who is outside gardening. Though the coprolalia of Tourette's sounds involuntary, more often than not the words are relevant to the situation at hand. Speaking to an obese woman, a Touretter might interject, "Fat pig!"; to an African

American in a purple sweatsuit, "Purple nigger!"; to just about any-one, "Fuck you!" Many people might have thoughts like these, but their prefrontal cortex—the executive area of their brains—is able to override them and shut them down. The current theory is that people with Tourette's have a problem in an area of the brain called the basal ganglia, which plays a role in making choices among several actions and inhibiting certain motor functions. The executive areas of their brains can fight against their limbic urges for a time—people can often delay but not suppress tics—but eventually the lower brain wins, and out comes "Fuck me up the asshole!"

Other disciplines have pursued the study of swearing as well. Not so long ago, in the 1930s and 1940s, linguists had to disguise any interest in obscenity, as did Allen Walker Read, who, we've seen, wrote an entire article about *fuck* without once ever mentioning the word, and who had to publish his collection of lavatory graffiti pri-vately. For decades, however, most linguists simply pretended that swearwords didn't exist. The standard word frequency list created in 1944 ranked the frequencies of various words within a sample of 18 million. Almost the only swearword among those 18 million was *shit*, as the list had been compiled from *Black Beauty*, *Little Women*, and issues of *Reader's Digest*. Another study of English usage, this one based on spoken telephone conversations in New York City, ex-cluded 25 percent of the recorded words from its sample because they were indecent. Linguists and psychologists now feel free to include the bad words in their samples of English. Psychologist Tim-othy Jay found that on average 0.7 percent of the words people use in a day are taboo ones. This sounds like a small percentage until it is compared with first-person plural pronouns (*we, us, our, ourselves*), which occur at a 1 percent rate. And Jay found that the rate of swearing varied, from 0 percent (a person who doesn't swear at all) to 3 percent (someone who says *motherfucker* quite a bit more than *we* and *us*). In 1969, psychologist Paul Cameron compiled word frequency lists in three different social settings. He found that when he compared them, the only words on all three lists that were not pronouns (*he, I*), articles (*the, a*), or prepositions (*to, from*) were *damn, hell, fuck,* and *shit*.

Scientists have discovered much about the emotional impact of swearwords through traditional psychological testing such as word recall tasks. If you are given a list of words, some of which are obscene and some of which are not, chances are the ones that will stick in your mind are obscene. When Timothy Jay gave people a list of thirty-six taboo and non-taboo words, the top five recalled were *nigger, bitch, pussy, cock,* and *slut*. Fewer subjects recalled *friend* and *cuddle*; nobody remembered *kiss, pity, crime, lung,* or *frame*. This confirms what we feel instinctively and have seen through brain imaging studies—taboo words are arousing, not in the sexual sense (though of course they can be that too) but in a more general physiological sense. These words excite the lower-brain circuitry responsible for emotion, which creates electrical impulses that can be measured in the skin. Reading Jay's taboo words caused higher skin conductance frequencies than did the non-taboo words, correlating pretty exactly with the recall of the terms.

Another piece of folk wisdom about swearing has recently found scientific support. If you ask people why they swear when they hurt themselves, they will likely say that it makes them feel better—it is cathartic in some way. Intrepid researchers have discovered that you can keep your hand immersed in extremely cold water for longer (an additional forty seconds) if you swear than if you say some neutral word. The psychologist Richard Stephens, who led the experiment, summed up his results: "I would advise people, if they hurt themselves, to swear."

Many people in the twentieth century and today have been following Stephens's advice, and not only when they've hurt themselves. In the past century, swearing manifested itself in the public sphere to a degree not seen since the vain oaths of the Middle Ages. Like the Victorian period, though, it was an era of the Shit. Twentieth-century speakers still used religious oaths frequently when they swore, but they were much less powerful, less shocking than the obscenities. In the mid-twentieth century, we started to see a change in this schema, however, as sexual obscenities themselves started to lose power to a new class of obscene words—the racial slurs.

Epilogue

In the thousands of years we've surveyed, we've seen people use many different swearwords to express the same things—aggression, insult, one-upmanship, and denigration, certainly, but also love and friendship, and the surprisingness or awesomeness of our experiences. Swearwords were and are perhaps the best words we have with which to communicate extremes of emotion, both negative and positive.

Over the centuries, these words have drawn strength from two main areas of taboo—religion and the human body, the Holy and the Shit. In ancient Rome, the Shit was in ascendance. Latin obscenity was not the same as contemporary English obscenity, though, given that Rome had a very different sexual schema, and that for Romans some kinds of obscenity themselves had a religious function. In the Bible, the Holy replaced the Shit, and oaths gained power—sincere oaths because they called on God as a witness, and vain oaths because they could injure him in various ways. Oaths remained the most shocking, most highly charged language in the Middle Ages, as taboos on touching God's body and impugning God's honor were stronger than those on revealing or mentioning parts of the human body. In the Renaissance, this began to change. Because of the rise of Protestantism and other factors we've discussed, the balance slowly began to shift away from the Holy and back to the Shit. By the mid-nineteenth century, we were firmly mired in the Shit—obscene words had become the most shocking, the worst words in the English language. This was the height of the civilizing process, the maximum extent of the shame threshold, with obscene body parts and words taboo as never before or since. It was at the end of the nineteenth century that obscene words finally started to be thought of as and called "swearing," though they had been fulfilling this function for many years before then. Most recently, the twentieth century witnessed the beginning of sexual obscenity's decline and the rise of a new kind of obscenity, racial epithets, which are now some of the most taboo words in the English language.

Just as there has always been swearing, there have always been attempts to stop or control it. Roman obscenity was supposed to be limited to particular genres of texts, or particular occasions—the religious rites of Priapus, or triumphal ceremonies, for example. Yahweh wanted his people to swear by him and by nobody else. Medieval authors of pastoral texts tried to convince, then command, people not to take God's name in vain. The English Parliament issued laws against oaths onstage and in everyday life during the seventeenth century; prosecutions for obscenity began during the eighteenth century. In the nineteenth century, euphemisms grew in popularity as obscene words were stigmatized and avoided as vulgar and low-class. The twentieth century saw the regulation of fighting words and more obscenity prosecutions, which, ironically, helped pave the way for the public use of obscene words that they were intended to curtail.

Some people have set their sights even higher—not on the control of swearing but on its elimination altogether. In 1973, Yugoslav philologist Olga Penavin predicted that swearing would simply go extinct with the spread of socialism. In a socialist utopia, there would be no conflict, and thus no need for swearwords, she reasoned. This didn't work out, obviously—Russian obscenities constitute almost an entire language of their own, called *mat*, and Serbians, Slovenes, Croats, Bosnians, and Macedonians can all understand *jebem ti mater* ("I fuck your mother"), though they theoretically speak different languages. In the 1950s and early 1960s, comedian Lenny Bruce had reversed Penavin's causation, promoting the idea that getting rid of swearing would end sexual repression, racism, and violence. Many of his routines were intended to make audience members aware of what he saw as the Puritanism that prevented them from enjoying sexuality without guilt. In a bit called "To Is a Preposition, Come Is a Verb," he tried to get people to think about why it is taboo in polite society to discuss topics that are ultimately pleasurable, while racism, violence, and intolerance—the "true obscenities," according to Bruce—can be discussed and often even indulged in without repercussions.

One of Bruce's most famous routines tried to strip racial slurs of their power to wound. During "Are There Any Niggers Here Tonight?" Bruce looked out into the audience and pretended to count the people who belonged to stigmatized groups: "That's two kikes and three niggers, and one spic. One spic, two, three spics. One mick, one mick, one spic, one hick thick funky spunky boogie." Bruce's repetition of these slurs almost turns them into rhyming nonsense words, and for a brief time they lose their charge, their ability to stigmatize and degrade.

Is this a good thing? Should we all in our own small ways be working toward Bruce's goal? Fuck, no. Eradicating the words with which we express hatred will not get rid of the emotion itself, producing some conflict-free, if not socialist, utopia. A world without swearing would not be a world without aggression, hate, or conflict, but a world bereft of a key means of defusing these emotions, of working them out. Swearing is an important safety valve, allowing people to express negative emotions without resorting to physical violence. This doesn't always work, of course, or the legal category of "fighting words" would not exist. But swearwords are the closest thing we have to violence without actual physical contact—they are cathartic, relieving pent-up emotions in ways that other words cannot. Take away swearwords, and we are left with fists and guns.

We may not have much say in the matter, however. It could be that the current efflorescence of swearing is in fact well on its way to accomplishing at least some of what Lenny Bruce wanted. All the swearing parrots of the Internet are pretty effectively sapping the charge from some of our worst obscenities. The more often we hear or use *fuck*, the less power it has to shock and offend. For ancient Romans, the highly charged taboo status of the sexual organs was encoded in their language—the genitalia were *veretrum* (parts of awe) or *verecundum* (parts of shame). In today's American slang, the genitalia are devalued as *junk*. We have already seen one group of swearwords—the religious oaths—lose most of their charge, beginning in the Renaissance, but as their power declined, the sexual obscenities were there to take up the slack. Now, as our sexual and excremental obscenities are becoming less taboo, where will we find new ones? What will the swearwords of the future be?

Our sexual and excremental terms may one day be considered as mild as religious oaths are today, but it seems safe to say that epithets will remain strong obscenities. It is becoming more and more taboo to essentialize anyone or anything in a single word as epithets do, whether that word sums up a person by race, mental acuity (*retard*), physical disability (*cripple*), or size (*fat*). Epithets are more limited than our most popular obscene verbs, however, lacking the grammatical flexibility of the *f*-word and, to some extent, *shit*. Our most highly charged epithets are so far quite closely tied to their referential meanings as well. *Nigger* almost always refers to a black or African American person, or is used of a person of a different race who is supposed to possess "black" characteristics. Most of our obscene words, in contrast, as we've seen, can be used nonliterally. It is possible that as epithets become stronger obscenities, they will likewise begin to lose their referential function. Perhaps one day *nigger* and *paki*, like *fuck*, will be able simply to express strong emotion, negative or positive, without calling to mind their denotative meanings. One day, perhaps, they may even be plugged into the *damn you* formula that gave us *fuck you*, producing the even less comprehensible *nigger you*. For hundreds of years, though, English had swearing that did not need the grammatical flexibility of verbs. Perhaps, then, epithets could be used as were oaths such as *by God's bones*. In the twenty-second century maybe we'll be swearing by the retard's toes.

Or perhaps we will find an entirely different zone of taboo that will give us a whole new set of verbs with which to swear. As we live longer, healthier lives, as more and more fifty-year-olds strive to look and act as if they are twenty-five, as the end of life comes to seem less a natural process and more a grave, possibly avoidable injustice, death itself may become obscene. Many societies have long had compli-cated sets of rules for handling dead bodies, speaking the names of the deceased, what can and cannot be done during mourning, and so on, but to generalize very broadly, these are often "traditional" cul-tures in which death is wept for but accepted as natural and inevi-table. In contemporary American and British culture, our taboos around dying are by and large weak, limited to a preference for euphemisms when referring to death—it is more polite to say "pass away" than "die"—and a general uncomfortableness around people whom it has touched. These taboos could become stronger the more we fool ourselves that we can "conquer" death by curing cancer, stop-ping our telomeres from breaking off, or popping fish oil capsules and eating less than twelve hundred calories a day. Dying and corpses, then, could become a source of new obscene words—"Fuck off and die," for example, would become simply "Die!"

This line of thinking ignores the fact that in America, and to some extent in Britain, a large number of people have found their way back to the Holy. Evangelical Christians, Mormons, and Ortho-dox Jews all try to keep "chaste" tongues by avoiding obscene language, but perhaps try even harder not to take the Lord's name in vain. As a member of an evangelical group at Oxford University put it: "It's offensive to God, basically, to take His name in vain. . . . I find that kind of swearing more offensive, probably, than the 'F-word' or whatever." (Members of this group, conscience-barred from using either oaths or obscene language, expressed insult and frustration with the word *pants*.) Perhaps as our sexual taboos weaken, the balance will return to the Holy for more of us, and our most highly charged words will again become those that injure God or tarnish his honor. In many Catholic countries, where the

Protestant Reformation never caught hold, oaths still are among the strongest swearwords. The most famous example is Québec, where religious oaths, called *sacres*, are more shocking than obscenities. These are derived from aspects of the Catholic Mass—*ostie* (the Host), *tabarnak* (the tabernacle, where the Host is stored on the altar), *câlice* (chalice), and *ciboire* (the ciborium, the container in which the Host is stored, in the tabernacle). They can be combined, too, to increase their charge, as in *ostie de tabarnak*. *Hostia* (the Host, again) is one of the most highly charged words in the Spanish language, as is, perhaps more obviously, a phrase such as *me cago en el copón bendito* ("I shit on the blessed chalice"), while *porco Dio* (God [is a] pig), and *porca Madonna* (the Madonna [is a] pig) are considered quite offensive in Italian. It could be that future English-language swearers will return to using such religious oaths, due to the increasing influence of evangelical and other religious groups in America.

So the next time someone calls you a ———— for taking too long at the ATM machine, stop, reflect, and be grateful. When someone swears to God that he or she will ———— your ———— ————, run away, maybe, but be a little bit happy too. Appreciate that our language has so many such useful words that can be employed in such a wide variety of ways. And if by chance you are moved to return an answer, decide which terms in obscenity's or oaths' rich store will best suit your purpose, then swear away, in the full knowledge of the beautiful history and importance of these words.

Postscript

As we've seen, swearing changes over time, albeit slowly. *Holy Sh*t* was first published three years ago, hardly enough time for new taboos to replace old ones, or for new swearwords to take hold. Since then, however, we have learned a few things.

Computational linguists and social scientists have been making increasing use of "big data" to understand swearing. Social media platforms such as Twitter provide large *corpora* (collections of words chosen as representative samples) which can be analyzed to reveal trends in language use. Linguists have been using corpora for decades, but they were often small, gathered laboriously from recordings of speech, legal records, literary works, and personal letters. In 1969, the *American Heritage Dictionary* was assembled using a corpus of just over 1,000,000 words, the first dictionary to be based on such a data set. In 2015, Jack Grieve, a computational linguist, used a set of 8.9 *billion* words to analyze language on Twitter. It is a testament to the power and usefulness of swearing (or perhaps to the relative youth of Twitter-users) that 1.15% of all words on Twitter are swearwords, almost twice the number in everyday speech. Even when you have only 140 characters with which to express yourself, swearwords are useful *af* ("as fuck").

Grieve looked at regional differences in patterns of swearing in the United States. The term *fuckboy* (a derogatory word with a wide range of meanings, from "asshole," to "wimp," to "guy who is only interested in women for sex") is almost exclusively a product of the East and the West coasts. In the South and Midwest, people tend to favor milder words, such as *crap, damn,* and *hell,* while Northerners prefer *asshole* and *cunt.* A group made of Mainers and people in parts of Montana and the Dakotas carry a torch for *bastard*. Texans and Mainers use *motherfucker* more than other Americans, but everybody likes to say *fuck*, although people in the middle, from Idaho to Kentucky, less so. Other academics have used similar collections of Twitter data to examine gender differences in British swearing (British men's favorite swearwords to tweet are *cunt*, *tit*, and *fuck*; British women prefer *bitch*, *bloody*, and *hell*. It's a draw with *ass*, *piss*, and *bugger*).

Language on social media does not necessarily represent the language of the broader population—people who use Twitter, for example, are mostly college educated and under 50. And the style and norms of discourse on social media are not the same as those for speech or other kinds of communication. Studying a corpus of billions of tweets or Facebook posts tells us mostly about language on Twitter and on Facebook. Nevertheless, easy access to large quantities of data is proving extremely useful for those interested in finding out more about how we swear today.

Other linguists have been busy studying taboo words themselves, and have found further confirmation that the *n*-word is, more and more, being used nonliterally. Taylor Jones and Christopher Hall argue that in some African-American speech communities, *nigga* (but not *nigger*) has undergone a process of "semantic bleaching," in which it has lost its original meaning and "is no longer marked for race or ethnicity." (This is a standard linguistic term, not a joke in very bad taste.) In these communities one might say, for example: "There's this *White/Asian/Black/African* nigga in my class, who...." *Nigga* is no longer even always reserved for humans—in their research (based partly on Twitter and Facebook posts), Jones and Hall found examples of sentences like: "My cat fell in the toilet; damn that nigga dumb" and "A wasp just stung me on some drive-by type shit, nigga just stung me and bounced."

This sort of nonliteral use is also gaining prevalence among young people of other races, even while the word retains its enormous capacity to shock and offend. In many cases, the word can be employed without incident—in high schools around the United States, "Nigga, please!" is a common and unremarkable response to something said by a student of any race. Every once in a while, though, the racial tensions inherent in the word break through the semantic bleaching that is beginning to allow it to be used this way. In 2014, a multiracial group of seniors hung a sheet from the roof of their Georgia high school to celebrate their graduation—"Nigga we made it," it announced. A national bout of soul-searching followed, with people on Twitter, on television, and in newspapers condemning the prank as a blatant act of racism in a county in Georgia where the population is only around 3% black and where interracial protesters holding a "march for brotherhood" in 1987 were greeted by the Ku Klux Klan with cries of "Nigger, go home!" Although nonliteral use of the *n*-word, particularly in its *-a* (as opposed to *-er*) form, is continuing to expand, the word is still far from possessing the linguistic flexibility of *fuck* or even *cunt*.

Perhaps surprisingly, the past three years have also turned up new evidence about the history of swearing. In 2015, retired British historian Paul Booth was reading through the archives of the Chester County Court, as one does when one is a retired historian, when he came across three references to a man who had been summoned to attend the court and who had finally been outlawed for unspecified crimes in 1310—Roger Fuckebythenavel (also spelled Fuckebythenavele and Fukkebythenavele). This is a potential first use of the word *fuck* in its sexual sense, 150 years or so earlier than previous accepted first uses.

The discovery is causing scholars to reevaluate other early traces of the *f*-word. There are scattered examples of *fuck* from the 13th to the 15th centuries, though linguists and historians have generally explained them away. Court rolls from 1278, for example, record a man called John le Fucker, imprisoned for a double murder. "Le Fucker" is usually thought to be a misspelling or variant of "le Fulcher"—"the solider"—a more common 13th-century surname. One of Edward I's servants bore the name "Fuckebegger"—a Henry of that name is listed in the royal pay rolls of 1286 as one of the king's palfreymen (charged with caring for the king's *palfreys*, or riding horses). This example, however, is most often thought to be an instance of *fuck* meaning "hit" or "strike"—related words such as the German *ficken* seem to have indicated a rubbing or striking motion. Henry's name, then, referred to bashing beggars, not sleeping with them.

There is also a Simon Fukkebotere (Fuckbutter) from around 1290, but his name is taken to refer to the thumping involved in churning butter and so is seen as another use of *fuck* to mean "hit." William Smalfuk (Smallfuck), also from around 1290, was not little or quick in any sexual sense, but had a small sail—a *fuk* is a type of sail, first cited in 1465. Finally, there is a place name whose potential sexual sense is more difficult to deny. Records from 1373 show a copse of woods near Bristol with the evocative name, "Fockynggroue." (By 1634 this had been transformed into "Pucking Grove.") But this too could, if pressed, be taken to refer to some sort of open air boxing ring as well as a place people went to find a bit of privacy.

In each of these cases, it is difficult to know for sure what "fuck" means. Even Roger Fuckbythenavel could have been named for some sexual proclivity or youthful error, or for the habit of walloping people in the stomach. The degree of confusion shows how intimately sex and violence were connected in the Middle Ages and indeed in the popular imagination today. At some point, the argument goes, the original proto-Indo-European word for hitting or rubbing began by analogy to refer to sex. The question is, When did this transition occur in English?

After 1475, there are many recorded uses of *fuck* in English, all of them with a clearly sexual meaning. There seem to be no instances, in contrast, where it unambiguously means anything else. We have only these early names, which come to us shorn of context, providing no clues to guide our interpretation. It is even quite possible that the modern view—that before the mid-fifteenth century, the *f*-word referred to physical violence—is a result of scholarly prejudice. As Allen Walker Read, great collector of American bathroom graffiti, put it, one "can't imagine people seriously giving *this* activity prominence, or any man seriously accepting the name." But given that medieval records are full of "obscene" surnames, nicknames, and place names—the Widecunts, the Clevecunts; the Modipintels ("arrogant cocks") and the Shitwellways—is it so unlikely that there were also some real Fuckers?

NOTES

Introduction

3 *except for one phrase:* S. Dieguez and J. Bogousslavsky, "Baudelaire's Aphasia: From Poetry to Cursing," *Neurological Disorders in Famous Artists*, ed. J. Bogousslavsky and M. G. Hennerici (New York: Karger, 2007), 2:135.

6 *one that "kidnaps our attention":* Steven Pinker, *The Stuff of Thought: Language as a Window into Human Nature* (New York: Viking, 2007), 339.

"You are all a bunch": Timothy Jay, *Cursing in America: A Psycholinguistic Study of Dirty Language in the Courts, in the Movies, in the Schoolyards and on the Streets* (Philadelphia: John Benjamins, 1992), 11.

7 *The Court agreed: Federal Communications Commission v. Fox Television Stations,* 556 U.S. 502; 129 S. Ct. 1800; 173 L. Ed. 2d 738 (2009). In 2012, the Court looked at another aspect of this case, telling the FCC that it is probably fine to regulate fleeting expletives but that it should go back and review its indecency policy. The Court has not reexamined whether it is constitutional to regulate broadcast indecency.

Some language experts have criticized: Jess Bravin and Amy Schatz, "Don't Read His Lips—You Might Be Offended," WSJ.com, November 4, 2008, criticizing the FCC's argument about expletives; Timothy Jay, "Do Offensive Words Harm People?" *Psychology, Public Policy, and Law* 15, no. 2 (2009): 81–101; 92; Adam Freedman, "Gentleman Cows in Prime Time," *New York Times*, May 3, 2009.

8 *The patient with the first reported case:* William Osler, "On the Form of Convulsive Tic Associated with Coprolalia, Etc.," *Medical News* LVII, no. 25 (December 20, 1890): 646; Hélio A. G. Teive et al., "Historical Aphasia Cases: 'Tan-tan,' 'Vot-vot,' and 'Cré Nom!'" *Arquivos de Neuro-Psiquiatria* 69, no. 3 (June 2011): 555–58.

"thy drasty rhyming is not": Geoffrey Chaucer, "The Tale of Sir Thopas," *The Riverside Chaucer*, ed. Larry Benson, 3rd ed. (Boston: Houghton Mifflin, 1987), 2119–20. All later Chaucer quotes are from this edition.

9 *referring to "terms of racial or ethnic opprobrium":* quoted in Geoffrey Hughes, *An Encyclopedia of Swearing: The Social History of Oaths, Profanity, Foul Language and Ethnic Slurs in the English-Speaking World* (Armonk, NY: M. E. Sharpe, 2006), 222.

10 *"To hear* nigger *is to try on":* Pinker, *Stuff of Thought,* 369.

it helps create a sense: Randall Kennedy, *Nigger: The Strange Career of a Troublesome Word* (New York: Vintage, 2003), 27–30.

"you 'take exception to the profanities'": quoted in "Profanity," *OED* online.

"Expletives he very early ejected": Samuel Johnson, "The Lives of the English Poets: Pope," *Works* (London: J. Nichols and Son, 1810), XI:195.

12 *"swearing really takes off":* Allie Townsend, "Study: Kids Swearing Earlier than Ever," *Time* NewsFeed, September 22, 2010, http://newsfeed.time.com/2010/09/22/study-kids-swearing-earlier-than-ever, accessed August 1, 2012.

13 *"What! my dears! then you have been looking for them?":* Henry Digby Beste, *Personal and Literary Memorials* (London: Henry Colburn, 1829).

twenty-four things wrong with swearing: James O'Connor, "What's Wrong with Swearing," CussControl.com, accessed August 1, 2012.

15 *the worrying trend of increased swearing:* "Swearing Teen Fiction Characters Have It All," *Times of India* (online), June 27, 2012.

"This Culture of Swearing": Sue MacGregor, "This Culture of Swearing Curses Us All," *Mail Online*, June 14, 2006, dailymail.co.uk.

"the growing frequency": Lee Siegel, "What the Internet Unleashes," in "Why Do Educated People Use Bad Words?" *Room for Debate* (blog), *New York Times*, April 12, 2010.

Some studies have shown that: Timothy Jay, "The Utility and Ubiquity of Taboo Words," *Perspectives on Psychological Science* 4, no. 2 (2009): 153–61.

Chapter 1

16 *"There's a horrible boor"*: Martial, *Epigrams*, ed. and trans. D. R. Shackleton Bailey, Loeb Classical Library 480, 3 vols. (Cambridge, MA: Harvard University Press, 1993), 3.82. Most translations of Martial in this chapter are from the Loeb edition, as is the Latin. This loose translation is mine, however.

17 *fascini*: J. N. Adams, *The Latin Sexual Vocabulary* (Baltimore: Johns Hopkins University Press, 1982), 63; David M. Friedman, *A Mind of Its Own: A Cultural History of the Penis* (New York: Free Press, 2001), 25.

   the "Big Six": This list of the "Big Six" comes from Ruth Wajnryb's *Expletive Deleted: A Good Look at Bad Language* (New York: Free Press, 2005), 55. Geoffrey Hughes's *Swearing: A Social History of Foul Language, Oaths and Profanity in English* (Oxford: Blackwell, 1991) has a slightly different list: *shit, piss, fart, fuck, cock*, and *cunt* (20).

   Its etymology is unknown: Alastair Minnis, "From *Coilles* to *Bel Chose*: Discourses of Obscenity in Jean de Meun and Chaucer," in *Medieval Obscenities*, ed. Nicola McDonald (Woodbridge, Suffolk: York Medieval Press, 2006), 156; Jan M. Ziolkowski, "Obscenity in the Latin Grammatical and Rhetorical Tradition," in *Obscenity: Social Control and Artistic Creation in the European Middle Ages*, ed. Jan M. Ziolkowski (Leiden: Brill, 1998), 44.

18 Cassell's Latin Dictionary *defines*: *Cassell's Latin Dictionary*, ed. D. P. Simpson (New York: Macmillan, 1968).

   obscene words are dirty: Jeffery Henderson, *The Maculate Muse: Obscene Language in Attic Comedy* (New York: Oxford University Press, 1991), 3.

19 *The Romans, on the other hand, strove*: The other image we have of the Romans is that of sex-mad degenerates who bay for blood at gladiatorial contests, which maybe doesn't sound so unfamiliar either.

   The Old English cwithe: Wajnryb, *Expletive Deleted*, 67; John Ayto, *Word Origins*, 2nd ed. (London: A. & C. Black, 2005).

   just as it gave con *to French*: Adolf Zauner, *Die romanischen Namen der Körperteile* (Erlangen: Junge & Sohn, 1902), 186.

   But the British were different: Nicholas Ostler, *Ad Infinitum: A Biography of Latin* (New York: Walker, 2007), 138–43.

20 *Gropecuntelane*: "Cunt," *OED* online, June 2012.

   Some proper names: Russell Ash, *Morecock, Fartwell & Hoare: A Collection of Unfortunate but True Names* (New York: St. Martin's Press, 2007),

100; Geoffrey Hughes, *An Encyclopedia of Swearing: The Social History of Oaths, Profanity, Foul Language and Ethnic Slurs in the English-Speaking World* (New York: M. E. Sharpe, 2006), 110.

20 *"Corus licks"*: Antonio Varone, *Erotica Pompeiana: Love Inscriptions on the Walls of Pompeii*, trans. Ria P. Berg (Rome: L'Erma di Bretschneider, 2002), 80.

"Jucundus licks": Ibid., 80.

"It is much better": Ibid., 60.

21 *might even employ a* picatrix: John Younger, *Sex in the Ancient World from A to Z* (New York: Routledge, 2005), 75.

"Why do you pluck": Martial, *Epigrams*, 10.90.

"Here I bugger": *Corpus Inscriptiones Latinarum* IV 3932; Varone, *Erotica Pompeiana*, 134–35.

22 *Rome had lots of nouns*: Adams, *Latin Sexual Vocabulary*, 231–39.

It was shit: I have translated *merda* as "shit" here, instead of using the Loeb "filth," as it seems better able to convey the slight shock Martial seems to be going for in using *merda* to end the epigram. *Epigrams*, 3.17.

23 *The houses of the wealthy might have private privies*: Richard Neudecker, *Der Pracht der Latrine: zum Wandel öffentlicher Bedürfnisanstalten in der kaiserzeitlichen Stadt* (Munich: Verlag Dr. Friedrich Pfeil, 1994); Ann Olga Koloski-Ostrow, "Finding Social Meaning in the Public Latrines of Pompeii," *Cura Aquarum*, ed. Nathalie de Haan and Gemma C. M. Jansen (Leiden: Stichting Babesch, 1996), 79–86; Alex Scobie, "Slums, Sanitation, and Mortality in the Roman World," *Klio* 68 (1986): 399–433.

24 *People called fullers*: Miko Flohr, *"Fullones* and Roman Society: A Reconsideration," *Journal of Roman Archaeology* 16 (2003): 447–50.

The basic Latin terms for urination: Adams, *Latin Sexual Vocabulary*, 245–49.

25 *Hic ego puellas multas futui*: Craig A. Williams, *Roman Homosexuality*, 2nd ed. (New York: Oxford University Press, 2010), 296–97.

Hic ego cum veni futui: Ibid., 28; Judith Harris, *Pompeii Awakened: A Story of Rediscovery* (London: I. B. Tauris, 2007), 122–23.

"Fortunatus, you sweet soul": Varone, *Erotica Pompeiana*, 68. (The English translation given for *perfututor* is "mega-fucker.")

"Because Antony fucks Glaphyra": Augustus's epigram appears in one of Martial's, 11.20.

26   *the penis is a weapon:* Adams, *Latin Sexual Vocabulary,* 19–22.

     sex is depicted as brutal: Ibid., 145–50.

     The opposing sides lobbed sling bullets: Judith P. Hallett, "*Perusinae Glandes* and the Changing Image of Augustus," *American Journal of Ancient History* 2 (1977): 151–71.

     Fututa sum hic: Harris, *Pompeii Awakened,* 122.

27   Lesbian *comes from the Greek:* Kenneth Dover, *Greek Homosexuality* (Cambridge, MA: Harvard University Press, 1989), 182–84.

     tribade *was still the ordinary word:* Charlotte Brewer, *Treasure-House of the Language: The Living OED* (New Haven: Yale University Press, 2007), 205.

     So I confess I thought: Martial, *Epigrams,* 1.90.

28   *Eupla laxa landicosa:* Adams, *Latin Sexual Vocabulary,* 96; Diana M. Swancutt, "*Still* Before Sexuality: 'Greek' Androgyny, the Roman Imperial Politics of Masculinity and the Roman Invention of the *Tribas,*" in *Mapping Gender in Ancient Religious Discourses,* ed. Todd Penner and Caroline Vander Stichele (Leiden: Brill, 2007), 30; Werner Krenkel, "Tribaden," *Wissenschaftliche Zeitschrift der Wilhelm-Pieck-Universität Rostock* 38 (1989): 49–58.

     most likely a misrepresentation: Scholars who have addressed Roman ideas of the *tribas* and whether they have any basis in reality include Judith P. Hallett, "Female Homoeroticism and the Denial of Roman Reality in Latin Literature," in *Roman Sexualities,* ed. Marilyn Skinner and Judith P. Hallett (Princeton: Princeton University Press, 1997), 255–73; Pamela Gordon, "The Lover's Voice in *Heroides* 15: Or, Why is Sappho a Man?" in *Roman Sexualities,* ed. Marilyn Skinner and Judith P. Hallett (Princeton: Princeton University Press, 1997), 274–91; Marilyn B. Skinner, *Sexuality in Greek and Roman Culture* (Oxford: Blackwell, 2005), 252–53; Bernadette J. Brooten, *Love Between Women: Early Christian Responses to Female Homoeroticism* (Chicago: University of Chicago Press, 1996).

     They thought that both the male and female partners: Fouad R. Kandeel and Jeannette Hacker, "Male Reproduction: Evolving Concepts of Procreation and Infertility Through the Ages," in *Male Reproductive Dysfunction: Pathophysiology and Treatment,* ed. Fouad R. Kandeel (New York: Informa Healthcare USA, 2007), 4; David M. Halperin, "Why Is Diotima a Woman? Platonic *Eros* and the Figuration of Gender," in *Before Sexuality: The Construction of Erotic Experience in the Ancient Greek World,* ed. David M. Halperin et al. (Princeton: Princeton University Press, 1990), 278–79.

28 *They were plenty misinformed about sex:* Ann Carson, "Dirt and Desire: The Phenomenology of Female Pollution in Antiquity," *Constructions of the Classical Body,* ed. James I. Porter (Ann Arbor: University of Michigan Press, 2002), 78–87; Adrian Thatcher, *God, Sex, and Gender: An Introduction* (Oxford: Wiley-Blackwell, 2011), 8–11, 29–31.

30 *Vir carried with it a set of cultural expectations:* Holt N. Parker, "The Teratogenic Grid," in *Roman Sexualities,* ed. Marilyn Skinner and Judith P. Hallett (Princeton: Princeton University Press, 1997), 47–65; Craig Williams, *Roman Homosexuality;* Jonathan Walters, "Invading the Body: Manliness and Impenetrability in Roman Thought," in *Roman Sexualities,* ed. Marilyn Skinner and Judith P. Hallett (Princeton: Princeton University Press, 1997), 29–46.

"Catching me with a boy": Martial, *Epigrams,* 11.43.

31 *irrumare:* Werner A. Krenkel, "Fellatio and Irrumatio," *Wissenschaftliche Zeitschrift der Wilhelm-Pieck-Universität Rostock* 29 (1980): 77–88; Amy Richlin, "The Meaning of *Irrumare* in Catullus and Martial," *Classical Philology* 76 (1981): 40–46.

Bene caca: John R. Clarke, *Art in the Lives of Ordinary Romans: Visual Representation and Non-Elite Viewers in Italy, 100 B.C.–A.D. 315* (Berkeley: University of California Press, 2003), 172.

32 *beginning one poem,* Pedicabo ego vos: Catullus, *Catullus, Tibullus, and Pervigilium Veneris,* trans. Francis Warre Cornish, Loeb Classical Library 6, rev. ed. (Cambridge, MA: Harvard University Press, 1988), 16.

33 *"Suillius, cross-examine your sons":* Williams, *Roman Homosexuality,* 180.

Integral to this priapic model: Amy Richlin, *The Garden of Priapus: Sexuality and Aggression in Roman Humor,* 2nd ed. (Oxford: Oxford University Press, 1992), 57; Williams, *Roman Homosexuality,* 169.

Many epigrams from the Priapea: *The Priapus Poems: Erotic Epigrams from Ancient Rome,* trans. Richard W. Hooper (Urbana: University of Illinois Press, 1999); Williams, *Roman Homosexuality,* 18–19.

Virgil . . . was more inclined to boys: Williams, *Roman Homosexuality,* 89; Suetonius, *The Lives of the Caesars* and *The Lives of Illustrious Men,* ed. J. C. Rolfe, vol. II, Loeb Classical Library 38 (Cambridge MA: Harvard University Press, 1970), Verg. 9.

34 *"I hate those embraces":* Ovid, *The Love Books of Ovid,* trans. J. Lewis May (London: J. Lane, 1925), 150.

34 *The emperor Claudius was:* Suetonius, *Lives of the Caesars*, Claud. 33.2.

Not everyone, however, was fair game: Julia Haig Gaisser, *Catullus* (Oxford: Wiley-Blackwell, 2009), 12–13; Williams, *Roman Homosexuality*, 17–19, 103–9.

25 to 40 percent of people were slaves: Different scholars occasionally give vastly different estimates of the number of slaves, but most estimates range from 25 to 40 percent of the population, as in Keith Hopkins, *Conquerors and Slaves* (Cambridge: Cambridge University Press, 1978), 99–132; Peter Lampe, *Christians at Rome in the First Two Centuries: From Paul to Valentinus* (London: Continuum, 2003), 172–73; Mary T. Boatwright, *Peoples of the Roman World* (Cambridge: Cambridge University Press, 2012), 22, 25; Arthur A. Ruprecht, "Slave, Slavery," in *Dictionary of Paul and His Letters*, ed. Gerald Hawthorne et al. (Downer's Grove, IL: InterVarsity, 1993), 881–83.

special clothing, the toga praetexta: Judith Lynn Sebesta, "Symbolism in the Costume of the Roman Woman," in *The World of Roman Costume*, ed. Judith Lynn Sebesta and Larissa Bonfante (Madison: University of Wisconsin Press, 2001), 46–53.

35 *necklace called a* bulla: Ann M. Stout, "Jewelry as a Symbol of Status in the Roman Empire," in *The World of Roman Costume*, ed. Judith Lynn Sebesta and Larissa Bonfante (Madison: University of Wisconsin Press, 2001), 77; Oskar Seyffert, *A Dictionary of Classical Antiquities*, trans. Henry Nettleship and J. E. Sandys (New York: Macmillan, 1901), 234.

This is in direct contrast to the Greeks: Williams Armstrong Percy, *Pederasty and Pedagogy in Archaic Greece* (Urbana: University of Illinois Press, 1996); Eva C. Keuls, *The Reign of the Phallus: Sexual Politics in Ancient Athens*, 2nd ed. (Berkeley: University of California Press, 1993), 274–99.

36 *As with stereotypes:* Williams, *Roman Homosexuality*, 191–208; Amy Richlin, "Not Before Homosexuality: The Materiality of the *Cinaedus* and the Roman Law Against Love Between Men," *Journal of the History of Sexuality* 3 (1993): 523–73; Rabun Taylor, "Two Pathic Subcultures in Ancient Rome," *Journal of the History of Sexuality* 7 (1997): 319–71.

"a man who daily is adorned": Gellius, *Noct. Att.* 6.12.5, quoted in Richlin, *Garden of Priapus*, 93.

The most surefire way to identify: Juvenal, "Satura IX," The Latin Library (online), accessed October 23, 2012: 133; Williams, *Roman Homosexuality*, 199; Younger, *Sex in the Ancient World*, 44; Catherine Edwards,

The Politics of Immorality in Ancient Rome (Cambridge: Cambridge University Press, 1993), 63–64; Carlin A. Barton, *The Sorrows of the Ancient Romans: The Gladiator and the Monster* (Princeton: Princeton University Press, 1993), 139.

37 *The* cinaedus *or* catamitus *is not gay:* Parker, "The Teratogenic Grid," 51–52; Williams, *Roman Homosexuality*, 218–30.

The worst insult you could throw at a Roman: Parker, "The Teratogenic Grid," 51–52; Swancutt, "*Still* Before Sexuality," 40–41.

the "most sacred part of the body": Cicero of Gabinius, quoted in Williams, *Roman Homosexuality*, 219.

"Zoilus, why are you": Martial, *Epigrams*, 2.42.

38 *"You sleep with well-endowed boys":* Martial, *Epigrams*, 3.73.

"They are twin brothers": Martial, *Epigrams*, 3.88.

What is the flip side of cunnilingus? Parker, "The Teratogenic Grid," 51–52.

41 *Even the Forum of Augustus:* Barbara Kellum, "The Phallus as Signifier: The Forum of Augustus and Rituals of Masculinity," in *Sexuality in Ancient Art*, ed. Natalie Boymel Kampen and Bettina Bergmann (Cambridge: Cambridge University Press, 1996), 170–83.

According to Freud: Sigmund Freud, *Totem and Taboo*, trans. A. A. Brill (New York: Moffat, Yard, 1918), 30.

42 *things that would taint a religious rite:* Richlin, *The Garden of Priapus*, 9; Celia Schultz, "Juno Sospita and Roman Insecurity in the Social War," in *Religion in Republican Italy*, ed. Celia E. Schultz and Paul B. Harvey (Cambridge: Cambridge University Press, 2006), 207–9; Otto Kiefer, *Sexual Life in Ancient Rome* (London: Constable, 1994), 113.

There was also the mysterious Mutunus Tutunus: Kiefer, *Sexual Life in Ancient Rome*, 109; Karen K. Hersch, *The Roman Wedding: Ritual and Meaning in Antiquity* (Cambridge: Cambridge University Press, 2010), 269–72.

Wedding guests would sing fescennine songs: Hersch, *The Roman Wedding*, 151–57.

an epithalamium . . . by Catullus: Catullus, *Poems 61–68*, ed. and trans. John Godwin (Warminster: Aris & Phillips, 1995), 24–39.

the ludi florales: Richlin, *The Garden of Priapus*, 10; Clarke, *Art in the Lives of Ordinary Romans*, 134–35.

43   *Obscene words were thought to be magical:* Henderson, *The Maculate Muse,* 13–14; William Fitzgerald, *Catullan Provocations: Lyric Poetry and the Drama of Position* (Berkeley: University of California Press, 1999), 61–64.

   Victorious generals were serenaded: Barton, *Sorrows of the Ancient Romans,* 142–43; Adams, *Latin Sexual Vocabulary,* 4.

   When Julius Caesar returned to Rome: Suetonius, *Lives,* vol. I, Caes. 49.

   Some verses were even more specific: Fitzgerald, *Catullan Provocations,* 62.

44   *does the government still have "good reason":* Adam Liptak, "TV Decency Is a Puzzler for Judges," *New York Times,* January 10, 2012.

   As Lenny Bruce supposedly noted: These lines are from the Dustin Hoffman movie about Bruce, *Lenny,* quoted in Pinker, *Stuff of Thought,* 346.

   Roman curses were much more elaborate: The best introduction is John Gager, *Curse Tablets and Binding Spells from the Ancient World* (Oxford: Oxford University Press, 1992).

   "Malchio son/slave of Nikon": Henk S. Versnel, "An Essay on Anatomical Curses," *Ansichten Griechischer Rituale,* ed. Fritz Graf (Stuttgart: B. G. Teubner, 1998), 223.

45   *Gladiators and charioteers:* Florent Heintz, "Circus Curses and Their Archaeological Contexts," *Journal of Roman Archaeology* 11 (1998): 337–42.

   On the back of Malchio's tablet: Versnel, "An Essay on Anatomical Curses," 223.

46   *the hierarchy of genres:* Adams, *Latin Sexual Vocabulary,* 2, 218–25; Michael Coffey, "The Roman Genre of Satire and Its Beginnings," *Latin Verse Satire: An Anthology and Reader,* ed. Paul Allen Miller (New York: Routledge, 2005), 327–31.

   The most taboo words: Varone, *Erotica Pompeiana;* Rex Wallace, *An Introduction to Wall Inscriptions from Pompeii and Herculaneum* (Wauconda, IL: Bolchazy-Carducci, 2005); J. A. Baird and Claire Taylor, eds., *Ancient Graffiti in Context* (New York: Routledge, 2011).

   "Oh wall, I am amazed": Wallace, *An Introduction,* xxiii.

   "The goldsmiths unanimously urge": Naphtali Lewis and Meyer Reinhold, eds., *Roman Civilization Selected Readings: The Empire* (New York: Columbia University Press, 1990), 2:237.

   "Dickhead recommends": John F. DeFelice, *Roman Hospitality: The Professional Women of Pompeii* (Warren Center, PA: Shangri-La Publications, 2001), 117.

47　*"Eulale, may you enjoy"*: Varone, *Erotica Pompeiana*, 164.

Since the surviving graffiti is so florid: For a quick summary of both the "lower classes" and the "well-educated" view, see Kristina Milnor, "Literary Literacy in Roman Pompeii: The Case of Vergil's *Aeneid*," *Ancient Literacies: The Culture of Reading in Greece and Rome*, ed. William A. Johnson and Holt N. Parker (Oxford: Oxford University Press, 2009), 291–92.

"Crescens's member is hard": Varone, *Erotica Pompeiana*, 87.

But scholars who study ancient literacy: William V. Harris, *Ancient Literacy* (Cambridge MA: Harvard University Press, 1989), 266.

Although he was a Roman citizen: For Martial's biography, see J. P. Sullivan, *Martial: The Unexpected Classic* (Cambridge: Cambridge University Press, 1991).

The patron-client relationship: Richard P. Saller, *Personal Patronage Under the Early Empire* (Cambridge: Cambridge University Press, 1982), 119–45; Richard P. Saller, "Patronage and Friendship in Early Imperial Rome: Drawing the Distinction," *Patronage in Ancient Society*, ed. Andrew Wallace-Hadrill (London: Routledge, 1989), 49–62; Michele George, "The 'Dark Side' of the Toga," *Roman Dress and the Fabrics of Roman Culture*, ed. Jonathan Edmondson and Alison Keith (Toronto: University of Toronto Press, 2008).

48　*"can't please without"*: Martial, *Epigrams*, 1.35.

"my little book": Ibid., 11.15.

"my page is wanton": Ibid., 1.4.

"a lascivious truth of words": Ibid., 1.1.

49　*"May I die, Priapus"*: Ziolkowski, "Obscenity," 43; *The Priapus Poems*, 67.

50　*"Then came Corinna"*: Christopher Marlowe, *The Complete Works*, ed. Fredson Bowers, 2nd. ed. (Cambridge: Cambridge University Press, 1981), 2:321.

The rhetorician Seneca instructs: Seneca, *Controversies* 1.2.23, quoted in Thomas K. Hubbard, *Homosexuality in Greece and Rome: A Sourcebook of Basic Documents* (Berkeley: University of California Press, 2003), 388.

Crepo, for instance, must be a polite: Adams, *Latin Sexual Vocabulary*, 249.

51　*"Dido and the Trojan leader"*: *The Essential Aeneid*, trans. Stanley Lombardo (Indianapolis: Hackett, 2006), 57.

51 *Cicero's letter about the word* mentula: Cicero, "Epistulae ad Familiares 9.22," The Latin Library (online), accessed July 23, 2012; "Letters to His Friends," trans. Evelyn Shuckburgh, The Perseus Project (online), accessed July 23, 2012.

52 *the external genital organs:* "Vulva," *Free Dictionary*, Farlex, Inc. (online), July 23, 2012.

   During its long tenure: Ostler, *Ad Infinitum*, 159–76.

   was used this way into the eighteenth century: Ibid., 292–301.

53 *"a language for male initiates":* Ibid., 193.

Chapter 2

55 *In the Bible, swearing:* The ancient Romans used oaths as well, but the swearing that has come down to us can be traced most directly back to the Bible. For more on Roman oath swearing, see "Jusjurandum" in *A Dictionary of Greek and Roman Antiquities*, ed. William Smith, William Wayte, and G. E. Marindin, vol. 1, 3rd ed. (London: John Murray, 1901).

   "Go from your country": I have generally used the New Revised Standard Version of the Bible (NRSV), most often in the New Oxford Annotated Bible version. When I use other translations, I will note them.

56 *first covenant with Abraham:* Jeff A. Benner, "The Revised Mechanical Translation of the Book of Genesis," *The Mechanical Translation of the Hebrew Bible*, Mechanical Translation Project (online), accessed August 9, 2010; Sheldon H. Blank, "The Curse, Blasphemy, the Spell and the Oath," *Hebrew Union College Annual* XXIII (1950–51): 73–95; Tony Cartledge, *Vows in the Hebrew Bible and the Ancient Near East*, Journal for the Study of the Old Testament Supplement Series 147 (Sheffield: Sheffield Academic Press, 1992); René Lopez, "Israelite Covenants in the Light of Ancient Near Eastern Covenants," part 1, *CTS Journal* 9 (2003): 92–111, and part 2, *CTS Journal* 10 (2004): 72–105; Nahum Sarna, *Understanding Genesis*, The Heritage of Biblical Israel 1 (New York: Jewish Theological Seminary of America, 1966); E. A. Speiser, *Genesis*, The Anchor Bible Commentary 1 (New York: Doubleday, 1964); John A. Wilson, "The Oath in Ancient Egypt," *Journal of Near Eastern Studies* 7, no. 3 (1948): 129–56; Yael Ziegler, *Promises to Keep: The Oath in Biblical Narrative* (Leiden: Brill, 2008).

57 *"If anyone have intercourse":* No. 199 in "The Code of the Nesilim, c. 1650–1500 BCE," *Internet Ancient History Sourcebook*, Internet History Sourcebooks Project (online), 1999, accessed August 9, 2010.

57 *what scholars call a self-curse:* Paul Sanders, "So May God Do to Me," *Biblica* 85 (2004): 91–98.

58 *"He can, and then he lifts it":* Harry G. Frankfurt, "The Logic of Omnipotence," *Philosophical Review* 73 (1964): 262–63.

This appears to be divine humor: For more about obscenity in the Bible, including prophetic scatology, see Jeremy F. Hultin, *The Ethics of Obscene Speech in Early Christianity and Its Environment*, Supplements to Novum Testamentum 128 (Leiden: Brill, 2008). For more about the covenant of circumcision, see Ralph F. Wilson, "The Covenant of Circumcision with Abraham (Genesis 17)." *Jesus Walk,* Joyful Heart Renewal Ministries (online), accessed August 9, 2010.

60 *As the Hellenistic Jewish philosopher Philo wrote:* Philo, *Questions and Answers on Genesis,* trans. Ralph Marcus, Loeb Classical Library, Philo Supplement 1 (Cambridge: Harvard University Press, 1953).

the most famous of which: For my discussion of the third commandment, the following commentaries were helpful: Waldemar Janzen, *Exodus,* Believers Church Bible Commentary (Waterloo, ON: Herald Press, 2000); Cornelis Houtman, *Exodus Vol. 1,* trans. Jonathan Rebel and Sierd Woudstra, Historical Commentary on the Old Testament (Kampen: Kok Publishing House, 1993); J. Philip Hyatt, *Commentary on Exodus,* New Century Bible (London: Oliphants, 1971); Noel D. Osborn and Howard A. Hatton, *A Handbook on Exodus,* UBS Handbook Series (New York: United Bible Societies, 1999); William H. C. Propp, ed., *Exodus 19–40: A New Translation with Introduction and Commentary,* The Anchor Bible Commentary 3 (New York: Doubleday, 2006); Douglas K. Stuart, *Exodus,* The New American Commentary 2 (Nashville: Broadman & Holman, 2006).

61 *As the catechism of the Catholic Church puts it: Catechism of the Catholic Church,* 2nd ed. (New York: Doubleday, 2003), 576.

"Telle us a fable anon": Geoffrey Chaucer, *The Riverside Chaucer,* ed. Larry D. Benson, 3rd ed. (New York: Houghton Mifflin, 1987), 287, line 29.

63 *God was one of hundreds of gods:* Two especially good books about the history of God's relationship to other ancient Near Eastern deities are Robert Wright, *The Evolution of God* (New York: Little, Brown, 2009), and Mark S. Smith, *God in Translation: Deities in Cross-Cultural Discourse in the Biblical World,* Forschungen zum Alten Testament 57 (Tübingen: Mohr Siebeck, 2008). Other texts that I consulted are: Jan Assman,

Of God and Gods: Egypt, Israel and the Rise of Monotheism (Madison: University of Wisconsin Press, 2008); Susanne Bickel, Silvia Schroer, René Schurte, and Christoph Uehlinger, eds., *Bilder als Quellen/Images as Sources: Studies on Ancient Near Eastern Artifacts and the Bible Inspired by the Work of Othmar Keel*, Orbis Biblicus et Orientalis Special Volume (Göttingen: Academic Press Fribourg, 2007); William G. Dever, *Did God Have a Wife? Archaeology and Folk Religion in Ancient Israel* (Grand Rapids, MI: William B. Eerdmans, 2005); Clyde E. Fant and Mitchell G. Reddish, *Lost Treasures of the Bible: Understanding the Bible Through Archaeological Artifacts in World Museums* (Grand Rapids, MI: William B. Eerdmans, 2008); W. Randall Garr, *In His Own Image and Likeness: Humanity, Divinity and Monotheism*, Culture and History of the Ancient Near East 15 (Boston: Brill, 2003); Roberta L. Harris, *The World of the Bible* (London: Thames and Hudson, 1995); Karel van der Toorn, ed., *The Image and the Book: Iconic Cults, Aniconism, and the Rise of Book Religion in Israel and the Ancient Near East*, Biblical Exegesis and Theology 21 (Leuven: Peeters, 1997); Greg Herrick, "Baalism in Canaanite Religion and Its Relation to Selected Old Testament Texts," Bible.org, July 24, 2004, accessed August 9, 2010.

64 *scientists used multispectral imaging:* "The Imaging of the Archimedes Palimpsest," *Archimedes: The Palimpsest Project* (online), October 29, 2008, accessed August 9, 2010.

   God goes by several different names: Mark S. Smith, *The Early History of God: Yahweh and the Other Deities in Ancient Israel*, 2nd ed, Biblical Resource Series (Grand Rapids, MI: William B. Eerdmans, 2002); Smith, *God in Translation*, in particular Chapter 3: Christopher Heard, "When Did Yahweh and El Merge?" *Higgaion*, November 6, 2006 (online), accessed August 9, 2010; "From Adonai to Yahweh: A Glossary of God's Names," *The Bible Study* (online), accessed August 9, 2010.

65 *When the Most High:* This passage is textually very difficult—there are many different versions in many different manuscripts. For more information about it, see Smith, *God in Translation*, 139.

66 *"the LORD's own portion":* As I have said above, *The New Oxford Annotated Bible* is based on the NRSV. It is interesting to note that even in this "monotheistic" reading, the verses imply that Yahweh would have given other peoples to other gods.

   The Bible contains several more instances of God appearing as just one of many gods. Yahweh participates in another divine council in Psalm

82: "God has taken his place in the divine council; in the midst of the gods he holds judgment"; or, in a more literal translation, "Elohim stands in the council of El; among the elohim he pronounces judgment." Here, *elohim* is used as both a singular noun and a plural one—it stands for the one and only Yahweh, but also for the other gods on the council. And El is named outright as the chief god of the council, more evidence that the Elyon we saw earlier probably refers to El. In another song, Moses asks, "Who is like you, O Lord, among the gods?" (Ex. 15:11).

66   *Scholars of a less determinedly monotheistic bent:* The scholars who see monotheism as developing slowly through the Bible are amply represented in these notes already, including Dever, Wright, and Smith. Catherine Keller names some scholars who argue that *elohim* refers to God and his heavenly court or to the Trinity in her "The Pluri-Singularity of Creation," in *Creation and Humanity: The Sources of Christian Theology*, ed. Ian A. McFarland (Louisville: Westminster John Knox Press, 2009). Many other scholars and amateurs who espouse these views can be found online as well; for example, James Patrick Holding, "Is the Bible Polytheistic?" Tekton Education and Apologetics Ministry (online), accessed August 9, 2010, and "Elohim = The Plural God," Believer's Web (online), May 5, 2003, accessed August 9, 2010.

68   *Vows are another important way:* See Cartledge, *Vows in the Hebrew Bible*.

69   *He takes over many of his rival:* Wright, *The Evolution of God*, 120–24.

70   *Yahweh also takes on many attributes of El:* "From Adonai to Yahweh: A Glossary of God's Names"; Wright, *The Evolution of God*, 110–15.

   Yahweh had perhaps the hardest time displacing: For more about Asherah, consult Dever, *Did God Have a Wife?*; Smith, *God in Translation*; and Wright, *The Evolution of God*, 118–20.

71   *"To [Y]ahweh [of] Teiman"*: Dever, *Did God Have a Wife?*, 162; Othmar Keel and Christoph Uehlinger, eds., *Gods, Goddesses and Images of God in Ancient Israel*, trans. Thomas H. Trapp (Minneapolis: Fortress Press, 1998), 210–82.

73   *"put your hand under my thigh"*: Meir Malul, "More on *Pahad Yishaq* (Genesis XXXI 42, 53) and the Oath by the Thigh," *Vetus Testamentum* XXXV, no. 2 (1985): 192–200.

75   *testis was also a "risqué and jocose" word:* Adams, *Latin Sexual Vocabulary*, 67.

77   *There is a famous statue:* Fant and Reddish, *Lost Treasures of the Bible*; Keel and Uehlinger, *Gods, Goddesses and Images of God*, 210–82, for

numerous images of goats feeding on trees, associated with Asherah and other goddesses.

77 *In the Sermon on the Mount:* For more on Matthew 5:33, see Jo-Ann A. Brant, "Infelicitous Oaths in the Gospel of Matthew," *Journal for the Study of the New Testament* 63 (1996): 3–20; R. T. France, *The Gospel of Matthew*, The New International Commentary on the New Testament (Grand Rapids, MI: William B. Eerdmans, 2007); Akio Ito, "The Question of the Authenticity of the Ban on Swearing (Matthew 5:33–37)," *Journal for the Study of the New Testament* 43 (1991): 5–13; Jerome, *Commentary on Matthew*, trans. Thomas P. Scheck, The Fathers of the Church 117 (Washington, DC: Catholic University of America Press, 2008); Ulrich Luz, *Matthew 1–7: A Commentary*, trans. James E. Crouch (Minneapolis: Fortress Press, 2007); Barclay M. Newman and Philip C. Stine, *A Translator's Handbook on the Gospel of Matthew*, UBS Helps for Translators (New York: United Bible Societies, 1988); John Nolland, *The Gospel of Matthew: A Commentary on the Greek Text* (Grand Rapids, MI: William B. Eerdmans, 2005); Manlio Simonetti, ed., *Matthew 1–13*, Ancient Christian Commentary on Scripture New Testament 1a (Downers Grove, IL: InterVarsity Press, 2001); Ben Witherington, *Matthew*, Smyth & Helwys Bible Commentary (Macon, GA: Smyth & Helwys, 2006); Augustine, *On the Sermon on the Mount, Book One*, trans. William Findlay, New Advent (online), accessed August 10, 2010; Thomas Aquinas, *Summa Theologica*, trans. Fathers of the English Dominican Province, New Advent (online), accessed August 10, 2010; Philipp Melanchthon, *Verlegung etlicher unchristlicher Artikel. . . . Werke*, ed. Robert Stupperich (Gütersloh: Bertelsmann, 1951), quoted in Luz, *Matthew 1–7*, 267.

Christ also seems to single out fighting words as worthy of divine condemnation. In the Sermon on the Mount, he explains that in the past, murder was outlawed, but that he would forbid anger itself, as well as insulting words that express anger: "if you are angry with a brother or sister, you will be liable to judgment; and if you insult [say *raca* to] a brother or sister, you will be liable to the council; and if you say 'You fool,' you will be liable to the hell of fire" (Matt. 5:21–22). This passage is notoriously difficult to interpret, however. *Raca* is an Aramaic word that apparently means "empty-headed" or "fool," and scholars are not sure how that term compares with the Greek for "fool" used in the final phrase. Is Christ making the point that *raca* and *fool* are terrible insults and should not be said in anger, or that Christians should not utter even such mild insults as *fool*? Scholars also do not know what to make of the scale of punishments Christ sets out. Are "judgment," "the council," and "the hell of fire" supposed to be equivalent, different ways for describing the same punishment, or increasingly awful?

78 *The Quakers, in contrast:* For an introduction to the Quakers, see Margery Post Abbott, Mary Ellen Chijioke, Pink Dandelion, and John William Oliver, *Historical Dictionary of the Friends (Quakers)* (Lanham, MD: Scarecrow Press, 2003) and Pink Dandelion, *An Introduction to Quakerism* (Cambridge, Cambridge University Press, 2007).

"plainer words than these": George Fox, *The Works of George Fox: Gospel Truth Demonstrated* (Philadelphia: Marcus T. C. Gould, 1831), vol. 5, part 2, 165.

80 *More than a thousand years later:* Idolatry is still a pressing concern in the New Testament, but more in terms of how to begin spreading Christ's message to the gentiles (non-Jews) after his death. There are still many other gods to choose from—Jesus lived in the Roman Empire, after all—but the near-hysterical fear that pervades the Hebrew Bible, that Israelites will go off and worship strange gods, is gone.

To the ancient Israelites, excrement: For the concept of defilement, see Mary Douglas, *Purity and Danger: An Analysis of Concepts of Pollution and Taboo*, 2nd ed. (New York: Routledge, 2002).

81 *NRSV, NIV, ESV:* NRSV = New Revised Standard Version; NIV = New International Version; ESV = English Standard Version; NASB = New American Standard Bible; ERV = Easy-to-Read Version.

82 *As these various translations show:* For more about biblical obscenity, including an argument that the compilers of the Talmud were ashamed of several words they found in the Hebrew Bible, you could have a look at Jeremy F. Hultin, *The Ethics of Obscene Speech in Early Christianity and Its Environment*, Supplements to Novum Testamentum 128 (Leiden: Brill, 2008).

Hebrew is like Latin: Joel M. Hoffman, *In the Beginning: A Short History of the Hebrew Language* (New York: New York University Press, 2004); Angel Sáenz-Badillos, *A History of the Hebrew Language*, trans. John Elwolde (Cambridge: Cambridge University Press, 1993).

83 *Biblical Hebrew is extremely euphemistic:* S. H. Smith, "'Heel' and 'Thigh:' The Concept of Sexuality in the Jacob-Esau Narratives," *Vetus Testamentum* XL, no. 4 (1990): 464–73.

84　*"In this chapter we have"*: Matthew Henry, "Commentary," Biblegateway. com, accessed August 10, 2010.

Scholar Ziony Zevit takes this euphemism: Scott F. Gilbert and Ziony Zevit, "Congenital Human Baculum Deficiency: The Generative Bone of Genesis 2:21–23," *American Journal of Medical Genetics* 101, no. 3 (2001): 284–85; John Kaltner, Steven L. McKenzie, and Joel Kilpatrick, *The Uncensored Bible: The Bawdy and Naughty Bits of the Good Book* (New York: Harper One, 2008), 1–11.

One biblical law is a case in point: Jerome T. Walsh, "You Shall Cut Off Her . . . Palm? A Reexamination of Deuteronomy 25:11–12," *Journal of Semitic Studies* 49 (2004): 47–48; Kaltner, McKenzie, and Kilpatrick, *The Uncensored Bible,* 99–106.

86　*in the immortal words of sixteenth-century Scottish poet:* The Poetical Works *of Sir David Lyndsay* (London: Longman, 1806), 161.

87　*"An idle word is one":* Jerome 146.

Chapter 3

Two books on medieval obscenity were very helpful to my thinking about this chapter: Nicola McDonald, ed., *Medieval Obscenities* (York: York Medieval Press, 2006), and Jan Ziolkowski, ed., *Obscenity: Social Control and Artistic Creation in the European Middle Ages,* Cultures, Beliefs and Traditions 4 (Leiden: E. J. Brill, 1998). I have modernized the spelling and punctuation of quotations when necessary for clarity.

88　*the Lindisfarne Gospels:* British Library, "Online Gallery Sacred Texts: Lindisfarne Gospels" (online), accessed May 12, 2010; Michelle P. Brown, *The Lindisfarne Gospels: Society, Spirituality and the Scribe* (London: British Library, 2003), 16–83.

the oldest surviving English version: Walter W. Skeat, ed., *The Gospel According to Saint Matthew* (Cambridge: Cambridge University Press, 1887).

"don't sard another man's wife": "Sard," *Middle English Dictionary,* 2001 ed. (online), accessed May 25, 2010. Thanks also to George Brown and Dorothy Bray for their help on *sard.*

89　*In a 1530 English-French dictionary:* John Palsgrave, *Lesclarissement de la langue francoyse,* ed. R. C. Alston, English Linguistics 1500–1800 190 (Menston, England: Scolar Press, 1969).

89   *And what these ordinary people learned:* Quotes from the Wycliffite Bible
come from Studylight.org, *The Wycliffite Bible* (online), accessed May 25,
2010; see also Mary Dove, *The First English Bible: The Text and Context of
the Wycliffite Versions* (Cambridge: Cambridge University Press, 2007).

In a 2000 ranking: Advertising Standards Authority, BBC, Broadcasting
Standards Commission, and the Independent Television Commission,
"Delete Expletives?" Ofcom.org, December 2000, accessed May 25,
2010.

90   *as we've seen Steven Pinker define a swearword:* Pinker, *Stuff of Thought*,
339.

91   *what the linguistic situation in England was:* Geoffrey Hughes, *A History of
English Words* (Malden, MA: Blackwell, 2000), 109–45; Seth Lerer,
Inventing English: A Portable History of the Language (New York: Colum-
bia University Press, 2007), 25–70; Richard M. Hogg, ed., *The Cam-
bridge History of the English Language*, vol. 1: *The Beginnings to 1066*
(Cambridge: Cambridge University Press, 1992); Norman Blake, ed.,
The Cambridge History of the English Language, vol. 2: *1066–1476* (Cam-
bridge: Cambridge University Press, 1992); Hans Sauer, "Glosses, Glos-
saries, and Dictionaries in the Medieval Period," in *The Oxford History of
English Lexicography*, ed. Anthony Paul Cowie (Oxford: Clarendon
Press, 2009), 1:17–40.

King Richard the Lionheart: Jean Flori, *Richard the Lionheart: King and
Knight*, trans. Jean Birrell (Edinburgh: Edinburgh University Press,
2006), 7.

92   *Aldred belongs to the end:* This classification of the Middle Ages is fairly
standard among historians. Mine comes most directly from Sauer,
"Glosses, Glossaries and Dictionaries," 17.

the "civilizing process": Norbert Elias, *The Civilizing Process: Sociogenetic
and Psychogenetic Investigations*, ed. Eric Dunning et al., trans. Edmund
Jephcott, rev. ed. (Oxford: Blackwell, 2000).

93   *The* Nominale sive Verbale: "Nominale sive Verbale," ed. Walter Skeat, in
Transactions of the Philological Society, 1903–1906 (London: Kegan Paul,
Trench, Trübner, 1906), 1–50.

Schetewellwey . . . Randulfus: These names can be found in the *Middle
English Dictionary*.

Blame Alexander Pope: Alexander Pope, trans. *The Odyssey of Homer*, ed.
George Musgrave, 2 vols. (London: Bell and Daldy, 1865).

94 *"Bastard, thine Epigrams to sport"*: John Davies, "The Scourge of Folly," in *The Complete Works of John Davies of Hereford*, ed. Alexander Grosart, 2 vols (Edinburgh: Edinburgh University Press, 1878).

Dictionaries and vulgaria: *Ortus Vocabulorum*, ed. R. C. Alston, English Linguistics 1500–1800 123 (Menston, England: Scolar Press, 1968). The *Pictorial Vocabulary* (747–814), the *Nominale* (675–744), Abbot Ælfric's vocabulary (104–67), and "a ners" (678) are found in Thomas Wright, *Anglo-Saxon and English Vocabularies*, ed. Richard Paul Wülcker, 2nd ed., vol. 1 (London: Trübner, 1884); *Catholicon Anglicum*, ed. Sidney J. H. Herrtage, EETS 75 (Millwood, NY: Kraus Reprint, 1973); *Promptorium Parvulorum*, ed. A. L. Mayhew, EETS Extra Series 52 (London: Kegan Paul, Trench, Trübner, 1908).

95 *"dum paro menpirium"*: Wright, *Anglo-Saxon and English Vocabularies*, 627.

Led, by a creative but false: Jack Anderson, review of *Watch this Space* and *Anitergium II Hohodowndownho*, by Phoebe Neville, *New York Times*, March 17, 1988.

Despite their name, vulgaria: *The Vulgaria of John Stanbridge and the Vulgaria of Robert Whittington*, ed. Beatrice White, EETS 187 (London: Kegan Paul, Trench, Trübner, 1932).

96 *"Courtesie" was another important part:* For more on medieval education, see Nicholas Orme, *Medieval Schools: From Roman Britain to Renaissance England* (New Haven: Yale University Press, 2006), and Nicholas Orme, *Education and Society in Medieval and Renaissance England* (London: Hambledon Press, 1989). Also *The Babees Book* (a collection of poetical and prose instructions for young children, showing the kinds of things that were thought to be important to learn), ed. Frederick J. Furnivall, EETS 32 (New York: Greenwood Press, 1969). And you might look as well at Chapter 3 of my dissertation, about the similar aims of early sixteenth-century education: "Strong Language: Oaths, Obscenities, and Performative Literature in Early Modern England," Ph.D. diss., Stanford University, 2003.

expulsion for "lying, swearing, and filthy speaking": *The Vulgaria of John Stanbridge and the Vulgaria of Robert Whittington*, xv.

"In women the neck of the bladder": Lanfrank's *"Science of Cirurgie,"* ed. Robert v. Fleischhacker (London: Kegan Paul, Trench, Trübner, 1894), 173. For other examples of medical texts using unmarked obscene

words, see "balocke codde," "pyntell," and "ars" in *The Middle English Version of William of Saliceto's Anatomia*, ed. Christian Heimerl (Heidelberg: Winter, 2008), 45, 47, 53; "the ersse" in John Arderne's *Treatises of Fistula in Ano*, ed. D'Arcy Power, EETS 139 (London: Kegan Paul, Trench, Trübner, 1910), 2; and Juhani Norri, *Names of Body Parts in English, 1400–1550* (Helsinki: Finnish Academy of Science and Letters, 1998).

96 *you should anoint him: Lanfrank's "Science,"* 176.

97 *"For on thy bed"*: Chaucer, "The Manciple's Tale," *The Riverside Chaucer*, 256, 311–12.

"We! hold thy tongue": quoted in Lynne Forest-Hill, *Transgressive Language in Medieval Drama: Signs of Challenge and Change* (Burlington, VT: Ashgate, 2000), 34.

"Take out that southern": "Southerne," *Middle English Dictionary*, accessed July 25, 2012.

98 Kekir *and* bobrelle: Wright, *Anglo-Saxon and English Vocabularies;* Thomas Ross, "Taboo-Words in Fifteenth-Century English," *Fifteenth Century Studies: Recent Essays*, ed. Robert F. Yeager (Hamden, CT: Archon Books, 1984), 137–60; *Middle English Dictionary*.

Pintel, tarse, *and* yerde: *Middle English Dictionary;* Ross, "Taboo-Words," 153; Eve Salisbury, ed., "A Talk of Ten Wives on Their Husbands' Ware," Teams Middle English Texts Series (online), accessed September 27, 2010.

99 *how did people insult each other:* For more on linguistic crimes such as defamation and scolding, see Sandy Bardsley, *Venomous Tongues: Speech and Gender in Late Medieval England* (Philadelphia: University of Pennsylvania Press, 2006); Edwin Craun, *The Hands of the Tongue: Essays on Deviant Speech*, Studies in Medieval Culture XLVII (Kalamazoo, MI: Medieval Institute, 2007), particularly the essay by Derek Neal, "Husbands and Priests: Masculinity, Sexuality, and Defamation in Late Medieval England"; Ruth Mazo Karras, "The Latin Vocabulary of Illicit Sex in English Ecclesiastical Court Records," *Journal of Medieval Latin* 2 (1992): 1–17; L. R. Poos, "Sex, Lies, and the Church Courts of Pre-Reformation England," *Journal of Interdisciplinary History* XXV, no. 4 (Spring 1995): 585–607; and J. H. Baker, *An Introduction to English Legal History*, 3rd. ed. (London: Butterworths, 1990).

100 *The Victorian legal scholar:* Frederic William Maitland, *Select Pleas in Manorial and Other Seignorial Courts*, vol. 1 (London: Bernard Quaritch, 1889).

100 *Late medieval accounts:* The Rokker case is described in Kim Phillips, *Medieval Maidens: Young Women and Gender in England, 1270–1540* (Manchester: Manchester University Press, 2003). Elizabeth Whyns's words are from Poos, "Sex, Lies, and the Church Courts," 593. Wybard's attack is found in Derek G. Neal, *The Masculine Self in Late Medieval England* (Chicago: University of Chicago Press, 2008).

"For harlots and servants": Morte Arthure, ed. Edmond Brock, EETS 8 (London: Kegan Paul, Trench, Trübner, 1871).

"the moralisation of status words": C. S. Lewis, *Studies in Words* (Cambridge: Cambridge University Press, 1967), 21–23.

101 *But the court records:* Court rolls provide a valuable record of real-life insults, but they have their limitations. It is likely that *whore* was the most common abuse recorded for women and *false* for men because defamation suits were most often brought about words that had the potential to cause real damage. Being tarred as unchaste could cost an unmarried woman a husband, or could cause a married woman to be hauled up before another court on charges of adultery; having a reputation as a dishonest man could cost a farmer or tradesman business. It is possible that other kinds of insults were rife but that they do not appear in the court rolls because they would have been an unsuccessful basis for a defamation suit. The fact that other linguistic crimes such as scolding and assault with contumelious words also employ the *whore/false* vocabulary would indicate otherwise, however.

Badges like this: Jos Koldeweij, "'Shameless and Naked Images:' Obscene Badges as Parodies of Popular Devotion," in *Art and Architecture of Late Medieval Pilgrimage in Northern Europe and the British Isles,* ed. Sarah Blick and Rita Tekippe (Leiden: Brill, 2005), 493–510; Susan Signe Morrison, "Waste Space: Pilgrim Badges, Ophelia and Walsingham Remembered," *Walsingham in Literature and Culture from the Middle Ages to Modernity,* ed. Dominic Janes and Gary Waller (Burlington VT: Ashgate, 2010), 49–66; Anthony Weir, "Satan in the Groin," Beyond-the-Pale.org.uk, accessed July 25, 2012.

103 *"shameless and naked images":* Morrison, "Waste Space," 57.

There was almost no such thing as privacy: Mark Girouard, *Life in the English Country House* (New York: Penguin, 1978); Diana Webb, *Privacy and Solitude in the Middle Ages* (London: Hambledon Continuum, 2006); Lena Cowen Orlin, *Locating Privacy in Tudor London* (Oxford: Oxford University Press, 2007); Ian Mortimer, *The Time Traveler's Guide to*

Medieval England (New York: Simon & Schuster, 2010); Margaret Wade Labarge, *A Baronial Household of the Thirteenth Century* (New York: Barnes and Noble, 1965); Maryanne Kowaleski, ed., *Medieval Domesticity: Home, Housing, and Household in Medieval England* (Cambridge: Cambridge University Press, 2008); C. M. Woolgar, *The Great Household in Late Medieval England* (New Haven: Yale University Press, 1999).

"it is impolite": quoted in Elias, *The Civilizing Process*, 110.

104 *"One should not, like rustics"*: quoted in ibid., 111.

We can reconstruct what a dinner: Melitta Weiss Adamson, *Food in Medieval Times* (Westport, CT: Greenwood Press, 2004).

"If you spit over the table": *The Boke of Curtasye* in Frederick James Furnivall, *Early English Meals and Manners* (London: Kegan Paul, Trench, Trübner, 1868), 175–205.

"belch near no man's face": Hugh Rhodes, *The Boke of Nurture for Men, Servants, and Children* (London, 1545), Early English Books Online, accessed July 25, 2012.

105 *"the floors too are generally spread"*: Erasmus, *The Correspondence of Erasmus: Letters 1356 to 153*, trans. R. A. B. Mynors and Alexander Dalzell (Toronto: University of Toronto Press, 1992), 10:471.

"Soon then Beowulf": *Beowulf: An Updated Verse Translation*, trans. Frederick Rebsamen (New York: Harper Collins, 2004), 1793–99.

"the sight of total nakedness": quoted in Elias, *The Civilizing Process*, 139.

106 *"Medieval people would be much less likely"*: Ruth Mazo Karras, *Sexuality in Medieval Europe: Doing unto Others* (New York: Routledge, 2005), 153.

In a 1366 case: P. J. P. Goldberg, ed., *Women in England c. 1275–1525* (Manchester: Manchester University Press, 1995), 62.

"What was lacking": Elias, *The Civilizing Process*, 60.

107 *"a shitten shepherd"*: Chaucer, "General Prologue," *The Riverside Chaucer*, 504.

A well-known comic set piece: Chaucer, "The Miller's Tale," *The Riverside Chaucer*, 687–743.

There is in fact a famous crux: Larry D. Benson, "The 'Queynte' Punnings of Chaucer's Critics," in *Studies in the Age of Chaucer, Proceedings of the New Chaucer Society, no. 1, 1984: Reconstructing Chaucer*, ed. Paul Strohm and Thomas J. Heffernan (Knoxville: University of Tennessee Press, 1985), 33, 36, 43.

107 *One manuscript of the poem actually does: The Canterbury Tales,* Cambridge Ii.3.26, Cambridge University Library, Cambridge.

108 *what are now called pastoral texts:* For an introduction to these texts, see Edwin Craun's *Lies, Slander and Obscenity in Medieval English Literature: Pastoral Rhetoric and the Deviant Speaker* (Cambridge: Cambridge University Press, 1997).

109 *When God punished him for eating the fruit:* St. Augustine, *City of God,* trans. P. Levine, vol. 4 (Cambridge, MA: Harvard University Press, 1965), Book 14, Chapters 23–24.

   do not discuss obscenity: "The terms *obscene* and *obscenity*—although they were part and parcel of the Latin rhetorical tradition from its formation through its transference to modern spoken languages—do not enter the lexica of the vernaculars until after the Middle Ages." Ziolkowski, *Obscenity,* 16.

   "These are the sins of the mouth": **Speculum Christiani,* ed. Gustaf Holmstedt, EETS 182 (Oxford: Humphrey Milford, Oxford University Press, 1933), 58.

110 *the "wose of synne": Jacob's Well,* ed. Arthur Brandeis, EETS 115 (London: Kegan Paul, Trench, Trübner, 1900), 1:53.

   "the seven heads": Ayenbite of Inwit or Remorse of Conscience, vol. 1, ed. Pamela Gradon, EETS 23 (London: Oxford University Press, 1965).

111 *"The devil tempts of this sin": Ayenbite,* 46.

   The danger of this sort of speech: R. Howard Bloch, "Modest Maids and Modified Nouns: Obscenity in the Fabliaux," in *Obscenity: Social Control and Artistic Creation in the European Middle Ages,* ed. Jan M. Ziolkowski (Leiden: Brill, 1998), 305.

   "Had we but world enough": Andrew Marvell, "To His Coy Mistress," in *The Oxford Book of English Verse: 1250–1900,* ed. Arthur Quiller-Couch (n.p., 1919), online at Bartleby.com, accessed September 27, 2010.

   The place to find obscenity in the Middle Ages is not in English but perhaps in French. The thirteenth-century literary genre called the *fabliau* contains tales with titles such as *Le Chevalier qui fist parler les Cons* ("The Knight Who Made Cunts Talk") and *Cele qui se fist foutre sur la fosse de son mari* ("The One Who Got Herself Fucked on Her Husband's Grave"), in which words such as *foutre* and *con* do seem to be "obscene" in the modern sense of the word. Several *fabliaux,* and the c. 1275 *The Romance of the Rose,* deal explicitly with the question of whether it is immodest of women

to use words such as *coillons* ("balls"), indicating that a taboo was developing against it. For men, though, no such taboo seems to have existed—
the injunctions are directed at women. Chaucer scholar Charles Muscatine
argues that the concept of obscenity was just starting to develop at this
time: "Much of the fabliau diction we might now consider obscene might
not have been so obscene in its own time. The fabliau language of sexuality . . . is much of the time surprisingly free of impudence or
self-consciousness. It often sounds like normal usage, the unreflec-
tive language of a culture that was relatively free of linguistic taboos, but
took pleasure of various kinds in the direct verbal evocation of sexuality. It
must have been the contemporaneous emergence of courtly norms of diction . . . that created, invented, or perhaps reinvented, in the twelfth and
thirteenth centuries a new sense of obscene or vulgar language." (281)
The *fabliaux* date from the time of the separation between England and
Normandy; the development of obscenity, which begins in the thirteenth
century in Norman French, starts later in English. See Charles Muscatine,
"The Fabliaux, Courtly Culture, and the (Re)Invention of Vulgarity," in
Obscenity: Social Control and Artistic Creation in the European Middle Ages,
ed. Jan M. Ziolkowski (Leiden: Brill, 1998), 281–92.

113 *England was a feudal society:* On the feudal system, see Jeffrey L. Forgeng
and Will McLean, *Daily Life in Chaucer's England*, 2nd ed. (Westport,
CT: Greenwood Press, 2009); W. L. Warren, *Henry II* (London:
Methuen, 1991); "Oath," in *Encyclopedia of the Middle Ages*, ed. André
Vauchez, Barrie Dobson, and Michael Lapidge, trans. Adrian Walford
(Chicago: Fitzroy Dearborn, 2000).

Just such a broken oath was the cause: On the Conquest, see Simon
Schama, *A History of Britain: At the Edge of the World?* (New York:
Hyperion, 2000), 86; Kari Ellen Gade, "Northern Light on the Battle of
Hastings," *Viator* 28 (1997); De Re Militari: The Society for Medieval
Military History (online), accessed June 28, 2010.

114 *through a process called compurgation:* On compurgation and trial by
ordeal, see Richard Firth Green, *A Crisis of Truth: Literature and Law in
Ricardian England* (Philadelphia: University of Pennsylvania Press,
1999); Frederic William Maitland, *The Constitutional History of England*
(Cambridge: Cambridge University Press, 1961); Baker, *An Introduction
to English Legal History*.

Christiana de Dunelmia: The Calendar of the Early Mayor's Court Rolls, ed.
H. A. Thomas (Cambridge: Cambridge University Press, 1924), xxx–xxxi.

115 *"worse is he than an homicide"*: Miles Coverdale, *A Christen Exhortation unto Customable Swearers* (London: W. Hill, 1548), 20.

116 *Lollardy began in England:* There was a contemporaneous Lollard-like movement in Bohemia, led by the preacher Jan Hus. Hus was a follower of John Wyclif, the theologian who inspired the Lollards. Hus was burned at the stake in 1415. Wyclif died before he could be executed, but his bones were dug up and burned in 1428. For more on the Lollards, see Anne Hudson, *The Premature Reformation: Wycliffite Texts and Lollard History* (Oxford: Clarendon Press, 1988) and her *Selections from English Wycliffite Writings,* rev. ed. (Toronto: University of Toronto Press, 1997).

117 *De Haeretico Comburendo: English Historical Reprints,* ed. W. Dawson Johnston and Jean Browne Johnston (Ann Arbor: Sheehan, 1896), 27.

   At her trial in 1429: John Foxe, *Actes and Monuments,* ed. George Townsend (New York: AMS Press, 1965); Norman P. Tanner, ed., *Heresy Trials in the Diocese of Norwich, 1428–31,* Camden Fourth Series 20 (London: Royal Historical Society, 1977).

118 *"the sacrament on the altar"*: Hudson, *Selections,* I.

   "I abjure and forswear": Foxe, *Actes and Monuments,* 540, 593.

   you shouldn't swear by creatures: Henry G. Russell, "Lollard Opposition to Oaths by Creatures," *American Historical Review* 51, no. 4 (1946): 668–84.

119 *William Thorpe, for example, was all ready:* Foxe, *Actes and Monuments,* 249–85.

   "false swearing become one of the most commonly": Hughes, *Swearing,* 60.

   In one example from 1303: Robert of Brunne, *Handlyng Synne,* ed. Frederick James Furnivall, EETS 119 and 123, 2 vol. (London: Kegan, Paul, Trench, Trübner & Co., 1901–3), 2700–734.

120 *Or, as Steven Pinker writes:* Pinker, *Stuff of Thought,* 341.

   The Pardoner addresses this kind of language: Chaucer, "The Pardoner's Tale," *The Riverside Chaucer,* 629–50.

   "it is not lawful to swear by creatures": "On the Twenty-Five Articles" in John Wyclif, *Selected Works,* ed. Thomas Arnold (Oxford: Clarendon Press, 1871), III:483.

121 Jacob's Well *discusses these oaths: Jacob's Well,* 153.

   Christ is seven feet tall: Hudson, *Selections,* I.

121 *The first pattern poem written in English:* Stephen Hawes, *The Conversyon of Swerers* (London, 1509), Early English Books Online, accessed May 15, 2012.

123 *An Easter Sunday sermon:* Woodburn O. Ross, ed., *Middle English Sermons*, EETS 209 (London: H. Milford, Oxford University Press, 1940), sermon 22.

The mechanism of this miracle: See Chapter 1 of Miri Rubin, *Corpus Christi: The Eucharist in Late Medieval Culture* (Cambridge: Cambridge University Press, 1991); Hudson, *Selections*, 142; and Eamon Duffy, *The Stripping of the Altars: Traditional Religion in England 1400–1580* (New Haven: Yale University Press, 1992), 91–130.

the tale of a monk who doubts: Handlyng Synne 9981–10072. Other such "miracle of the Host" stories can be found in *Mirk's Festial*, ed. Theodor Erbe, EETS 96 (extra series) (London: Kegan, Paul, Trench, Trübner, 1905), 170–71; 173, and *The Mirrour of the Blessed Lyf of Jesu Christ*, ed. Lawrence F. Powell (Oxford: Clarendon Press, 1908), 308–9. See also Duffy, *The Stripping of the Altars*, 91–109, for a useful contextualization of these stories in terms of medieval lay experience of the Mass.

124 *There was once a man who swore constantly: Gesta Romanorum*, ed. Sidney Herrtage, EETS 33 (extra series) (London: Kegan, Paul, Trench, Trübner, 1879), 409–10. The phrase "complaint against swearers" is Rosemary Woolf's. See her *English Religious Lyric in the Middle Ages* (Oxford: Clarendon Press, 1968), 395, for more examples of these complaints. See also Elaine Scarry, *The Body in Pain: Making and Unmaking the World* (New York: Oxford University Press, 1985) for an analysis of how societies often have recourse to the human body as the most effective means to legitimate cultural constructs and other "truths" because of its "sheer material factualness" (14).

126 *"The body of Christ":* Duffy, *The Stripping of the Altars*, 91–92.

"even [to] touch": Ibid., 110.

"A bell was rung": Ibid., 97.

"holding up of the hands": Ibid., 103.

127 *"no state can stand":* John Downame, *Four Treatises, tending to dissuade all Christians from 4 no lesse hainous then common sinnes* (London, 1608).

Catholic pastoral literature expresses great anxiety: G. R. Owst, *Literature and Pulpit in Medieval England* (New York: Barnes & Noble, 1961), 416.

Chapter 4

129 *Gregorian calendar:* The Gregorian calendar is the one in use throughout most of the world today. It replaced the Julian calendar, in which the dates of the equinoxes were moving earlier and earlier due to a slightly inexact calculation of the length of the year. Britain and its possessions finally adopted the Gregorian calendar in 1752.

The 1585 Act: 27 Eliz.c.2 in Charles Dodd and M. A. Tierney, *Dodd's Church History of England, from the Commencement of the Sixteenth Century to the Revolution in 1688,* vol. 4 (London: C. Dolman, 1839–43).

130 *"I will waste no time reading it":* The quip is variously attributed to Benjamin Disraeli or Moses Hadas.

131 *Henry VIII had halfheartedly:* For more about how the English populace was affected by these changes, see Eamon Duffy, *The Stripping of the Altars: Traditional Religion in England 1400–1580* (New Haven: Yale University Press, 1992).

132 *the bull* Regnans in Excelsis: Pius V, "Regnans in Excelsis," Papal Encyclicals Online, accessed February 14, 2011.

After this, English penal laws: "Penal Laws," *Catholic Encyclopedia,* ed. Charles G. Herbermann et al. (1907–1912), online at New Advent, accessed February 14, 2011. The statutes are: 1571—13 Eliz. c. 1 and 13 Eliz. c. 2; 1581—23 Eliz. c. 1; 1587—35 Eliz. c. 2.

133 *souls in Purgatory might:* Duffy, *The Stripping of the Altars,* 338.

There are several accounts of Southwell's life, capture, and trial, including Christopher Devlin, *The Life of Robert Southwell: Poet and Martyr* (London: Longmans, Green, 1956); Pierre Janelle, *Robert Southwell: A Study in Religious Inspiration* (London: Sheed and Ward, 1935); and F. W. Brownlow, *Robert Southwell,* Twayne's English Authors Series 516 (New York: Twayne, 1996).

the crown's chief and most insidious weapon: For the oath ex officio, see Janelle, *Robert Southwell;* Devlin, *Life of Robert Southwell;* and Christopher Hill, *Society and Puritanism in Pre-Revolutionary England* (New York: Schoken Books, 1964), 348.

134 *"to a conscience that feareth God":* Hill, *Society and Puritanism,* 330.

The "Bloody Question": Scott R. Pilarz, *Robert Southwell and the Mission of Literature 1561–1595: Writing Reconciliation* (Burlington, VT: Ashgate, 2004), 236, and Alice Hogge, *God's Secret Agents: Queen Elizabeth's*

Forbidden Priests and the Hatching of the Gunpowder Plot (New York: HarperCollins, 2005), 232.

135 *Southwell was accused of telling:* Southwell's teachings on equivocation are found in Janelle, *Robert Southwell*, 81; for more on Jesuit views of equivocation, see Perez Zagorin, *Ways of Lying: Dissimulation, Persecution, and Conformity in Early Modern Europe* (Cambridge, MA: Harvard University Press, 1990), 169–70; Robert Parsons, *A Treatise Tending to Mitigation*, English Recusant Literature 1558–1640 (Ilkley, England: Scolar Press, 1977), 340.

"if this doctrine should be allowed": Brownlow, *Robert Southwell*, 20; Janelle, *Robert Southwell*, 81–82.

136 *"not without some note and touch":* William Camden, *The History of the Most Renowned and Victorious Princess Elizabeth, Late Queen of England* (1688), 344. For Southwell's death, see Devlin, *Life of Robert Southwell*, 323; Pilarz, *Robert Southwell*, 278–80; and Hogge, *God's Secret Agents*, 188–90.

137 *"they may charge us":* Christopher Bagshaw, *A Sparing Discoverie of Our English Jesuits* (1601), 11–12.

138 *God is not "bodily":* Hudson, *The Premature Reformation*, 281.

The Thirty-Nine Articles: Gavin Koh, ed., *The Thirty-Nine Articles of Religion*, November 29, 1999, http://gavvie.tripod.com/39articles/articles.html, accessed March 19, 2011.

139 *Robert Parsons scoffed:* Robert Parsons, *The Third Part of a Treatise, Intitled of Three Conversions of England* (St. Omer, 1604), 134.

Protestant swearing was thought to rip apart: William Vaughn, *The Spirit of Detraction, Conjured and Convicted in Seven Circles* (London, 1611), 123.

140 *The sheer number of oaths people were required to take:* For more on the conflicting oaths, see Hill, *Society and Puritanism*, 382–419.

"they force us to take": quoted in Ibid., 411.

142 *"Supernatural sanctions became less necessary":* Ibid., S 399.

"it paid a man": Ibid., 418.

The scientist Robert Boyle: Robert Boyle, *A Free Discourse Against Customary Swearing* (London: John Williams, 1695); Michael Hunter, *Robert Boyle 1627–1691: Scrupulosity and Science* (Woodbridge, Suffolk: Boydell Press, 2000), 64–68.

142 *She liked to sprinkle her speech with:* Peter Brimacombe, *All the Queen's Men: The World of Elizabeth I* (New York: St. Martin's Press, 2000), 118; Alison Weir, *The Life of Elizabeth I* (New York: Ballantine 1999), 166, 427.

143 *John Harington called it "obscenousnesse":* John Harington, "An Apologie of Poetrie," preface to Ludovico Ariosto, *Orlando Furioso* (1591), in *Ancient Critical Essays upon English Poets and Poesy*, ed. Joseph Haslewood (London: Robert Triphook, 1815), II:138–39.

145 *He ends his 1598 erotic poem:* John Marston, "The Metamorphosis of Pigmalion's Image," *Poems*, ed. Arnold Davenport (Liverpool: Liverpool University Press, 1961).

   a much less titillating mock encomium: Thomas Nashe, *Nashe's Lenten Stuff*, ed. Charles Hindley (London: Reeves and Turner, 1871), 14.

146 *"all things that are to be eschewed":* Thomas Thomas, *Dictionarium linguae Latinae et Anglicanae* (London, 1587).

   Huge numbers of dictionaries: Janet Bately, "Bilingual and Multilingual Dictionaries of the Renaissance and Early Seventeenth Century," in *The Oxford History of English Lexicography*, ed. Anthony Paul Cowie (Oxford: Clarendon Press, 2009), 1:41.

147 *"we shall also bore":* Desiderius Erasmus, *Copia: Foundations of the Abundant Style*, trans. Betty I. Knott, in *Collected Works of Erasmus* (Toronto: University of Toronto Press, 1978), 24:302.

   "a thousand more Latin words": Thomas Elyot, *Dictionary* (London, 1538), sig. Aiiir. For Elyot's ideas of who is a good author, see his 1531 *The Boke Named the Governour*, ed. R. C. Alston, English Linguistics 1500–1880, 246 (Menston, England: Scolar Press, 1970), 51.

   look for his "many commendable": Elyot, *Governour*, 51v.

148 *"there may hap by evil custom":* Ibid., 17r.

   Elyot broaches this conflict in a Latin epistle: Elyot, *Dictionary*, "Lectoribus vere doctis."

149 *"a womans wycket":* For more on wickets, see James T. Henke, *Gutter Life and Language in the Early "Street" Literature of England: A Glossary of Terms and Topics Chiefly of the Sixteenth and Seventeenth Centuries* (West Cornwall, CT: Locust Hill Press, 1988).

150 *Other lexicographers abandoned didactic responsibility:* John Florio, *A Worlde of Wordes* (1598), Anglistica & Americana 114 (Hildesheim: Georg Olms Verlag, 1972); Palsgrave, *Lesclarcissement de la Langue Francoyse*.

151 *La Cazzaria:* For more on this work, see Ian Moulton, *Before Pornography: Erotic Writing in Early Modern England* (Oxford: Oxford University Press, 2000), 147–48.

"*O d fuckin Abbot*": Edward Wilson, "A 'Damned F … in Abbot' in 1528: The Earliest English Example of a Four-Letter Word," *Notes and Queries* 40, no. 1 (1993): 29–34; Jesse Sheidlower, *The F Word*, 3rd ed. (New York: Oxford University Press, 2009), 139–40.

152 "*He clappit fast, he kist and chukkit*": William Dunbar, "In Secreit Place This Hyndir Nycht," in *The Makars: The Poems of Henryson, Dunbar and Douglas*, ed. Jacqueline Tasioulas (Edinburgh: Canongate Books, 1999), 569.

"*Non sunt in cœli*": Thomas Wright and James Orchard Halliwell, eds., *Reliquiae Antiquae: Scraps from Ancient Manuscripts* (London: John Russell Smith, 1845), 1:91; Sheidlower, *The F Word*, 83.

153 Naff, *for example, is not:* Michael Quinion, "Naff," World Wide Words, January 26, 2008 (online), accessed July 27, 2012.

If it's not an acronym: Sheidlower, *The F Word*, viii–xii.

154 *In the sixteenth century, the insults:* These examples are from Bridget Cusack, ed., *Everyday English 1500–1700* (Ann Arbor: University of Michigan Press, 1998), 12, 22, 26, as well as from Colette Moore, "Reporting Direct Speech in Early Modern Slander Depositions," in *Studies in the History of the English Language: A Millennial Perspective*, ed. Donna Minkova and Robert Stockwell (Berlin: Mouton de Gruyter, 2002).

155 For more great real-life Renaissance insults, see B. S. Capp, *When Gossips Meet: Women, Family and Neighborhood in Early Modern England* (Oxford: Oxford University Press, 2003), 189.

"*Skaldit skaitbird*": "The Flyting of Dumbar and Kennedie," in *The Makars: The Poems of Henryson, Dunbar and Douglas*, ed. Jacqueline Tasioulas (Edinburgh: Canongate Books, 1999), 338–51.

156 "*advance in the frontiers of shame*": Norbert Elias, *The Civilizing Process: Sociogenetic and Psychogenetic Investigations*, ed. Eric Dunning et al., trans. Edmund Jephcott, rev. ed. (Oxford: Blackwell, 2000), 118.

Even confession, the most secret: Duffy, *The Stripping of the Altars*, 288, 570; see also Mary C. Mansfield, *The Humiliation of Sinners: Public Penance in Thirteenth-Century France* (Ithaca: Cornell University Press, 1995).

157 *Reading too was very often not private:* Heidi Brayman Hackel, *Reading Material in Early Modern England: Print, Gender, and Literacy* (Cambridge: Cambridge University Press, 2005), 46.

Historian Victor Skipp: Skipp's analysis quoted in Lena Cowen Orlin, *Elizabethan Households: An Anthology* (Washington, DC: Folger Shakespeare Library, 1995), 81–82.

158 *Around 1330, fireplaces:* Bill Bryson, *At Home: A Short History of Private Life* (New York: Doubleday, 2010), 58–59.

Privies were also spaces: Girouard, *Life in the English Country House,* 56–57; John Harington, *The Metamorphosis of Ajax,* ed. Elizabeth Story Donno (London: Routledge and Kegan Paul, 1962), 57, 82, 85, 89, and most of the book, really; Tony Rivers, Dan Cruickshank, Gillian Darley, and Martin Pawley, *The Name of the Room: A History of the British House and Home* (London: BBC Books, 1992), 93–95; Lucinda Lambton, *Temples of Convenience and Chambers of Delight* (London: Pavilion Books, 1995), 6–14.

159 *"His head, and his necke":* "Sirreverence," *OED* (online).

the family at Chilthorne Domer: Lambton, *Temples of Convenience,* 38.

160 *For true privacy, a wealthy person:* Girouard, *Life in the English Country House,* 56.

People of the middling and lower sorts: Orlin, *Elizabethan Households,* 3.

"evolving civility showed itself": Nicholas Cooper, "Rank, Manners and Display: The Gentlemanly House, 1500–1750," *Transactions of the Royal Historical Society,* sixth series, 12 (2002): 297.

others reverse the causation: See Orlin, *Locating Privacy,* 66–111 for a great summary of scholarly views of architecture as the cause of the new desire for privacy and for qualifications of it.

162 As we can see from the multiseat privies, however, shame had not advanced to quite to the levels of today. Privacy, and the shame it engendered, was in many cases more notional than actual. Especially for the middling and lower sorts, accommodations in London were often crowded, with nothing but paper walls or a few boards creating the new rooms of the Great Rebuilding. Court records still contain numerous eyewitness accounts of adultery or fornication, such as that of John Morris, whose elderly neighbor was able to observe him in flagrante with a girl (not his wife) by peeping through the apparently sizable gap between the door frame and his front door, or Sara Bonivall and John

Crosbie (also fornicators), who were seen through a hole in the wall that separated Crosbie's house from his adjoining neighbor's. In cases like these, it seems that early modern people in London might have even had *less* privacy than in the Middle Ages, when London itself was not as crowded with people looking for work, and when people remaining in the country could have sought out a bush more private than urban bedrooms. See Orlin, *Locating Privacy*, 152–55,

162 *"one should not sit"*: quoted in Elias, *The Civilizing Process*, 117.

In life, she liked to show her breasts: For Hurault and Elizabeth, see Valerie Traub, *The Renaissance of Lesbianism in Early Modern England* (Cambridge: Cambridge University Press, 2002), 139.

163 *There was a hierarchy of chambers:* Rivers et al., *The Name of the Room*, 73–74.

John Harington relates: Harington, *Metamorphosis*, 91, 98.

165 *Thomas Speght's 1598 edition: The Workes of our Antient and lerned English Poet, Geffrey Chaucer* (London, 1598), Early English Books Online. The preface I quote was actually written by Francis Beaumont, the playwright famous for his theatrical collaborations with John Fletcher, but since it appears in Speght's edition, for simplicity's sake I refer to it as Speght's preface.

166 *It is thus something of a surprise to read: The Whole Works of Homer* (London, 1616), Early English Books Online. Chapman had previously published several editions of the *Iliad* alone and called someone a "Windfucker" there too. My point is that it is surprising to find that word in a work that is supposed to be the definitive edition of a respected author.

here is a tiny, tiny sampling: All quotes are from *The Riverside Shakespeare*, ed. G. Blakemore Evans (Boston: Houghton Mifflin, 1974). *The Merry Wives of Windsor:* IV, I; III, iii; *Henry V:* III, iv; *Hamlet:* III, ii; "tun-dish" in *Measure for Measure:* III, ii; "bauble" in *Romeo and Juliet:* II, iii; "cod's head" in *Othello:* II, i. Gordon Williams gives the most plausible interpretation, that the "cod's head" refers to a foolish husband, and the "salmon's tail," a delicacy, to a lover. See his *A Dictionary of Sexual Language and Imagery in Shakespearean and Stuart Literature*, 3 vols. (London: Athlone Press, 1994), 493.

167 *Shakespeare never employs a primary obscenity:* In Act II, scene I of *Romeo and Juliet*, Mercutio teases Romeo by wishing that Rosaline "were an open-" *something*. It is clear from the text that Mercutio means

"open-arse," a medlar, but no edition of the play prints the word, prefer-
ring the euphemism "open et caetera" (Q1) or, as in the Folio, leaving it
blank, "O that she were an open, or thou a Poprin Pear." I think the actor
must have said "open-arse" on stage, given the kind of obscene language
Shakespeare's contemporaries were employing, although it is also possible that the actor could have hinted at "arse" yet not said it. For more on
this, see the following chapter.

167 *Other Renaissance dramatists:* "windfucker": *Epicene, or the Silent Woman*
(1609), I, iv; "Turd in your teeth": *Bartholomew Fair* (1614, pub. 1631),
I, iv; "Marry, shit o' your hood": *Bartholomew Fair*, IV, iv; "Kiss the
whore": *Bartholomew Fair*, V, v.

168 *Plays were licensed for performance:* For more about the master of the
revels, see Richard Dutton, *Mastering the Revels: The Regulation and Censorship of English Renaissance Drama* (London: Macmillan, 1991).

   In The Famous Victories: *The Famous Victories of Henry the Fifth* (London, 1598), Early English Books Online.

169 For more about the expurgation of oaths in Shakespeare, see Gary Taylor's "'Swounds Revisited," in *Shakespeare Reshaped, 1606–1623*
(Oxford: Clarendon Press, 1993), 51–106. I have simplified what is actually a complicated situation.

   *Sir Henry Herbert is so concerned: The Dramatic Records of Sir Henry Her-
bert,* ed. Joseph Quincy Adams (New Haven: Yale University Press,
1917), 22.

   Herbert once burns a play: Scholars debate whether he burned the play
solely because of the obscenity. Most think that he probably had another
reason, e.g., anti-Catholic satire that was presented in a bawdy way. See
Richard Dutton, *Licensing, Censorship and Authorship in Early Modern
England* (New York: Palgrave, 2000), 51–61.

   The first acknowledged case: Karen Harvey, *Reading Sex in the Eighteenth
Century: Bodies and Gender in English Erotic Culture* (Cambridge: Cambridge University Press, 2004), 36–38; Deana Heath, *Purifying Empire:
Obscenity and the Politics of Moral Regulation in Britain, India, and Australia* (Cambridge: Cambridge University Press, 2010), 51. Curll is the first
person prosecuted for "obscene libel," an entirely new category that
made obscenity subject to legal regulation under common law. Printers
had suffered fines for printing "obscene and lascivious books" before,
starting around 1680, but this had been as a result of the pre-publication

licensing system. Rochester's *Sodom* (1684) and *The School of Venus* (1680) were banned as obscene and lascivious as a result.

170 *a religious group from the 1650s:* For more on the Ranters, see Christopher Hill, *The World Turned Upside Down: Radical Ideas During the English Revolution* (New York: Penguin Books, 1991); A. L. Morton, *The World of the Ranters: Religious Radicalism in the English Revolution* (London: Lawrence & Wishart, 1970); J. C. Davis, *Fear, Myth, and History: The Ranters and the Historians* (Cambridge: Cambridge University Press, 1986).

"The fellow creature which sits next": The Ranters Ranting (London 1650), 4, Early English Books Online.

"it put the woman into such a fright": The Ranters Ranting, 6.

Chapter 5

173 *In 1673, John Wilmot:* All Rochester poems are from *John Wilmot, Earl of Rochester: The Poems and Lucina's Rape,* ed. Keith Walker and Nicholas Fisher (Malden, MA: Wiley-Blackwell, 2010).

175 *"boxing the Jesuit":* Francis Grose, *A Classical Dictionary of the Vulgar Tongue* (London: S. Hooper, 1785), 18.

176 *Rochester abducted the fourteen-year-old Elizabeth:* Walker and Fisher, introduction to *John Wilmot,* xviii; Arthur Malet, *Notices of an English Branch of the Malet Family* (London: Harrison & Sons, 1885), 48–49.

177 *they are now ranked among the mildest:* Tony McEnery, *Swearing in English: Bad Language, Purity and Power from 1586 to the Present* (London: Routledge 2006), 36, 50, and n. 59.

In a 2006 study of speakers: Timothy Jay, "The Utility and Ubiquity of Taboo Words," *Perspectives on Psychological Science* 4, no. 2 (2009): 156.

178 *"My Lord, why, what the Devil?"* Alexander Pope, *The Rape of the Lock,* 2nd ed. (London: Bernard Lintott, 1714), 37.

Francis Grose's 1785 Classical Dictionary: Grose, *A Classical Dictionary,* 182, 43, 61.

Eighty years later: John Hotten, *The Slang Dictionary: or, The Vulgar Words, Street Phrases, and "Fast" Expressions of High and Low Society,* 3rd ed. (London: John Camden Hotten, 1865).

"How do you do, sir?" Basil Hall, *Fragments of Voyages and Travels,* second series (Edinburgh: Robert Cadell, 1832), II:234.

179   *religion occupied a less central role:* For more on the decline of religion in
       the eighteenth century, see Roy Porter, *English Society in the Eighteenth
       Century* (London: Penguin, 1990) and Joss Marsh, *Word Crimes: Blas-
       phemy, Culture, and Literature in Nineteenth-Century England* (Chicago:
       University of Chicago Press, 1998).

       "The terrors of supernatural vengeance": Keith Thomas, *Religion and the
       Decline of Magic* (London: Weidenfeld & Nicolson, 1971), 65.

       But in 1847, Lionel de Rothschild, a Jew: "Bank to Westminster: Lionel de
       Rothschild's Journey to Parliament, 1847–1858," The Rothschild Archive
       (online), accessed July 29, 2012; *Reports of State Trials,* ed. John E. P. Wal-
       lis, new series (London: Eyre and Spottiswoode, 1898), VIII:114.

180   *In 1880, the people of Northampton chose someone:* Marsh, *Word Crimes,*
       135; Adolphe S. Headingley, *The Biography of Charles Bradlaugh,* 2nd ed.
       (London: Freethought, 1883), 177.

       "the sacredness of oaths": "Popery in the Nineteenth Century," *Black-
       wood's Edinburgh Magazine,* February 1851, 252.

181   *"that from the earliest times of a Christian Legislature":* The Annual Register,
       or a View of the History and Politics of the Year 1850 (London: F. & J. Riv-
       ington, 1851), 183.

       "Deny the existence of God": The Westminster Review, vol. CXIII, January-
       April 1880, American ed. (New York: Leonard Scott), 183.

       As literary critic and historian: Marsh, *Word Crimes,* 50.

182   *Rothschild finally took his seat in Parliament:* The Jewish Encyclopedia: A
       Descriptive Record, ed. Isidore Singer (New York: Funk and Wagnalls,
       1906), 5:172.

       in 1888 he secured the passage: Edward Royle, *Radicals, Secularists and
       Republicans: Popular Freethought in Britain, 1866–1915* (Manchester:
       Manchester University Press, 1980), 266.

       George Washington undercut: Forrest Church, *So Help Me God: The
       Founding Fathers and the First Great Battle over Church and State* (New
       York: Houghton Mifflin Harcourt, 2008), 448. Some scholars deny that
       Washington actually added the words. For this view, see Peter R. Hen-
       riques, "'So Help Me God': A George Washington Myth that Should Be
       Discarded," George Mason University's History News Network (online),
       accessed July 29, 2012.

184   *"the naked and plaine truth":* John Aubrey, *Aubrey's Brief Lives,* ed. Oliver
       Lawson Dick (Jaffrey, NH: David R. Godine, 1999), cxiii, 107, 271.

184 *"he calls a fig a fig"*: Desiderius Erasmus, *Adages*, trans. R. A. B Mynors, in *Collected Works of Erasmus*, ed. Craig R. Thompson (Toronto: University of Toronto Press, 1974), 33:132, 133.

"will strike the hearer as rather": Desiderius Erasmus, *Copia: Foundations of the Abundant Style*, trans. Betty I. Knott, in *Collected Works of Erasmus* (Toronto: University of Toronto Press, 1978), 24:309.

"Telling of a Roman army": D. J. Enright, *Fair of Speech: The Uses of Euphemism* (Oxford: Oxford University Press, 1985), 38.

The Greek actually means: Erasmus, *Adages*, 384.

In a 2005 study: Eric Rassin and Simone van der Heijden, "Appearing Credible? Swearing Helps!" *Psychology, Crime & Law* 11, no. 2 (June 2005): 177–82.

186 *"hardly anyone called a spade"*: Marsh, *Word Crimes*, 218.

"Generally, people now call": William Dean Howells, *Criticism and Fiction* (New York: Harper and Brothers, 1891), 154.

"Call a spade a spade": Henry Alford, *A Plea for the Queen's English*, 2nd ed. (New York: Dick & Fitzgerald, 1864), 278.

John Ruskin, the eminent Victorian art critic: For Ruskin, I consulted Timothy Hilton, *John Ruskin: The Early Years, 1819–1859* (New Haven: Yale University Press, 1985); Wolfgang Kemp, *The Desire of My Eyes: The Life and Work of John Ruskin*, trans. Jan van Heurck (London: Harper Collins, 1990); Peter Gay, *The Education of the Senses* (New York: Oxford University Press, 1984); Phyllis Rose, *Parallel Lives: Five Victorian Marriages* (New York: Knopf, 1983).

187 *Other scholars have argued:* Matthew Sweet, *Inventing the Victorians* (London: Faber, 2001), 216.

He described Turner's erotic works: Maev Kennedy, "Infamous Bonfire of Turner's Erotic Art Revealed to Be a Myth," *Guardian*, December 31, 2004; Sarah Lyall, "A Censorship Story Goes up in Smoke," *New York Times*, January 13, 2005.

189 *"Then owls and bats"*: Robert Browning, "Pippa Passes," in *The Major Works*, ed. Adam Roberts (Oxford: Oxford University Press, 2005), IV.ii.96. Browning's "twat" has been covered in Jesse Sheidlower, *The F Word*, 3rd ed. (New York: Oxford University Press, 2009), xv; Patricia O'Conner and Stewart Kellerman, *Origins of the Specious: Myths and Misconceptions of the English Language* (New York: Random House,

2009), 90–91; and Peter Silverton, *Filthy English: The How, Why, When, and What of Everyday Swearing* (London: Portobello, 2009), among others.

189 *"Give not male names then to such things"*: Martial, *Ex Otio Negotium, or Martiall His Epigrams Translated,* trans. Robert Fletcher (London, 1656).

190 *It appears in Thomas Wright's:* Thomas Wright, *Dictionary of Obsolete and Provincial English* (London: H. G. Bohn, 1857).

   And in 1888, a concerned reader: H. W. Fay, "A Distressing Blunder," *The Academy,* no. 841 (June 16, 1888): 415.

191 *trousers, "an article of dress"*: quoted in Jeffrey Kacirk, *The Word Museum: The Most Remarkable English Words Ever Forgotten* (New York: Simon & Schuster, 2000), 98.

192 *"When at Niagara Falls"*: Capt. Frederick Marryat, *A Diary in America: With Remarks on Its Institutions* (New York: Wm. H. Colyer, 1839), 154.

193 *There is scholarly debate about the number:* Sweet, *Inventing the Victorians,* xiv–xv; Karen Lystra, *Searching the Heart: Women, Men, and Romantic Love in Nineteenth-Century America* (New York: Oxford University Press, 1989), 56–57.

195 *"euphemisms, words and phrases"*: Noah Webster, ed., *The Holy Bible* (New Haven: Durrie & Peck, 1833), iv.

   Even John Farmer and William Henley: "Bender," in John Farmer and William Henley, eds., *Slang and Its Analogues Past and Present,* 7 vols. (London, 1890–1904).

   In the 1874 edition of his Slang Dictionary: John Hotten, ed., *Slang Dictionary,* rev. ed. (London: Chatto and Windus, 1874).

   "In the papers": Henry Alford, *A Plea for the Queen's English,* rev. ed. (New York: George Routledge & Sons, 1878), 251, 248.

196 *"not once unsheathed"*: John Cleland, *Fanny Hill, or Memoirs of a Woman of Pleasure,* ed. Peter Wagner (New York: Penguin Books, 1985), 112–13.

197 *"The tree of Life"*: quoted in Alison Syme, *A Touch of Blossom: John Singer Sargent and the Queer Flora of Fin-de-Siècle Art* (University Park: Pennsylvania State University Press, 2010), 26; Karen Harvey, *Reading Sex in the Eighteenth Century: Bodies and Gender in English Erotic Culture* (Cambridge: Cambridge University Press, 2004), 90.

198 *Of perspiration:* quoted in *OED.*

Linguists Keith Allan and Kate Burridge: Keith Allan and Kate Burridge, *Forbidden Words: Taboo and the Censoring of Language* (Cambridge: Cambridge University Press, 2003), 33. See especially Chapter 2, "Sweet Talking and Offensive Language."

199 *"not even this word, it seems":* Leigh Hunt, *The Autobiography of Leigh Hunt* (London: Smith, Elder, 1891), 376.

When an actress spoke it: Adrian Frazier, *Playboys of the Western World: Production Histories* (Dublin: Carysfort Press, 2004), 13–16.

"Presumptuous Piss-pot": "On Melting Down the Plate: Or, the Piss-pot's Farewell," *Poems on Affairs of State,* pt. III (London, 1698), 215.

Consider the toilet: These euphemisms come from the *OED;* Richard W. Bailey, *Nineteenth-Century English* (Ann Arbor: University of Michigan Press, 1996); and Andreas Fischer, "'Non Olet': Euphemisms We Live by," *New Perspectives on English Historical Linguistics II* (Amsterdam: John Benjamins, 2004), 91–108.

200 *"The newly wedded country gent":* quoted in Bailey, *Nineteenth-Century English,* 168.

201 *Gardez l'eau . . . bourdalou:* Naomi Stead, "Avoidance: On Some Euphemisms for the 'Smallest Room,'" in *Ladies and Gents: Public Toilets and Gender,* ed. Olga Gershenson and Barbara Penner (Philadelphia: Temple University Press, 2009), 128.

202 toilet *came to indicate:* Stead, "Avoidance," 129–30; *OED.*

Toiletgate: John Harris, "Common People," *Guardian,* April 16, 2007.

"I find it almost impossible": Sarah Lyall, "Why Can't the English Just Give Up That Class Folderol?" *New York Times,* April 26, 2007.

203 *"No freshman shall mingo":* William Bentnick-Smith, *The Harvard Book: Selections from Three Centuries* (Cambridge, MA: Harvard University Press, 1982), 162.

205 *"During World War I":* Catherine O'Reilly, *Did Thomas Crapper Really Invent the Toilet? The Inventions That Changed Our Homes and Our Lives* (New York: Skyhorse, 2008), xii; personal communication, Simon Kirby.

A. J. Splatt and D. Weedon: "Nominative Determinism," *Wikipedia,* June 30, 2012, accessed July 29, 2012.

"Excretion was an accepted and semipublic event": quoted in Fischer, "'Non Olet,'" 105.

206 *"the transition from a society of estates or orders"*: Suzanne Romaine, ed., *The Cambridge History of the English Language*, vol. IV: *1776–1997* (Cambridge: Cambridge University Press, 1998), 13.

For more about this great social transition, see T. C. W. Blanning, *The Oxford History of Modern Europe* (Oxford: Oxford University Press, 2000).

"The middle class ... sought an identity": McEnery, *Swearing in English*, 84.

207 *"How shamefully rich"*: Richard Chenevix Trench, *On the Study of Words*, 2nd ed. (New York: Blakeman & Mason, 1859), 40.

"purity of speech, like personal cleanliness": George Perkins Marsh, *Lectures on the English Language* (New York: Scribner, 1860), 645.

"Few things are in worse taste": Alfred Ayers, *The Verbalist*, rev. ed. (New York: D. Appleton, 1896), 103–4.

208 *"evidence of hypercorrection"*: McEnery, *Swearing in English*, 49.

209 *"in good sooth"*: William Shakespeare, *Henry IV, Part One*, Act III, scene i.

210 *"the great Australian adjective"*: Geoffrey Hughes, *Swearing: A Social History of Foul Language, Oaths and Profanity in English* (Oxford: Blackwell, 1991), 171.

"is often classed as profane or obscene": Thomas H. B. Graham, "Some English Expletives," *Gentleman's Magazine*, July-December 1891, 199.

211 *"a few seconds of stunned disbelieving silence"*: Geoffrey Hughes, *An Encyclopedia of Swearing: The Social History of Oaths, Profanity, Foul Language and Ethnic Slurs in the English-Speaking World* (Armonk, NY: M. E. Sharpe, 2006), 372.

"not pygmalion likely": Ibid., 392.

"un epithet difficult to define": "Bloody," in Farmer and Henley, eds., *Slang and Its Analogues*.

212 *"We cannot disguise to ourselves"*: Julian Sharman, *A Cursory History of Swearing* (London: Nimmo and Bain, 1884), 178.

213 *"God damn him"*: *A Collection of State-Trials and Proceedings* (London: Benj. Motte and C. Bathurst, 1735), 7:349.

"get thee gone": Rabelais, *Gargantua and Pantagruel*, trans. Thomas Urquhart, ed. Charles Whibley (London: David Nutt, 1900), 135.

"B—st [blast] and b-gg-r": "Bugger," *OED*.

"Damn 'em bugger you": Jacob A. Hazen, *Five Years Before the Mast, or, Life in the Forecastle* (Philadelphia: G. G. Evans, 1854), 254.

213 *"Take the bugger off":* William G. Shaw, "State v. McDonnell," *Reports of Cases Argued and Determined in the Supreme Court of the State of Vermont,* vol. 32, new series, vol. 3 (Rutland: Geo. A Tuttle, 1861), 495.

"Previous to this the soil had": Henry Lamson Boies, *History of De Kalb County, Illinois* (Chicago: O. P. Bassett, 1868), 391.

"came out and met him": Journal of the Senate of Ohio, at the First Session of the Thirty-Ninth General Assembly (Columbus: Samuel Medary, 1840), 529.

214 *a low-class prostitute with whom: My Secret Life* (Amsterdam, 1888), 2:256.

"a term of contempt": Frederick Thomas Elworthy, *The West Somerset Word-Book* (London: Trübner, 1886), 663.

the "feminization of ambisexual terms": Hughes, *Swearing,* 220–23.

216 *"G—d—your books":* Sheidlower, *The F Word,* 73; Hughes, *Encyclopedia,* xxii.

"For all your threats": Sheidlower, *The F Word,* 73; Henry Spencer Ashbee, *Catena Librorum Tacendorum, by Pisanus Fraxi* (London, 1885), 319–21.

one Mr. Baker had told him: Sheidlower, *The F Word,* 89–90.

In 1836 Mary Hamilton: Joy Damousi, *Depraved and Disorderly: Female Convicts, Sexuality and Gender in Colonial Australia* (Cambridge: Cambridge University Press, 1997), 75.

An 1857 abolitionist work: Sheidlower, *The F Word,* 140; *The Suppressed Book About Slavery!* (New York: Carleton, 1864), 211.

217 *"Shit, that't nothen":* Congressional Serial Set: The Miscellaneous Documents of the House of Representatives for the Second Session of the Fiftieth Congress, 18 vols. (Washington, DC: Government Printing Office, 1889), 299.

218 *In 1894, a New York man murdered:* "New York v. Thomas Kerrigan," *Court of Appeals* (New York: Evening Post Job Printing House, 1894).

"the 'bad language' of the present day: Graham, "Some English Expletives," 199.

219 *The entry on* swearing: *Chambers's Encyclopædia: A Dictionary of Universal Knowledge,* vol. 10 (London: William and Robert Chambers, 1892). This entry is in contrast to those of earlier editions of the *Encyclopaedia,* where swearing was characterized only as profane use of religious oaths.

219 *"We say that it is no worse"*: "The Obscenity Spook," *Liberty*, vol. IV, no. 26 (July 30, 1887).

220 *Gordon Williams argues persuasively*: Gordon Williams, *A Dictionary of Sexual Language and Imagery in Shakespearean and Stuart Literature*, 3 vols. (London: Athlone Press, 1994), 350.

"a velvet salute": Harris's List of Covent-Garden Ladies: Sex in the City n Georgian Britain, ed. Hallie Rubenhold (Stroud, Gloucestershire: Tempus, 2005), 156.

221 *There were many vulgar slang words*: Many of these come from Farmer and Henley, *Slang and Its Analogues*, under "prick."

222 *Mrs. B-ooks*: *Harris's List of Covent-Garden Ladies*, 90–91.

Betsy Miles: Ibid., 154.

When the List *describes*: Ibid., 127.

Tit *as a variant of* teat: Thomas Wright, *Anglo-Saxon and English Vocabularies*, ed. Richard Paul Wülcker, 2nd ed. (London: Trübner, 1884), 1:159.

223 *"a dictionary by which the pronunciation"*: Samuel Johnson, "The Plan of an English Dictionary," *The Works of Samuel Johnson, LL.D.* (London: F. C. and J. Rivington et al., 1823), 10:28.

"As an independent nation": Noah Webster, *Dissertations on the English Language* (Boston: Isaiah Thomas, 1789), 20.

224 *"comparatively few terms of abuse"*: Hughes, *Swearing*, 135.

Abusive terms for other: These racial and ethnic slurs come from Farmer and Henley, *Slang and Its Analogues*; the *OED*; and Irving Lewis Allen, *The Language of Ethinic Conflict: Social Organization and Lexical Culture* (New York: Columbia University Press, 1983).

Chapter 6

227 *Some scholars have argued*: Geoffrey Hughes, *Swearing: A Social History of Foul Language, Oaths and Profanity in English* (Oxford: Blackwell, 1991), 199; Geoffrey Hughes, *An Encyclopedia of Swearing: The Social History of Oaths, Profanity, Foul Language and Ethnic Slurs in the English-Speaking World* (Armonk, NY: M. E. Sharpe, 2006), 439, 486; Ruth Wajnryb, *Expletive Deleted: A Good Look at Bad Language* (New York: Free Press, 2005), 141.

228 *soldiers used* fucking *so often*: John Brophy and Eric Partridge, eds., *Songs and Slang of the British Soldier: 1914–1918* (London: Eric Partridge at the Scholartis Press, 1930), 16.

228   *"It became so common"*: Ibid., 17.

      "are ugly, in form and in sound": Ibid., 15.

      "'Oo's the bloody shit": Frederic Manning, *The Middle Parts of Fortune: Somme and Ancre* (Minneapolis: Filiquarian, 2007), 309.

229   *"Sir, he called me"*: Robert Graves, *Goodbye to All That: And Other Great War Writings*, ed. Steven Trout (Manchester: Carcanet, 2008), 66.

      "So you're the young man": Hughes, *Encyclopedia*, "Soldiers and Sailors." This story is possibly apocryphal, as the line has also been attributed to Dorothy Parker.

      though he had to cut his: Jesse Sheidlower, *The F Word*, 3rd ed. (New York: Oxford University Press, 2009), xxii.

      In 1928 Allen Walker Read: Allen Walker Read, *Classic American Graffiti: Lexical Evidence from Folk Epigraphy in Western North America* (Waukesha, WI: Maledicta, 1977), 55, 51, 45.

230   *"Fuck 'Em All"*: Les Cleveland, "Soldiers' Songs: The Folklore of the Powerless," The Vietnam Veterans Oral History and Folklore Project (online), accessed July 31, 2012.

      "the floodgates opened": Hughes, *Swearing*, 200.

      "a change of emphasis": Tony McEnery, *Swearing in English: Bad Language, Purity and Power from 1586 to the Present* (London: Routledge 2006), 121.

231   *his groundbreaking article*: Allen Walker Read, "An Obscenity Symbol," *American Speech* 9, no. 4 (1934): 264–78.

      "the filthiest, dirtiest, nastiest": quoted in Randall Kennedy, *Nigger: The Strange Career of a Troublesome Word* (New York: Vintage Books, 2003), 23.

      "probably the most offensive word": "Nigger," Dictionary.com, accessed July 30, 2012.

232   *The real, less well-known scandal*: Leonard J. Leff and Jerold L. Simmons, *The Dame in the Kimono: Hollywood, Censorship, and the Production Code*, rev. ed. (Lexington: University Press of Kentucky, 2001), 98–108; Kennedy, *Nigger*, 90; "The Depiction of African-Americans in David Selznick's 'Gone with the Wind,'" American Studies at the University of Virginia (online), accessed July 30, 2012; Leonard J. Leff, "*Gone with the Wind* and Hollywood's Racial Politics," *Atlantic*, December 1999.

      The 1930 Motion Picture Production Code: "Motion Picture Production Code of 1930 (The Hays Code)," ed. Matt Bynum, ArtsReformation. com, accessed July 31, 2012. The code was amended shortly before the film's release in 1939 to discourage but not forbid the use of racial slurs, including *nigger*. See "The Production Code of the Motion Picture Industry (1930–1967)," ed. David P. Hayes, http://productioncode. dhwritings.com/multipleframes_productioncode.php, accessed July 31, 2012.

232 *a genteel elderly white woman:* Lynne Tirrell, "Derogatory Terms: Racism, Sexism, and the Inferential Role Theory of Meaning," in *Language and Liberation: Feminism, Philosophy, and Language,* ed. Christina Hendricks and Kelly Oliver (Albany: State University of New York Press, 1999), 45.

233 *David Howard:* Kennedy, *Nigger,* 94–96.

234 *The fighting-words doctrine:* Chaplinsky v. New Hampshire, 315 U.S. 568; 62 S. Ct. 766; 86 L. Ed. 1031 (1942).

235 *Connie Watkins screamed: Watkins v. State,* 2010 Ark. App. 85 (2010).

When a police officer asked: Kaylor v. Rankin, 356 F.Supp.2d 839 (2005).

In Michigan, Thomas Leonard: Leonard v. Robinson, 477 F.3d 347 (2007).

Whore, harlot, *and* jezebel: *State v. Ovadal,* 2004 WI 20; 269 Wis. 2d 200; 675 N.W.2d 806 (2004).

236 *Jerry Spivey:* Kennedy, *Nigger,* 52–57; In re *Jerry Spivey, District Attorney* 345 N.C. 404; 480 S.E.2d 693 (1997).

The North Dakota supreme court: In the Interest of A.R., a Child v. R., a Minor Child, 2010 ND 84; 781 N.W.2d 644 (2010).

an appeals court in Arizona: In re *John M.,* 201 Ariz. 424; 36 P.3d 772 (2001).

The n-word does not always fit: People v. Livio, 187 Misc. 2d 302; 725 N.Y.S.2d 785 (2000).

237 *The other key case: Cohen v. California,* 403 U.S. 15; 91 S. Ct. 1780; 29 L. Ed. 2d 284 (1971).

238 *The situation is different in Britain*: See Public Order Act 1986, c. 64, and The Crime and Disorder Act 1998, c. 37.

Welsh university student: Luke Salkeld, "Off to Jail in Cuffs," *Daily Mail,* March 27, 2012.

"You must be fucking barmy": William Oddie, "Liam Stacey's Drunken Racist Tweets," CatholicHerald.co.uk, March 30, 2012; "Liam Stacey Twitter Racism Against Fabrice Muamba, Don't Lose the Evidence," Youtube.com, posted by mattvandam1, March 17, 2012, accessed July 31, 2012.

239 *Stiddard had called:* Luke Salkeld, "Next Time Just Call him a Fat B******,"
Daily Mail, January 16, 2007.

Ulysses *is now seen as a classic:* See Shane Sherman, "*Ulysses* by James Joyce," TheGreatestBooks.org, accessed July 31, 2012.

"the most infamously obscene": These three quotes come from Elizabeth Ladenson, *Dirt for Art's Sake: Books on Trial from* Madame Bovary *to* Lolita (Ithaca, NY: Cornell University Press, 2007), 79.

240 *"I'll wring the bastard fucker's":* James Joyce, *Ulysses* (1922), accessed via BompaCrazy.com, 504.

"God fuck": Ibid., 506.

"Bugger off": Ibid., 505.

"And she saw a long Roman candle": Ibid., 349.

241 *alert reader John Sumner:* Robert Denning, ed., *James Joyce: The Critical Heritage,* vol. 1: *1907–1927* (London: Routledge, 1970), 18; Ladenson, *Dirt for Art's Sake,* 71–106; Bennett Cerf, *At Random: The Reminiscences of Bennett Cerf* (New York: Random House, 2002), 90–99.

242 *The trial happened in 1933: The United States of America v. One Book Entitled Ulysses,* 5 F. Supp. 182, 72 F.2d 705 (1934).

the Hicklin Rule: Wayne Overbeck and Genelle Belmas, eds., *Major Principles of Media Law* (Boston: Wadsworth, 2012), 419–24; Joseph Kelly, *Our Joyce: From Outcast to Icon* (Austin: University of Texas Press, 1998), 131–33.

"whether the tendency": Joel Feinberg, *Offense to Others: The Moral Limits of the Criminal Law* (New York: Oxford University Press, 1985), 171.

243 *"If I use the taboo words":* quoted in Hughes, *Swearing,* 191.

The book had been published in several editions: John Sutherland, *Offensive Literature: Decensorship in Britain, 1960–1982* (London: Junction Books, 1982), 10–31; Michael Squires, "Introduction," in D. H. Lawrence, *Lady Chatterley's Lover,* ed. Michael Squires (Cambridge: Cambridge University Press, 2002).

244 *"Th'art good cunt":* Lawrence, *Lady Chatterley's Lover,* 177–78.

245 *"The word shit, uh":* "The Following Is a Verbatim Transcript of 'Filthy Words,'" University of Missouri–Kansas City School of Law (online), July 31, 2012.

Legally, indecency is: "Obscenity, Indecency, and Profanity," FCC.gov, July 31, 2012.

245 *The FCC threatened: Federal Communications Commission v. Pacifica*, 435 U.S. 966; 98 S. Ct. 1602; 56 L. Ed. 2d 57 (1978).

247 *three of the top ten hit songs:* Jon Pareles, "From Cee Lo Green to Pink, Speaking the Unspeakable," *New York Times*, March 15, 2011.

Much of rap music deals with: Jay-Z, *Decoded* (New York: Spiegel & Grau, 2010); Tim Strode and Tim Wood, eds., *The Hip Hop Reader* (New York: Pearson Longman, 2008).

"Lighters": Bad Meets Evil, "Lighters," *Hell: The Sequel (Deluxe Version)*, Aftermath, 2011, compact disc.

248 *Rap battling evolved most directly from:* Elijah Wald, *The Dozens: A History of Rap's Mama* (New York: Oxford University Press, 2012).

Hustling, as rapper Jay-Z: Jay-Z, *Decoded*, 18.

On July 10, 1890: William Osler, *On Chorea and Choreiform Affections* (London: H. K. Lewis, 1894), 79–81.

249 *Tourette's syndrome is characterized:* Timothy Jay, *Why We Curse: A Neuro-Psycho-Social Theory of Speech* (Philadelphia: John Benjamins, 2000), 63–80. See also Douglas W. Woods et al., *Treating Tourette Syndrome and Tic Disorders: A Guide for Practitioners* (New York: Guilford Press, 2007); Howard I. Kushner, *A Cursing Brain: The Histories of Tourette Syndrome* (Cambridge, MA: Harvard University Press, 1999); Lowell Handler, *Twitch and Shout: A Touretter's Tale* (New York: Dutton, 1998).

The problem was thought: For the various theories of what causes Tourette's, see Kushner, *A Cursing Brain*, 45–118.

250 *what goes on in "normal" brains:* Jay, *Why We Curse*, 33–62; Steven Pinker, *The Stuff of Thought: Language as a Window into Human Nature* (New York: Viking, 2007), 331–37; Diana Van Lancker Sidtis, "Formulaic and Novel Language in a 'Dual Process' Model of Language Competence," in *Formulaic Language*, ed. Roberta Corrigan et al. (Philadelphia: John Benjamins, 2009), 2:445–72; Diana Van Lancker Sidtis, "Where in the Brain Is Nonliteral Language?" *Metaphor and Symbol* 21, no. 4 (2006): 213–44.

251 *The standard word frequency list:* Paul Cameron, "Frequency and Kinds of Words in Various Social Settings, or What the Hell's Going On?" *Pacific Sociological Review* 12, no. 2 (Autumn 1969): 101–4.

this one based on spoken telephone conversations: David B. Morris, "The Neurobiology of the Obscene: Henry Miller and Tourette Syndrome," *Literature and Medicine* 12, no. 2 (Fall 1993): 194–214.

251 *on average 0.7 percent of the words people use:* Timothy Jay, "The Utility and Ubiquity of Taboo Words," *Perspectives on Psychological Science* 4, no. 2 (2009), 155.

    psychologist Paul Cameron complied word frequency lists: Morris, "The Neurobiology of the Obscene," 196.

252 *the top five recalled were:* Timothy Jay, "Recalling Taboo and Nontaboo Words," *American Journal of Psychology* 121, no. 1 (Spring 2008): 83–103.

    Another piece of folk wisdom about swearing: Richard Stephens, John Atkins and Andrew Kingston, "Swearing as a Response to Pain," *Neuro-Report* 20 (2009): 1056–60.

Epilogue

254 *swearing would simply go extinct:* Bernard Nezmah, "Fuck This Article: The Yugoslav Lexicon of Swear-Words," *Central Europe Review* 2, no. 41 (November 27, 2000).

    Russian obscenities constitute almost an entire language: Victor Erofeyev, "Dirty Words," *New Yorker*, September 15, 2003, 42.

255 *"To Is a Preposition, Come Is a Verb":* Lenny Bruce, "To Is a Preposition, Come Is a Verb," Famous Trials: The Lenny Bruce Trial 1964 (online) , July 31, 2012.

    "Are There Any Niggers Here Tonight": Lenny Bruce, "Are There Any Niggers Here Tonight?" *Warning Lenny Bruce Is Out Again*, Sicsicsic, 2004, compact disc.

258 *where religious oaths, called* sacres: Clément Légaré and André Bougaïeff, *L'Empire du Sacre Québécois* (Sillery, Québec: Presses de L'Université du Québec, 1984); "Swearing in Quebec: If You Profane Something No One Holds Sacred, Does It Make a Swear?" *Economist*, November 24, 2011; "Quebec French Profanity," *Wikipedia*, July 24, 2012 (online), accessed July 31, 2012.

Postscript

259 American Heritage Dictionary: Patrick Hanks, "The Impact of Corpora on Dictionaries," in *Contemporary Corpus Linguistics*, ed. Paul Baker, 2009 (New York: Continuum, 2012), 214.

In 2015, Jack Grieve: Jack Grieve, "Trees and Tweets," *Jack Grieve's Homepage*, January 3, 2015, accessed January 28, 2016.

1.15% of all words on Twitter: Wenbo Wang, Lu Chen, et al. "Cursing in English on Twitter," *Proceedings of the 17th ACM Conference on Computer Supported Cooperative Work & Social Computing* (2014): 415-424.

regional differences in patterns of swearing: Jack Grieve, "Trees and Tweets," *Jack Grieve's Homepage*, July 16, 2015, accessed January 28, 2016.

260   *gender differences in British swearing*: Michael Gauthier, Adrien Guille, et al. "Text Mining and Twitter to Analyze British Swearing Habits," http://mediamining.univ-lyon2.fr/people/guille/publications.php, accessed January 28, 2016.

people who use Twitter: Maeve Duggan, Nicole B. Ellison, et al. "Demographics of Key Social Networking Platforms," PewResearch.org, January 9, 2015, accessed January 28, 2016.

in some African-American speech communities: Taylor Jones and Christopher Hall, "Semantic Bleaching and the Emergence of New Pronouns in AAVE," *LSA Annual Meeting Extended Abstracts* (2015), vol. 6, 10:1-5.

261   *"Nigga we made it"*: Krissah Thompson and Dave Sheinin, "Redefining the Word: A Controversial Banner," *Washington Post.com*, November 9 2014, accessed February 2, 2016.

retired British historian Paul Booth: Mike Pearl, "We Interviewed the Historian Who Just Found the Oldest Use of the Word 'Fuck,'" *Vice.com*, September 12, 2015, accessed February 2, 2016; "The Earliest Use of the F-Word Discovered," *Medievalists.net*, September 10, 2015, accessed February 2, 2016.

John le Fucker. *Calendar of the Close Rolls Preserved in the Public Records Office: Edward I: A.D. 1272-1279* (London: Public Record Office, 1900), 451; The National Archives of the UK, C 54/95, last entry on membrane 11.

Fuckebegger: *Records of the Wardrobe and Household, 1286-1289*, ed. Benjamin Byerly and Catherine Byerly (London: H.M. Stationery Office, 1986), 151; Marc Morris (Longshanks1307), "Here's one of Edward I's palfreymen in a pay roll from 1286," February 10, 2014, 4:38 AM, Tweet.

262   *the German ficken*: *Deutsches Wörterbuch von Jacob Grimm und Wilhelm Grimm* (1854), *Wörterbuchnetz.de*, accessed February 11, 2016.

Fukkebotere...Smalfuk: Kate Wiles, "On the Origin of *Fuck*," *So Long as It's Words*, February 12, 2014, accessed February 2, 2016.

Fockynggroue: Richard Coates, "*Fockynggroue* in Bristol," *Notes and Queries* 54.4 (2007): 373-376; Roger Leech, *The St. Michael's Hill Precinct of the University of Bristol: Medieval and Early Modern Topography*. (Bristol: Bristol Record Society, 2000), 35.

the original proto-Indo-European word: Roger Lass, "Four Letters in Search of an Etymology," *Diachronica* 12:1 (1995): 99-111.

As Allen Walker Read: Allen Walker Read, *Milestones in the History of English in America*, Publications of the American Dialect Society 86 (Durham, NC: Duke University Press, 2002), 285.

263   *the* Modipintels: For more examples, see the MED, *Middle English Dictionary, Middle English Compendium (University of Michigan)*; Keith Briggs, "OE and ME *cunte* in Place-names," *Journal of the English Placename Society* 41 (2009): 26-39.

CREDITS

INDEX

Printed in the USA
CPSIA information can be obtained
at www.ICGtesting.com
BVHW052323150823
668545BV00005B/11